Paise for

THE VAGABOND'S WAY

"Rolf Potts, the author who inspired wanderlust in many, has mastered the art of 'engaged travel,' which makes you see home with fresh eyes."
—*The New York Times*

"The book is set up as a series of meditations—travel quotes that Potts reflects on and reacts to. . . . The result of this formula is a book that's snackable, weighty, and fun all at once. The premier travel writer of a generation offering travel inspiration in short bursts and fun anecdotes? Sign. Us. Up."
—*Uproxx*

"Rolf Potts has long been a road warrior and a deep thinker about travel. In *The Vagabond's Way,* he distills decades of hard-won insight into bite-sized morsels, and the result is a wise, generous, and profound book. It is a gift for anyone engaged in the journey."
—Andrew McCarthy, *New York Times* bestselling author of *Brat* and *The Longest Way Home*

"In an age of bucket lists, Instagram posts, and one-up travel, Rolf Potts is a breath of fresh air. This book reminds us that the essence of travel isn't necessarily linear—it's the moments of beauty and insight that happen spontaneously along the way, rather than the plans and the destination."
—Peter Hessler, *New York Times* bestselling author of *River Town*

"Thought-provoking, encouraging, and inspiring, these one-page reflections on the power and pleasures of travel will make even a homebody yearn to hit the road."
—Gretchen Rubin, *New York Times* bestselling author of *The Happiness Project* and host of the *Happier with Gretchen Rubin* podcast

"It is so refreshing to read Rolf Potts's new book, *The Vagabond's Way: 366 Meditations on Wanderlust, Discovery, and the Art of Travel*. Rolf captures the wisdom of the world's most storied travelers, then builds on it based on his own life of vagabonding. Read one meditation per day (a bonus meditation for leap year) or read it all in one sitting. Either way, it will make you think, then inspire you to get up and go."
     —Stephanie Pearson, contributing editor, *Outside*

"In this wise, wonder-struck book, travel-writing legend Rolf Potts distills a lifetime of wandering and reading into a series of irresistible songs for the open road. An inspiring vade mecum for new travelers and experienced vagabonds both."
     —Kate Harris, author of *Lands of Lost Borders*

"*The Vagabond's Way* won't help you find the best deals on flights or hotels or take viral Instagram photos. It will inspire you, challenge you, and remind you why we travel in the first place: to see the world, and ourselves, just a bit differently. Don't read this book in one sitting. Dip into it, as I did, savoring each page as you would having a cup of coffee with a kind and wise friend."
     —Eric Weiner, *New York Times* bestselling author of
     The Geography of Bliss and *The Socrates Express*

"Filled with his wisdom from decades of travel, Rolf Potts's *The Vagabond's Way* will inspire you to travel more deeply and think differently about the world."
     —Matthew Kepnes, author of *Ten Years a Nomad*

"Spot on and eminently readable, this is the book I wish I'd had when I started my travel career many decades ago."
     —Tim Cahill, founding editor, *Outside*

THE VAGABOND'S WAY

THE
VAGABOND'S
WAY

366 Meditations on Wanderlust,
Discovery, and the Art of Travel

ROLF POTTS

BALLANTINE BOOKS
NEW YORK

LIBRARY OF CONGRESS CATALOGING-IN-PUBLICATION DATA
Names: Potts, Rolf, author.
Title: The vagabond's way: 366 meditations on wanderlust, discovery, and the art
of travel / Rolf Potts.
Description: New York: Ballantine Books, 2022.
Identifiers: LCCN 2022010159 (print) | LCCN 2022010160 (ebook) |
ISBN 9780593497470 (paperback) | ISBN 9780593497463 (ebook)
Subjects: LCSH: Travel—Philosophy. | Travel—Psychological aspects.
Classification: LCC G151 .P693 2022 (print) | LCC G151 (ebook) |
DDC 910/.01—dc23/ eng20220611
LC record available at https://lccn.loc.gov/2022010159
LC ebook record available at https://lccn.loc.gov/2022010160

For Kiki

Every day is a journey, and the journey itself is home.

—Matsuo Basho

CONTENTS

HOW TO USE THIS BOOK

In studying classic works of literature from across the centuries, one finds that the most affecting travel tales depict journeys as a metaphor for life itself. These stories don't presume to tell us where to go or what to do, but they do show how journeys can enlarge one's way of being in the world. These tales don't prescribe rules for living; they simply inspire us, by their very example, to live in a more engaged and dynamic way. Indeed, the purest approach to getting the most out of a journey has never revolved around itemized lists of travel strategies: The vagabond's way has always involved a simple and open attitude, a mindset that is inseparable from the way we pay attention to life itself.

This older, more philosophical way of understanding our journeys is too often overlooked in our time, when the act of travel is marketed as a lifestyle accessory. In presenting far-flung landscapes as "destinations," the travel industry encourages us to think of places as consumer products—a faintly interchangeable mix of landscapes against which we can shop, dine, and take photos. By this standard, Nepal and Greece offer a "mountains-and-monasteries" product, whereas Rome and Mexico City serve up "museums-and-cathedrals" travel options, and Sri Lanka and the Dominican Republic tout competing "sand-and-sea" selections. The more we're encouraged to see the world through a commercial lens, the less likely we are to seek out the humbler qualities—patience, receptivity, introspection—that compel us to experience the world in a life-enriching way.

At its best, travel is embraced not as a flashy backdrop for our lifestyle ambitions, but as an act that touches every aspect of our being. Travel is not a swaggering declaration of self, undertaken to impress other people; it is a quiet inquiry, requiring awareness, resilience, and openness to change. Travel is not a hard science that can be cracked open with some algorithmic formula; it is a nuanced art, expressed through joyous, ragged-edged, mindful practice. Travel is not some consumer product you buy into; it is something that you gift to yourself.

Over the course of 366 one-page meditations (one for each day of a leap year), *The Vagabond's Way* mimics the progression of a journey—travel inspiration and planning, getting started on the road, expanding one's comfort zone, learning from the quiet complexities of the journey, and circling back home. As with a journey, these meditations are best approached slowly, one day at a time, reflecting on each day's nuances before moving on to the next. Though this book can technically be read from cover to cover in a few days, it is designed to be taken in incremental doses, in the same manner that one might visit the gym or dance studio—steadily benefiting from the daily ritual over the course of a year.

The Vagabond's Way is about the mindset that can enlarge each day on the road, however long the journey might be. Though some of the historical and literary allusions in these pages refer to travels that spanned multiple continents over the course of many years, its insights apply as readily to short-term, close-to-home journeys. And while the word *vagabond* is traditionally defined as "a person who wanders from place to place without a fixed home," this book affirms that travel is as much a way of being as it is an act of movement.

Some travel themes reappear in these pages, in slightly different form, numerous times over the course of the year. Often, these recurring themes reinforce the kinds of issues the travel industry would have us ignore—issues like traveling light, going slow, letting go of rigid plans, staying open to surprise, embracing boredom, celebrating disorientation, shutting off our technology, spending less money, wandering away from tourist zones, looking beyond cultural stereotypes, and developing travel habits that benefit local economies. These thematic repetitions are deliberate, and serve as a kind of gentle refrain that encourages the reader to consider and reconsider these travel virtues.

At its best, this book will not just explore ideas about mindful travel; it will make you *want* to travel (and, in doing so, to enrich your life in ways you don't yet understand).

If, midway through reading this book, you fling it aside because it doesn't quite fit into the luggage for a journey you've concluded you can no longer postpone, it has done its job.

January/February

DREAMING AND PLANNING
THE JOURNEY

AN INARTICULATE ACHE TO TRAVEL IS WORTH PAYING ATTENTION TO

Homesickness is a feeling many know and suffer from; I, on the other hand, feel a pain less well known, and its name is "Outsickness." When the snow melts, the stork arises, and the first steamships race off, then I feel the painful travel unrest.

—Hans Christian Andersen, in an 1856 letter

Though the English word *wanderlust*—defined as "a strong desire to travel"—was borrowed from German in the early twentieth century, it actually has a slightly different connotation in its original tongue. The word *lust* implies "desire" in both languages, but while the German word *wandern* is often assumed to have a direct relation to the English word *wander,* its literal translation means "to hike." A more descriptive German expression of the desire to travel is, in fact, *fernweh,* which combines *fern,* meaning "distant," with *weh,* meaning "ache."

Fernweh is perhaps best apprehended as "farsickness," a kind of antonym to homesickness, or *heimweh.* In this way, *fernweh* can be understood as a quieter and more personal urge than wanderlust—a persistent longing to escape the confinement of the familiar and give oneself over to unseen places and experiences. *Fernweh* is the ache to widen one's horizons, to be at home in the unfamiliar—to begin anew, and reinvent oneself in the context of the as-yet-unknown.

While there is a certain vagueness to being homesick for the road—of longing to experience what you can't quite describe, since it has yet to happen—a logical way to honor your feelings of *fernweh* is to quietly start planning a journey. In seeking to embrace unseen lands, you'll allow yourself to embrace unseen parts of yourself.

AN INTANGIBLE SENSE OF WONDER IS A GREAT REASON TO TRAVEL

The best travel experiences are simple. They can't be planned. It's just a feeling of something genuine—knowing you're lucky to be in exactly that place at exactly that instant.
—Shannon Leone Fowler, "Kindness of Strangers" (2020)

In the fifteenth century, an Arabic manuscript entitled *The Book of Hidden Pearls* was said to contain directions to a hidden oasis known as Zerzura. Rumored to be located in the desert region west of the Nile, Zerzura was said to feature peaceful inhabitants, abundant gardens, and pristine white buildings.

Though no copies of *The Book of Hidden Pearls* existed by the time European Egyptologists began to dig for antiquities in Northern Africa, the location of Zerzura became a fixation for many early-twentieth-century travelers in the region. In 1929, Hungarian explorer Laszlo Almasy (who later became the fictionalized protagonist of Michael Ondaatje's 1992 novel *The English Patient*) spent more than a year searching for Zerzura with a convoy of Ford Model A trucks, but found nothing beyond a few uninhabited rain oases.

In his 1935 book *Libyan Sands*, British explorer Ralph Bagnold (who had accompanied Almasy on the 1929 expedition) asserted that Zerzura was less significant as a mythical desert oasis than as a metaphor for the intangible sense of wonder that comes with an encounter with the unfamiliar. "I like to think of Zerzura . . . [as] an indefinite thing, taking different shapes in the minds of different individuals according to their interests and wishes," he wrote, ". . . an excuse for the childish craving so many grown-ups harbor secretly to break away from civilization."

As with Zerzura, sometimes our motivations for travel—the goals we have in mind for a given journey—are less important than the wondrous meanderings that await us on the road.

FIND WAYS TO MAKE YOUR TIME ON EARTH MIRACULOUS

Since time is the one immaterial object which we cannot influence—neither speed up nor slow down, add to nor diminish—it is an imponderably valuable gift.
—Maya Angelou, *Wouldn't Take Nothing for My Journey Now* (1993)

Japanese conceptual artist On Karawa's "Today" series, which began in 1966 and lasted for decades, consisted of several thousand hand-painted canvases that simply depicted the calendar date on which the painting was made. His "I Got Up" series consisted of postcards recording his daily wake-up time (as well as the date and his location) from 1968 to 1979. Another series consisted of telegrams sent to various friends over the course of several years, each bearing the lone phrase "I Am Still Alive."

Though Karawa isn't the only artist to have used a personal lens to explore the notion of time and its passing, the droll simplicity of his work has an uncanny way of accentuating the fleeting nature of aliveness. At the risk of oversimplifying the ancient Greek understanding of time, Karawa's stubborn focus on the uniformity of *chronos* (sequential time) helps us understand that life's most essential textures reside in *kairos* (decisive moments of action). Strip *chronos* of *kairos,* and one is left with a sense for how short our span of aliveness on earth can be.

Pondering Karawa's work might well compel us to spend our days with a more deliberate sense of *kairos*—to break out of the fears and habits that keep us trapped in routines, as *chronos* ticks away, and embrace life as a miracle, rich in as-yet-unseen experiences.

LEAVING ON A JOURNEY IS A TIME-HONORED HUMAN RITE

We have only to follow the thread of the hero path. . . . Where we had thought to travel outwards we shall come to the center of our own existence; where we had thought to be alone we shall be with all the world.
—Joseph Campbell, *The Hero with a Thousand Faces* (1949)

Comparative mythologist Joseph Campbell is popularly remembered not for his academic achievements, but for his influence on the *Star Wars* movie franchise, which over the years has lovingly stolen its story templates from Campbell's writings about the "monomyth." Also known as the "Hero's Journey," the monomyth is a narrative archetype, common to cultures around the world, involving a protagonist who experiences a "call to adventure," leaves the comfort of the familiar for unknown horizons, encounters challenges and wonders in distant places, and returns home transformed.

The Hero's Journey formula made *Star Wars* popular with audiences because it explores ideals that are intrinsic to how we humans make narrative sense of who we are, who we want to be, and what in life is important. Myths predate humanity's rational understanding of the world, and—unlike more modern ideologies and institutions—they don't prescribe solutions so much as encourage action as a way to find purpose and fully engage with being alive.

In leaving home we don't just seek new places: We seek truer versions of ourselves. In confronting a journey's challenges, we don't just face fears and navigate obstacles: We encounter a new level of awareness and a heightened sense of aliveness. In coming back renewed and enlightened, we don't just see a once-familiar place in a new way: We arrive home better positioned to give back to the communities we left behind.

A JOURNEY IS A GOOD PRETEXT
TO SEEK CHANGE IN LIFE

When someone makes a decision, he is diving into a strong current that will carry him to places he had never dreamed of when
he first made the decision.

—Paulo Coelho, *The Alchemist* (1988)

For as long as people have taken journeys, the desire to see new places has always been mixed up with a desire for personal transformation. When the German poet Johann Wolfgang von Goethe traveled to Italy in the late eighteenth century, he considered the journey to be as inward-focused as it was outward. "My purpose in making this wonderful journey is not to delude myself, but to discover myself in the objects I see," he wrote. "Nothing, above all, is comparable to the new life that a reflective person experiences when he observes a new country. Though I am still always myself, I believe I have been changed to the very marrow of my bones."

For many people, the decision to depart on a long-dreamed-of journey is tied in with life transition—not just the time-honored travel impetus of school graduation, but the end of an employment contract, the end of a relationship, or the beginning of a new sense of life purpose. At home, we spend so many hours trapped in routines and obligations—sitting at desks, sitting in traffic-clogged commutes, sitting in front of entertainment screens—that we lose track of who we are and who we might become. On the road, away from those routines and obligations, we can, at the very least, find perspective.

Hence, travel is not just a pretext to behold sights and have experiences you previously knew only in your imagination; it's a chance to try out new versions of yourself as you come into a relationship with new places.

GIVE YOURSELF PERMISSION TO SEE THE WORLD FIRSTHAND

The world is wilder in all directions, more extravagant and bright. We are making hay when we should be making whoopee; we are raising tomatoes when we should be raising Cain or Lazarus.

—Annie Dillard, *Pilgrim at Tinker Creek* (1974)

Early in the twentieth century, a number of academic treatises sought to prove that wanderlust was in fact a form of neurosis. "Society has created its vagabonds, as it has created other defective classes," declared a 1907 Vassar College study cited in Dave Seminara's 2021 book *Mad Travelers*. One decade later, Seminara added, a Carnegie Institution paper asserted that people suffering from "feeble inhibitions" were unable to control their nomadic desires, and that "the more intellectual part of the population" asserted its civilizational superiority by taming its wandering impulses.

The idea that wanderlust should be regarded as a kind of mental illness never fully caught on in America, though long-term travel was seen as a transgressive act up through the "Hippie Trail" subculture of the 1970s, when hitting the road was considered a way of "dropping out" of society. As had been the case half a century earlier, however, living a nomadic life didn't make for a deviant lifestyle choice so much as a soul-expanding one. As the protagonist of James Michener's 1971 Hippie Trail novel *The Drifters* observed: "The 'drop-outs' that concerned me most were those adults who'd stayed home and made a virtue of their productivity."

Though the desire to travel long-term is no longer assumed to be a sign of neurosis (or countercultural resistance), it still flies in the face of conventional social wisdom. Your friends and neighbors will always offer up reasons that travel is selfish, or irresponsible, or best relegated to the distant future. Fortunately, the freedom to travel doesn't hinge on societal permission: It's something you give yourself.

DON'T SET LIMITS ON WHO CAN TRAVEL (INCLUDING YOU)

The Inuit traveled for generations by sledge or boat, and the knowledge they accumulated was used by European travelers to "discover" their regions.

—Tabish Khair, *Other Routes* (2005)

Reading old travel accounts makes one wonder about the fellow wanderers mentioned in passing by the presumed protagonists of the journeys. When Portuguese explorer Bartolomeu Dias left Lisbon for the Cape of Good Hope in 1487, for example, he brought along four African women to help explain his mission to locals encountered en route. Historians give us a clear sense for Dias's adventures, yet one is left wondering what happened to the woman who was put ashore in what is now Namibia with instructions to ask after the whereabouts of the legendary Christian king Prester John.

While centuries of literature would have us believe that travel is the exclusive birthright of well-funded ruling-class adventurers, most all classic travel accounts hint at the existence of less-privileged companions. Japanese noblewoman Sei Shonagon traveled with working-class servants in her tenth-century *Pillow Book;* Moroccan explorer Ibn Battuta sailed with Chinese concubines in his fourteenth-century *Travels.* Herman Melville based his novel *Moby-Dick* on the real-life voyage of the *Essex,* which counted seven black freedmen among its twenty-one-person crew; *Deadwood Dick,* the 1907 memoir by the formerly enslaved Nat Love, hints at the fact that as many as one in four cowboys wandering the American West were black.

The notion that travel is reserved for the privileged and the wealthy has always been a fiction. From the time of the ancient nomads, when women, men, and children all traveled together, sharing the duties of lives lived in motion, journeys have always been the prerogative of whoever has endeavored to take them, by whichever means were at their disposal.

THE BEST AGE TO TRAVEL IS WHATEVER AGE YOU ARE NOW

Without thinking too much about it first, pack a pillow and a blanket and see as much of the world as you can. One day it will be too late.

—Ghosh to Ashoke, in Jhumpa Lahiri's *The Namesake* (2004)

I was in my late twenties when I visited Europe for the first time. My journal entries from that initial journey, as I traveled from hostel to hostel in places like Latvia and Greece and Austria, were almost comical in their faint concern that I had perhaps grown "too old" to properly appreciate the European backpacker trail.

Decades later, having backpacked around Europe in my thirties and forties as well, I can see that the anxieties of my late twenties were not well founded. While there are (and, no doubt, always will be) a plethora of young people on indie-travel circuits worldwide, the freedom to wander doesn't hinge on age so much as attitude.

In fact, around the same time I was worrying about being in my late twenties as I traveled Europe, Australian ethnographer Klaus Westerhausen published a study asserting that age had ceased to be a core factor in backpacker culture. "There are those in their fifties and older engaging in long-term travel and adopting a way of life that previously had been the preserve of youth alone," he wrote. "[Travel] is open to all who subscribe to similar norms and values, irrespective of age or background."

This in mind, don't let concerns about your age—be you in your teens or your seventies—keep you from putting your travel dreams into action. The best age to travel is whatever age you are right now.

TRAVEL ALLOWS YOU TO TRY ON NEW VERSIONS OF YOURSELF

> We are not who we think we are when we are elsewhere. We can even become another person entirely. . . . We can surprise ourselves as well as being surprised.
>
> —Lucy R. Lippard, *On the Beaten Track* (2000)

Though English travel writer Bruce Chatwin garnered literary acclaim for his meditations on the nomadic life in books like *The Songlines* and *In Patagonia,* his own love of travel mixed an intellectual fascination with nomadism with his simple desire to escape the narrow social definitions of who he was supposed to be back home. "If you travel, you escape being labeled with class stereotypes," he said in a 1987 *Granta* interview. "I come from a very middle-class family. . . . Travel was an immense relief—it got rid of the pressure from above and from below. If you're out on the road, people have to take you at face value."

Indeed, if there is an advantage to embracing a nomadic life, it's that it leaves you less beholden to the obligations and expectations that define your workaday life. Away from the dull histories and constraints of how you're perceived back home, you are allowed to play games with your sense of self on the road—to expand your comfort zone, seek new experiences, and try on new versions of who it is you might like to be.

"Abroad, we are free of caste and job and standing; people cannot put a tag to us," wrote Pico Iyer in 2001. "Freed of inessential labels, we have the opportunity to come into contact with essential parts of ourselves—which may explain why we may feel most alive when far from home."

TIME IS PRECIOUS (BECAUSE TIME IS PASSING)

Why of your own accord postpone your real life to the distant future? Why wait for a place in the will of some wealthy old man, when you can be rich here and now?

—Seneca, *Letters from a Stoic* (65 C.E.)

When I visited Sumatra for the first time, I took a long-haul shared taxi from the Medan airport to the volcanic shores of Lake Toba. The trip took the better part of a day, but the driver kept everyone in the cab entertained by blasting *dangdut*—perky Indonesian folk songs that sounded like a cross between electropop techno and Bollywood show tunes.

Though most of the *dangdut* songs were sung in Bahasa, one English tune caught my attention. "It's now or never," the Indonesian singer crooned, "I ain't gonna live forever. I just want to live while I'm alive." The existential vibe of this lyric stuck with me, and when I later went online to track down the song's backstory, I discovered that it was not in fact a Sumatran folk song but a cover of "It's My Life," by the New Jersey pop-metal band Bon Jovi.

The idea that life is fleeting and needs to be embraced in the here and now is a notion that predates both pop-metal and *dangdut*. From the ancient book of Ecclesiastes, which declares that "it is *now* that God favors what you do," to poet Maya Angelou's assertion that "life is going to be short, no matter how long it is," the notion of "time wealth" has always been central to the philosophical notion of a well-lived life.

Actualizing this time wealth is often as simple as realizing that the purest form of treasure in life is, indeed, your time. Make plans accordingly.

MAKE THE MOST OF THE DAYS YOU'RE GIVEN

> Were you to live three thousand years, or even thirty thousand,
> remember that the sole life which a man can lose is that which
> he is living at the moment.
>
> —Marcus Aurelius, *Meditations* (180 C.E.)

In the 1993 movie *Groundhog Day*, the plot revolves around Phil Connors, a cynical TV weatherman played by Bill Murray, who gets stuck in a time loop while reporting from Punxsutawney, Pennsylvania. Doomed to live the same day again and again until he comes to terms with the moral potential of his own life, Phil Connors is thus forced to find—and embody—his best self over the course of thousands of repeated days.

Groundhog Day was a hit at the box office, but over time its most ardent fans have proven to be theologians and philosophers, who see the story as an existential allegory. "The curse is lifted when Bill Murray blesses the day he has just lived," wrote critic and historian Rick Brookhiser. "And his reward is that the day is taken from him. Loving life includes loving the fact that it goes."

In a way, we are all living an inversion of Bill Murray's *Groundhog Day* curse. Because we can't relive any of our given days, we're forced to make the most of the days we're given. And, because our time is scarce, we should take care not to postpone our fullest lives. If you dream of taking a far-flung journey, now is the time to start looking for ways to make it happen.

TRAVEL IS PART OF A LIFE WELL-LIVED

There is wisdom in turning as often as possible from the familiar to the unfamiliar: it keeps the mind nimble, it kills prejudice, and it fosters humor.

—George Santayana, "The Philosophy of Travel" (1964)

When Ulysses S. Grant's widow, Julia, wrote her memoirs, she counterbalanced recollections of her husband's tenure as a Civil War general and politician with memories of the round-the-world journey they undertook when his second presidential term ended. Nearly a third of Julia's book is dedicated to the journey, which took the couple on a meandering route through western and northern Europe, around the Mediterranean (including Spain, Italy, Turkey, and Jerusalem), and on to India, Thailand, China, and Japan.

Though as president Grant was understated and serious, he became more relaxed and extroverted on the road, seeking out the company of commoners, even as he rubbed shoulders with the likes of Queen Victoria, Pope Leo XIII, and Victor Hugo. In Italy he and Julia climbed Mount Vesuvius; in Egypt they sailed from Cairo to Luxor (Ulysses later recalled those weeks on the Nile as "among the happiest in my life"); in India they rode elephants and visited the Taj Mahal.

While the Grants' tour was seen by some contemporaries as an attempt to shore up his international savvy for future political ambitions, Ulysses himself viewed the journey as the actualization of a long-held dream and the capstone to an already full life. Upon returning home after a two-and-a-half-year journey, Grant declared that he enjoyed the simple novelty and vulnerability that came with traveling through unfamiliar lands. "A year and a half ago, I was homesick," he told reporters. "But the variation of scene and the kindness I met have done away with that feeling."

SEEK TO LIVE THE QUESTIONS NOW

You have brains in your head.
You have feet in your shoes.
You can steer yourself
any direction you choose.
—Theodor Seuss Geisel, *Oh, the Places You'll Go!* (1990)

etters to a Young Poet, Rainer Maria Rilke's classic book of life advice, began as correspondence with a nineteen-year-old Austrian military cadet. Though the young man had approached Rilke in the hope of getting feedback for his poetry, the elder Austrian broadened his advice to include insights about pursuing truth, finding love, and seeking a fuller range of human experience. "Don't search for the answers, which could not be given to you now, because you would not be able to live them," Rilke wrote. "Live the questions now. Perhaps then, someday far in the future, you will gradually, without even noticing it, live your way into the answer."

While Rilke's book is frequently gifted at graduations, my own college graduation yielded a curiously analogous advice compendium: *Oh, the Places You'll Go!*, the final book written by children's author Dr. Seuss. As with *Letters to a Young Poet*, Dr. Seuss's book addresses the reader directly as it dispenses insights for the journey of life. Though cheerful and upbeat, *Oh, the Places You'll Go!* also warns of bad times—of the fears and loneliness and confusions that can arise from any effort to seek a more interesting and engaged life.

The most ominous location in the Dr. Seuss story is "The Waiting Place," where people passively wait for things to happen rather than actively choosing to live their best lives. Like Rilke, Dr. Seuss thus encourages the reader to embrace uncertainty and be alive in the now—to find joy in not yet knowing exactly where you will go or what will happen when you get there.

THE FREEDOM TO TRAVEL DOESN'T HINGE ON MATERIAL WEALTH

Since time is all we have, we must measure its preciousness in units of freedom. Nothing else will do.
—James Wood, paraphrasing Martin Hägglund, in "Your Time Is Everything" (2019)

Skepticism about the connection of material wealth to a well-lived life goes back at least to the fourth century B.C.E., when the Greek philosopher Epicurus noted that "the acquisition of riches has been for many men not an end, but a change, of troubles."

This ancient notion has been borne out by the research of modern-day economists and psychologists. According to British economist Richard Layard, who studied economic growth in countries like Brazil and South Korea, money doesn't affect personal happiness within a given society past the first $10,000 of per capita income. In the United States, a 2012 Boston College study of households with a net worth of $25 million or more concluded that this wealth did not correspond to higher levels of happiness than those reported by middle-class folks.

Interestingly, researchers found that investing resources into experiences and relationships (rather than things) did correlate with a higher level of happiness. A 2014 Cornell University study found that inexpensive communal experiences, such as hiking, budget travel, and attending concerts, brought more life satisfaction—both in anticipation and in retrospective memory—than purchases like expensive electronics and luxury cars.

This in mind, "buying time" to make your dream travels happen isn't so much a matter of accumulating capital as of recalibrating your worldview to make better, more life-enriching use of the time you already own. That is, the truest form of wealth is expressed not in the things you own, but in the freedom to spend your time in a manner that enhances your life.

TRAVEL IS A WAY TO GAIN PERSPECTIVE ON WHAT "SUCCESS" IS

If you are too obsessed with success, you will forget to live. If you have learned only how to be a success, your life has probably been wasted.

—Thomas Merton, *Love and Living* (1979)

In 2005, when comedian Dave Chappelle departed for South Africa after having turned down $50 million to renew his Comedy Central TV show, American media was rife with speculation that he was suffering from either drug addiction or mental illness. Chappelle later expressed befuddlement at these rumors, noting that his time in Africa had allowed him to reflect on his own spiritual self-interests. "I was in this very successful place," he said in a 2017 interview, "but the emotional content of it didn't feel like anything I imagined success should feel like. I just didn't feel right."

If the decision to turn down $50 million caused people to question Chappelle's sanity, it likely had less to do with the comedian's mental health than with the material metric by which we measure "success" in the United States. As the writer and mystic Thomas Merton had pointed out a few decades earlier, "People may spend their whole lives climbing the ladder of success only to find, once they reach the top, that the ladder is leaning against the wrong wall." If the ladder of success leaves a person feeling ambivalent about the material trappings of wealth, it's perfectly fair for that person to find a quieter, more personal definition of what success can be.

One gift of travel is that, in compelling us to prioritize what we experience over what we own, it offers a useful perspective on how we might choose to measure our own success.

January 16

DON'T LET HABITS LIMIT LIFE'S POSSIBILITIES

> We relax back into the molds of habit. They are secure, they
> bind us and keep us contained at the expense of freedom.
> —Robyn Davidson, *Tracks* (1980)

In recalling his one-year sojourn in Italy, American author Anthony Doerr reflected on the ways habit helps us manage our way of being in the world. "Without habit, the beauty of the world would overwhelm us," he wrote in his 2008 memoir *Four Seasons in Rome*. "Imagine if we only got to see a cumulonimbus cloud or Cassiopeia or a snowfall once a century; there'd be pandemonium in the streets." Yet, Doerr added, while habit helps us get through the day in a more efficient manner, it can also limit our sense of what is possible. "Habit is dangerous, too," he wrote. "The act of seeing can quickly become unconscious and automatic."

Indeed, one of the reasons travel can lead to a sense of awakening is that leaving our home habits allows us to see things with eyes undimmed by familiarity. At home, we tend to toy with our own habits by creating low-stakes possibility within the familiar—activities like going to bars to meet new people, or dabbling in novel fads or hobbies—but on the road, away from our routines, our life becomes inseparable from possibility itself.

In a sense, it is not until we leave the constraints of our habit-driven lives that we can discover the raw energy and wildness that lies beyond our domesticated way of interacting with the world. In departing what is familiar and predictable—in leaving ourselves open to new challenges and surprises—we find ourselves embracing fuller, freer lives.

DON'T LET THE RITUALS OF STATUS LIMIT YOUR LIFE OPTIONS

We buy things we don't need, with money we don't have, to impress people we don't like.

—Chuck Palahniuk, *Fight Club* (1996)

At the beginning of David Fincher's 1999 movie *Fight Club,* Edward Norton's protagonist—feeling alienated by the dull realities of American office-drone life—finds his only sense of purpose in buying new lifestyle accessories. A strange set of circumstances introduces Norton to Brad Pitt's Tyler Durden, who has an aphoristic way of summarizing their plight. "Advertising has us chasing cars and clothes, working jobs we hate so we can buy things we don't need," he says. "The things you own end up owning you."

Though not initially a hit, *Fight Club* eventually became a cult sensation, compelling its viewers to ponder the limitations of American consumerist life. Curiously, while the movie itself was a dark-hearted satire—with its characters seeking meaningful existence in basement fistfights and increasingly dark pranks—many fans took its message at face value. In the decade after the movie's release, literal fight clubs were reported to have sprung up in places like Silicon Valley, a Seattle megachurch, and Princeton University.

While it might feel obvious to suggest that Ed Norton and Brad Pitt's characters would have been better served by a yearlong round-the-world journey than the diminishing returns of low-stakes fisticuffs, the very idea makes for an interesting thought experiment. In an age when far too many people still abide by status rituals like conspicuous consumption, fashion, and the mindless acquisition of new things, the most sensible way to resist such compulsions might not be to punch strangers in the face, but to buy a plane ticket (or strap on a pair of walking shoes) and humbly seek out more meaningful horizons.

DON'T TAKE YOUR HOURS ON EARTH
FOR GRANTED

Each of your breaths is a priceless jewel, since each of them is irreplaceable and, once gone, can never be retrieved. Do not be like the deceived fools who are joyous because each day their wealth increases while their life shortens.

—Al-Ghazali, *Beginning of Guidance* (1109 C.E.)

The Western notion of a mechanical clock ticking off standardized minutes and hours is a comparatively recent invention, dating back to the monasteries of the Middle Ages. For monks, creating a synchronous clock that ran independent of the sun was useful for coordinating night prayers. As the centuries progressed, the idea of time as a mathematical (rather than organic) concept was fully embraced by the realm of commerce, giving rise to mechanization, industrialization, and the modern world as we know it today.

Where humans' notion of time was once pegged to the sun and its metaphors, our understanding of time eventually became beholden to the logic and metaphors of machinery. Tellingly—perhaps because the ancients were more connected to an older, more eternal notion of time—the sundials of the Roman Republic were inscribed with mottos extolling the existential tenor of the hours they measured: *lente hora, celeriter anni* (an hour passes slowly, but the years go by quickly); *festina lente* (make haste, slowly); *memento vivere* (remember to live); *carpe diem* (seize the day).

In planning and prioritizing the events of your life, your dream travels included, seek to embrace this more ancient, organic notion of time. "Remember what time is," Ryan Holiday wrote in *Stillness Is the Key*. "It's your life, it's your flesh and blood, that you can never get back."

TRAVEL IS NOT ABOUT ESCAPE, BUT ENGAGEMENT

For me, travel has rarely been about escape. The motivation is to go—to meet life, and myself, head-on along the road.
—Andrew McCarthy, *The Longest Way Home* (2012)

American poet Louise Glück narrates her 1992 poem "Field Flowers" from the perspective of a flower, which takes humans to task for dreaming about heaven rather than being fully present in nature. "Better than earth?" the flower chides. "How would you know, who are neither here nor there, standing in our midst?" Glück's observation about humans' tendency to obsess about the hypothetical perfection of distant realities has a parallel in the way we often frame travel as an "escape" from the lives we live at home. This is a common way of describing journeys (a popular 1990s travel magazine called itself *Escape*), but thinking of travel purely as a contrast to the banal constraints of the familiar overlooks the ways that travel can be in dynamic conversation with the familiar.

In an essay called "On Travel as a Cure for Discontent," the Roman philosopher Seneca pointed out that no journey is a true escape, since we bring our own shortcomings and idiosyncrasies along with us. "Each man flees himself," he wrote. "But to what end if he does not escape himself?" In other words, the best journeys aren't tied up in the kinds of whimsical distractions and self-indulgences that provide contrast to the lives we've created back home; done mindfully, travel actively enhances the lives we've cultivated back home.

RUMORS OF THE DEATH OF TRAVEL
HAVE BEEN EXAGGERATED

Even locked in our homes during the pandemic, the gaze we turned on our own cities was touristic, for the city that flashed onto our screens in our confinement fulfilled the dream of every tourist—a place without other tourists, which is to say: without ourselves.

—Marco D'Eramo, *The World in a Selfie* (2021)

Alexander Kinglake's 1844 travel memoir *Eothen* is considered a classic, in part because it didn't showcase the kind of scientific or historical erudition that featured in contemporary English travel books. In describing a horseback journey through the Ottoman Empire, Kinglake ignored matters of political and scientific gravitas, focusing instead on the fanciful diversions—things like the drinking habits of Syrian monks, or the curious abundance of fleas in Tiberias—that made the journey fascinating for him.

Part of what made *Eothen*'s informal tone so remarkable was that Kinglake was traveling at a time when the Ottoman Empire was suffering an outbreak of bubonic plague. Though other authors might have used this detail to ratchet up the narrative drama, Kinglake treated it as another irritating (if occasionally perilous) travel obstacle—outlining his strategies to avoid the dreaded quarantine hospitals in Serbia, poking fun at Europeans' paranoia about contagion in Constantinople, and marveling at Egyptians' hospitality in the face of the disease in Cairo.

Though *Eothen* doesn't leave the reader eager to set out on a journey in a time of plague, it does underscore how travel has always existed in tandem with cycles of global uncertainty. Despite media speculation about the "death of travel" whenever a pandemic (or war, or natural disaster) upends world stability, taking a journey will always be an option for those willing to leaven their travel plans with equal doses of patience, precaution, flexibility, and optimism.

TRAVEL CAN BE A CLASSIC RITE OF PASSAGE IN LIFE

We find ourselves in strange places, doing strange things and we know not why, strange things that seem insignificant at the time and yet prepare us for who we one day will be. . . . We each have a certain destiny and the real adventure in life is to discover it; to discover how we may fully develop into who we are.

—Eddy L. Harris, *Native Stranger* (1992)

In West Sumatra's Minangkabau Highlands, young people undergo a coming-of-age ritual known as *merantau*, which involves leaving the community to seek *rantau* (roughly "anywhere but here"), form new relationships, learn practical skills, and accrue life experiences. Though *merantau* literally translates as "wandering," its functional meaning is more along the lines of "go make yourself useful." In leaving home, Minangkabau youth thus aim to become more effective members of society when they return home.

The closest thing we have to *merantau* in the industrialized world is heading off to university after secondary school—an institutionalized way to create separation from home, learn new concepts, test self-sufficiency, and ease transition into a new life phase. Some British youth embark on a travel-intensive "gap year" just before university, and young German craftspeople have a pre-employment travel rite called *wanderjahr*, but these coming-of-age rites aren't a societal expectation so much as a private option.

Fortunately for those of us in the industrialized world, the rites of passage that accompany a journey need not be confined to one's youth. Regardless of how old you are, life on the road allows you to separate yourself from the comforts of the familiar, meet people you might never encounter otherwise, embrace the process of self-discovery, and return home transformed. Invariably, the rejuvenated sense of life purpose that flows out of the journey comes with the realization that creating purpose is itself a lifelong endeavor.

MANY HAVE TRAVELED THE ROAD
BEFORE YOU

History without travel is unthinkable. First, humanity overspread the earth through the process of migration; later, through exploration and resettlement, the movement began towards the one world which we now inhabit.

—Peter Whitfield, *Travel: A Literary History* (2012)

When British writer Robert Byron visited the ancient ruins of Persepolis in Iran in the 1930s, he marveled at the idea of all the travelers who'd come there before him. "In the old days you arrived by horse," he wrote in his 1937 book *The Road to Oxiana*. "You made a camp there, while the columns and winged beasts kept their solitude beneath the stars, and not a sound or movement disturbed the empty moonlit plain. You thought of Darius and Xerxes and Alexander. You were alone with the ancient world."

Though Byron evoked this in part to illustrate the anticlimax of arriving at Persepolis by car, his observation underscores that, as travelers, we find our way in the footsteps of generations of wanderers who've come before us. Journeying has been a key motif in humanity's oldest literature, going back to the *Odyssey* and the book of Exodus. Many of the basic metaphors used to describe storytelling structure—terms like *quest* and *picaresque*—have roots in travel. Trade, migration, exploration, diaspora, and pilgrimage have, throughout history, shaped humanity's understanding of the world, and of our place in it.

In leaving on a journey you're joining a long tradition of pilgrims and vagabonds (and *bhikkhus* and *goliards* and *sannyasins*) who have traveled the road before you. Nomadism is the original, prehistoric condition of humankind, long predating our attachments to settled places. In giving yourself over to the obstacles and serendipities of the road, you are returning to a decidedly ancient way of being in the world.

TRAVEL CAN BE A WAY OF
CULTIVATING HAPPINESS

> There is no happiness for him who does not travel. The fortune
> of he who is sitting, sits; it rises when he rises; it sleeps when he
> sleeps; it moves when he moves. Therefore wander!
> —Mahidasa Aitareya, in a hymn from the *Rig Veda* (c. 800 B.C.E.)

When a young Swiss traveler named Nicolas Bouvier drove a Fiat 500 sedan from Geneva to Afghanistan in the mid-1950s, he felt a curious welling of emotion as he dealt with the workaday challenges of driving across Central Asia. Reflecting on his long hours of navigating muddy roads, his cold nights spent sleeping outdoors, and his quiet ritual of brewing tea each morning, he realized he would cherish these moments in his memory. "The word 'happiness' seems too thin and limited to describe what has happened," he wrote in his 1963 memoir, *The Way of the World.* "In the end, the bedrock of existence is not made up of family, or work, or what others say or think of you, but of moments like these, when you are exalted by a transcendent power that is more serene than love."

What's remarkable about Bouvier's recollection is how—in trying to describe these otherwise unremarkable moments of his journey—he evokes a counterintuitive notion of how happiness can be cultivated. In embracing the joys and hardships of his multi-month drive, Bouvier wasn't just creating memories; he was creating meaning. Happiness, he realized, is not a product to be acquired and fine-tuned; it is a *by-product* of a life that is being lived in a fully engaged way.

Travel is thus best understood not as a color-by-numbers formula for creating happiness so much as a pretext for discovering it in unexpected moments.

TRAVEL CAN BRING YOU TRUE NEWS
OF THE WORLD

> The Internet now makes facts so effortless to obtain that there is
> the illusion of knowledge where none actually exists. . . . The
> public is increasingly removed from the intangible essences and
> minutiae of distant places that explain the present, and thus
> forewarn of the future.
>
> —Robert D. Kaplan, "Cultivating Loneliness" (2006)

The phrase "man bites dog" dates back to the rise of popular newspaper journalism in the nineteenth century, when it was accepted that an unusual event (a man biting a dog) was more newsworthy than a common one (a dog biting a man). Though meant as a critique of journalism's capacity to give an accurate depiction of the world, "man bites dog" continues to be an apt metaphor in an age of clickbait news headlines.

In 2006, shortly before the social media "attention economy" doubled down on the inherent sensationalism of news reporting, author Robert D. Kaplan wrote an essay for the *Columbia Journalism Review* arguing that travel writing was as essential as news reporting in getting a sense for what life is like in distant countries.

"Travel writing is more important than ever as a means to reveal the vivid reality of places that get lost in the elevator music of 24-hour media reports," Kaplan wrote. "Rather than interrogate strangers, which is essentially what reporters do, the travel writer gets to know people, and reveals them as they reveal themselves." Whereas news reports fixate on wars, famines, and catastrophes, he added, travel writers are free to convey the "individual beauty, honesty, and friendliness" that they find in distant places.

As individual travelers, we have the privilege of looking beyond secondhand reports of the world, and bearing personal witness to a world that is far friendlier and more welcoming than what we see in the man-bites-dog tenor of news headlines.

FOR A MORE CREATIVE BRAIN, TRAVEL

> There are deeper reasons to travel—itches and tickles on the underbelly of the unconscious mind. We go where we need to go, and then try to figure out what we're doing there.
> —Jeff Greenwald, *Shopping for Buddhas* (1990)

In his 2009 book *Answers from the Heart*, Vietnamese monk Thich Nhat Hanh recalls meeting an American Buddhist scholar who suggested he could write more poems if he spent less time tending to the lettuce in his garden. "Everyone can grow lettuce," she told him, "but not everyone can write poems like you do." Nhat Hanh replied: "If I don't grow lettuce, I can't write poems."

Just as gardening can enable poetry, travel is a ritual act that stimulates human creativity in ways unrelated to the act itself. In a 2015 *Atlantic* article entitled "For a More Creative Brain, Travel," journalist Brent Crane noted that going to unfamiliar new places can enhance our cognitive flexibility. "New sounds, smells, language, tastes, sensations, and sights spark different synapses in the brain and may have the potential to revitalize the mind," he wrote. "Cognitive flexibility is the mind's ability to jump between different ideas, a key component of creativity." Crane also quoted American neuroscientist Mary Helen Immordino-Yang, who found that cross-cultural travel in particular can strengthen a traveler's sense of self. "Our ability to differentiate our own beliefs and values is tied up in the richness of the cultural experiences that we have had," she told him.

In this way, travel strengthens our neuroplasticity by the simple act of turning us into cultural and geographical novices. By the very process of encountering new sights, smells, concepts, and landscapes firsthand, we are able to look beyond who we are and get a glimpse of who we could become.

THERE IS NO SHAME IN TRAVELING FOR THE SHEER FUN OF IT

To do things for fun smacks of levity, immorality almost, in our utilitarian world. But I must admit that for my own part I traveled single-mindedly for fun.

—Freya Stark, *The Valley of the Assassins* (1934)

Young people are often seen by their elders as less than serious and given to self-indulgent frivolity, but I've actually found the opposite to be the case when giving public lectures about long-term travel. Whereas midcareer professionals and even retirees are not ashamed to admit that they aim to travel for the sheer fun of it, I've found that university students in particular feel they need an educational or volunteer-service pretext to spend a few months on the other side of the world.

Sincere as these young aspiring travelers may be, learning or serving need not be mutually exclusive with having fun. In fact, many a journey undertaken with whimsical or recreational motives ultimately transforms into a deeply educational and philanthropic enterprise. As Lord Stanhope advised his Grand Tour–bound son in 1750, "Pleasures are not time lost, provided they are the pleasures of a rational being."

Indeed, given the right attitude, one need not have earnest-minded travel motives for the journey to eventually become an illuminating endeavor. As often as not, the most transformative and life-affecting travel experiences flow out from—not in contrast to—a desire to enjoy each day of the journey. In wandering the world attuned to our own passions, we make ourselves more receptive to what people and places can teach us.

WHY YOU GO SOMEPLACE IS LESS IMPORTANT THAN JUST GOING

Photographer Yousuf Karsh and his wife were having lunch with astronaut Neil Armstrong after a photo session. Armstrong politely questioned the couple about the many different countries they had visited. "But Mr. Armstrong," protested Mrs. Karsh, "you've walked on the moon. We want to hear about your travels." "But that's the only place I've ever been," replied Armstrong apologetically.

—From the *Little, Brown Book of Anecdotes* (1985)

For the aristocratic Roman tourists who traveled the Mediterranean seaboard two millennia ago, choosing which places to visit was the least difficult aspect of the journey. "For those first tourists, the whole point of travel was to go where everyone else was going," wrote Tony Perrottet in his 2002 book *Pagan Holiday*. "Sightseeing was a form of pilgrimage."

While Western tourists have developed a far more individualistic system of travel motivations over the past two thousand years, postmodern pilgrimage may well come in the form of movie tourism—of *Star Wars* buffs who visit the Moroccan desert to feel as if they're on the desert planet Tatooine, or *Game of Thrones* fans who stroll the streets of Dubrovnik imagining they're at King's Landing. Yet just as an interest in the Indiana Jones films might lead to an appreciation for Nabataean history (or Bedouin cuisine) while envisioning *The Last Crusade* in Jordan's rock city Petra, most engaged travelers find far more than they'd dreamed of seeing when they were first deciding where in the world they might wander.

If in doubt, the reasons that inspire you to visit certain places are far less important than leaving yourself open to what you discover when you arrive there. To paraphrase a sentiment attributed to *Alice in Wonderland* author Lewis Carroll: "If you're never exactly sure where you're going, any road will take you there."

MAKING TIME IS MORE VITAL
THAN MAKING MONEY

> We are brainwashed by our economic system until we end up in
> a tomb beneath a pyramid of playthings that divert our atten-
> tion from the sheer idiocy of the charade. The years thunder by.
> The dreams of youth grow dim.
>
> —Sterling Hayden, *Wanderer* (1963)

John Muir is best known as an environmental philosopher whose conservation efforts led to the creation of America's national park system. Before his name became synonymous with the Yosemite Valley, however, he earned a reputation as a successful businessman. Specifically, Muir thrived managing his father-in-law's California orchards, at one point making a handsome profit from exporting grapes to Hawaii.

Instead of reinvesting his fortune into more ambitious entrepreneurial enterprises, however, Muir elected to sock away his dividends, retire from the agriculture trade, and live a life more aligned with this passion for exploring nature. "I made the choice to become a tramp," Muir would joke when asked about the business deals he was missing out on. Once, when a friend asked him if he envied the ever-growing wealth of the railroad magnate E. H. Harriman, Muir quipped, "I am already richer than Harriman. I have all the money I want, and he hasn't."

As Muir knew, success in life hinges less on accomplishment itself than on the attitude with which we make the most of our accomplishments. All too often, we postpone our deepest travel dreams for fear that we cannot afford them, when in fact the freedom to travel (or actualize any experience-focused dream) isn't the result of a hypothetical sum of riches: It is the result of a conscious decision to use whatever money we've saved up to create enough time to make our dreams happen.

CULTIVATING A KIND OF POVERTY MAKES TRAVEL POSSIBLE

In my hut this spring
There is nothing—
There is everything.

—Yamaguchi Sodo, from *Haiku Poems* (1683)

A story from the Buddhist tradition involves a farmer who, upset that his cows had run away, stumbled across the Buddha in a panic to find them. When the distraught man had moved on, the Buddha turned to his disciples, saying, "Dear friends, you should be very happy. You don't have any cows to lose." In his 2006 book *Reconciliation*, Thich Nhat Hanh suggested that we take out paper and write down the names of our "cows"—the possessions (and longed-for possessions) we think might be crucial to our well-being—and see if we're capable of releasing them. "If we look deeply," he wrote, "we may realize that these things are obstacles to our true joy and happiness."

The notion of winnowing your possessions through the principles of "strategic poverty" also appears in the letters of the first-century C.E. Roman philosopher Seneca the Younger, who wrote to his friend Lucilius with the following challenge: "Set aside a certain number of days, during which you shall be content with the scantiest and cheapest fare, with coarse and rough dress, saying to yourself the while: 'Is this the condition that I feared?'" Inevitably, living with less doesn't result in poverty so much as a perspective on what in life is really necessary.

As you consider the ways that dreamed-of journeys might enhance your life, remember that it is not money alone that affords the freedom to travel, but the willingness to "release your cows"—that is, to cultivate the kind of strategic poverty that will enable you to live a life rich in experience.

January 30

ANTICIPATING THE JOURNEY IS
A PART OF THE JOURNEY

----

*When I travel, I get nervous like for a date. Will the city like me?
Am I wearing the right dress? It's a little sick in the belly but that
can turn into a fire if things go well.*

—Jessa Crispin, in a 2015 interview

In her 2021 memoir *Between Two Kingdoms*, American author Suleika Jaouad recounted a friend's theory that discrete journeys actually consist of three separate trips—the trip of anticipation, the trip that plays out on the road, and the trip that is remembered afterward. "The key is to try to keep all three as separate as possible," he tells her. "The key is to be present wherever you are right now."

After the travel phase of a trip is in motion, it's easy to forget how relevant and affecting its anticipation—that initial emotional stage of the journey—can be. Psychologists have found that the happiness one finds on the road begins while you're still at home, dreaming about the landscapes and cuisines and people that await you. Indeed, one of my more thankless jobs when I was young involved mowing lawns in the dreary Seattle drizzle as I saved up for my first vagabonding trip—yet that experience was inseparable from the ebullience I felt as I accumulated the money to make my long-held travel dreams a reality.

"Not just unphotographable, anticipation frequently goes unacknowledged, or at the least, unappreciated," wrote Thomas Swick in his 2016 book *The Joys of Travel*. "Still, we are all familiar with it: the thrill of picking a destination, singling out a country, a city, or an island, and then picturing ourselves there, unburdened and happy. We start the countdown to our departure. We now have someplace to look forward to."

THE BIGGEST DANGER OF TRAVEL
MIGHT BE DECIDING NOT TO GO

Fear is inevitable, I have to accept that, but I cannot allow it to paralyze me.

—Isabel Allende, *The Sum of Our Days* (2008)

For as long as would-be travelers have yearned to journey to distant places, there have been people telling them that wandering in other lands is self-indulgent and dangerous. Such sour advice does not always arise from good-faith motivations. In medieval Europe, for example, the Church saw travel as a threat to its own rules and hierarchies. "Wandering was a form of pollution, of social mixing, and a disarticulation of established distinctions and categories," Eric J. Leed wrote in his 1991 book *The Mind of the Traveler*.

Often, we are conditioned to fear travel not because it's more dangerous than life at home, but because it has the potential to jar us out of our own comfortable routines and prejudices. Travel can at times be challenging, but it is through overcoming challenges that we grow into fuller, more capable versions of ourselves. Indeed, the biggest danger in considering a journey might not be the hypothetical scenarios we fear, but the more immediate temptation to stay home and let those fears limit who we might become.

"What gives value to travel is fear," French philosopher Albert Camus wrote in his journal in 1935. "It is the fact that, at a certain moment, when we are so far from our own country . . . we are seized by a vague fear, and an instinctive desire to go back to the protection of old habits. This is the most obvious benefit of travel. At that moment we are feverish but also porous, so that the slightest touch makes us quiver to the depths of our being. . . . Travel, which is like a greater and graver science, brings us back to ourselves."

A JOURNEY BEGINS THE MOMENT
YOU DECIDE TO DO IT

- -

Travel is mostly about dreams—dreaming of landscapes or cities, imagining yourself in them, murmuring the bewitching place
names, and then finding a way to make the dream come true.
—Paul Theroux, "Great American Roadtrip" (2009)

Were I to pinpoint when my first vagabonding trip began, it would not be the morning I headed out on Oregon Route 99W in a Volkswagen Vanagon. Nor was it the months I'd spent saving money from a Seattle landscaping job and building a fold-out bed in the van. In retrospect, the trip really began three years earlier, in the summer of my twentieth year, when I decided I was going to make a long-term road trip across North America a reality.

I'd been working the graveyard shift in a Wichita supermarket that summer. Anxious at the prospect of a lifetime of work, I concluded I needed to get my pent-up travel dreams out of my system. On my off nights, I sat alone in the living room of my parents' house, stringing beads into a handmade necklace and envisioning the dizzy possibilities my USA adventure might hold.

A few years later, two and a half months into my van journey, I met an Ohio-born college girl named Valerie and kissed her as the sun came up over a beach in Florida. As the daylight flared across the Atlantic, I took the beaded necklace from my own neck and draped it over hers, telling her I'd been dreaming of her when I'd made it.

As besotted with romantic bravado as that youthful moment was, I had, in my own way, been telling Valerie the truth. To this day, I believe that all life-affecting journeys, and the unexpected wonders they promise, become real the moment you decide they will happen.

PUT YOUR DREAMS INTO ACTION NOW

> For all of the most important things, the timing always sucks. . . .
> Conditions are never perfect. "Someday" is a disease that will
> take your dreams to the grave with you. If it's important to you,
> just do it and correct course along the way.
> —Tim Ferriss, *The 4-Hour Workweek* (2007)

In her 2011 book *The Top Five Regrets of the Dying*, which was based on interviews with scores of hospice patients, Australian palliative care nurse Bronnie Ware noted that the most common regret among people facing death was that they had lived too much of their lives based on others' expectations. "When people realize that their life is almost over and look back clearly on it, it is easy to see how many dreams have gone unfulfilled," Ware wrote. "Health brings a freedom very few realize, until they no longer have it."

One of the biggest impediments to travel dreams is the notion that these dreams can be put off until a later time in life—that, instead of finding creative ways to carve out time to make a long-term journey happen in the near future, folks wait for milestones like retirement to dictate their departure plans. Even young people who aren't yet committed to a vocation can be reluctant to embrace their dream travels for fear of being less employable at the outset of their adult careers. Thus relegated to an intangible time known as "someday," many dream trips never happen.

When Kenyan marathoner Eliud Kipchoge was asked to reflect on his life philosophy by the *New York Times* in 2018, he put a playful spin on a proverb that dates back to ancient Chinese times. "The best time to plant a tree was 25 years ago," he quipped. "The second-best time to plant a tree is today."

LIFE IS A FINITE ENDEAVOR (SO IF YOU DREAM OF TRAVEL, TRAVEL)

Live, don't know how long,
And die, don't know when;
Must go, don't know where;
I am astonished I am so cheerful.
—Verses attributed to Holy Roman Emperor Maximilian I (c. 1500)

Not long after Adam Yauch of the seminal hip-hop group Beastie Boys died of parotid cancer in 2012, his bandmate Mike D elected to pack up his family and seek a nomadic life in Asia. "After what happened with Adam, I realized that life can be short," he said in a 2018 *New York* magazine interview. "Especially being a parent, the moments I appreciate most are when I'm with my kids and we're all experiencing something together."

The death of a friend or loved one has famously compelled people to embark on personal journeys, from the titular protagonist's wanderings in the four-thousand-year-old Mesopotamian *Epic of Gilgamesh* through the long-haul hike Cheryl Strayed recounted in her 2012 memoir *Wild*. Indeed, witnessing the mortality of people close to us sharpens the urgency to live more fully in the face of our own mortality. "Life would suddenly seem wonderful to us if we were threatened to die," novelist Marcel Proust told a French newspaper in 1922. "Just think of how many projects, travels, love affairs, studies, it—our life—hides from us, made invisible by our laziness which, certain of a future, delays them incessantly."

Fortunately, pondering our own mortality need not be seen as a fixation on death so much as a fixation on life and the potential it contains. As Eleanor Roosevelt wrote in her 1960 book *You Learn by Living*: "The purpose of life is to live it, to taste experience to the utmost, to reach out eagerly and without fear for newer and richer experience."

EMBRACING TIME IS MORE IMPORTANT THAN "OPTIMIZING" IT

The commodification of time sets the terms of almost the whole of the American conversation, time in its current usages—overtime, downtime, spending time, saving time, killing time, buying time—is nearly always a synonym for money.
—Lewis H. Lapham, "Captain Clock" (2014)

The ancient Roman philosopher Seneca often evoked the inevitability of death in urging the reader not to postpone the most important things in life. "Who reckons the worth of each day," he wrote, "who understands that he is dying daily?" Seneca's reasoning was tied to the Latin concept of *memento mori,* or "remember death"—the notion that our time in life is a limited resource, and we should take care in how we spend (or squander) it.

Because Seneca had an aphoristic way of putting things, it's common to see his quotes making the online rounds in meme form. "No one sets a value on time; all use it lavishly as if it cost nothing," one Seneca meme reads. "It is not that we have a short space of time, but that we waste much of it," reads another.

Curiously, when I see Seneca's quotes in meme form online, they're often used to illustrate the need for time optimization rather than time wealth—to urge people to streamline their approach to time, rather than to live more fully within its riches. Granted, time optimization can be useful, but the whole concept of time as Seneca understood it was different from the mechanized abstractions that dominate our twenty-first-century understanding of time.

The first step in finding the time to travel comes in uncoupling our understanding of time from utilitarian abstraction and seeing it as the very substance of life. Freed from the compulsion to "use" time, we thus find ways to embrace it.

INVENT A MISSION, THEN PLAN
YOUR TRAVELS AROUND IT

- -

> Travel is still the most intense mode of learning. If you get the chance to travel, just do it.
>
> —Kevin Kelly, in a 2018 interview

In the early 1970s, a New Jersey teenager named Kevin Kelly dreamed of photographing the wonders of Asia for *National Geographic*. When a phone call to the magazine's office yielded little interest, Kelly decided to quit college and travel there anyway. Departing for Taiwan with one change of clothes and five hundred rolls of film, his self-initiated photo assignment wound up taking him around Asia for most of the decade. While his fellow backpackers partied their days away and aimlessly wandered from place to place, Kelly's journey had a focus. "I had given myself an assignment," he recalled later. "I was out all day, taking photos and exploring, traveling hard, always moving."

At a moment in history when the rise of mass tourism has come to offer all manner of entertainments for travelers, sometimes the best strategy for embracing a journey is to seek interests rather than diversions. An entire subgenre of travel books is about inventing a self-directed quest (seeking out fortune-tellers in Asia; drinking *kava* in the South Pacific; hitchhiking through Ireland carrying a mini-fridge), and invariably these journeys are less about the quest itself than what the authors learn along the way.

Kevin Kelly never became a full-time photographer—he went on to help pioneer internet culture in California, co-founding *Wired* magazine in 1993. Yet he credits his Asia journey with transforming his way of being in the world. "What you get by achieving your goals is not as important as what you become by achieving your goals," he said. "Photography made me get out. It was my excuse to get out and see the world."

FIND A PLACE YOU CARE ABOUT, AND MAKE A PILGRIMAGE

Pilgrimage has always been a pretext. It's a way to have a trip with some higher motive.
— Gideon Lewis-Kraus, *A Sense of Direction* (2012)

One of the ironies of Gideon Lewis-Kraus's pilgrimage memoir *A Sense of Direction* was that the author was initially more interested in the idea of pilgrimage than in taking a specific one. "Pretty much anything can be described as a pilgrimage," he noted in a 2012 interview. "People talk about pilgrimages to Graceland, or Cooperstown, or to see *Saturn Devouring His Son* at the Prado . . . so one of the challenges I faced was how to limit the discussion." Lewis-Kraus eventually settled on the Camino de Santiago in Spain, followed by the Shikoku pilgrimage in Japan and the Rosh Hashana pilgrimage in Ukraine. "What it ultimately came down to, for me, was the idea of pilgrimage as pretext," he said. "It's an arduous trip where the eventual arrival is generally beside the point, at least in retrospect."

Since ancient times, part of the point of taking a pilgrimage was seeking to experience the corporeal reality of a place you've venerated in your imagination. For Buddhists or Muslims this might mean Bodh Gaya or Mecca, though the same principle can apply to painters seeking Frida Kahlo's La Casa Azul in Mexico City, poets traveling to visit Basho's grave at Japan's Gichu-ji temple, or golfers journeying to play a round at Scotland's Old Course at St. Andrews.

As you think about where in the world you might want to travel, think of people and places you care about, and consider honoring them with pilgrimages. Part of the point in making a journey of veneration is, after all, the effort it requires, and the meanderings it engenders along the way.

TRAVEL IS NOT A STANDARDIZED
CONSUMER PRODUCT

> The modern American tourist . . . has come to expect both more
> strangeness and more familiarity than the world naturally offers.
> He has come to believe that he can have a lifetime of adventure
> in two weeks and all the thrills of risking his life without any real
> risk at all.
>
> —Daniel Boorstin, *The Image* (1962)

Ever since the rise of crowdsourced travel-planning apps like Trip-Advisor and Yelp in the 2010s, humor websites have occasionally featured roundups of the sites' most asinine destination reviews. Apparently, app users have complained that the Atlantic Ocean is too salty, that the people of Spain speak too much Spanish, that the *Mona Lisa* is "just a little painting," that the Grand Canyon is "just a big hole in the ground."

Moronic as these reviews sound, there is something just as fatuous in the broader compulsion to regard travel as a consumer experience rather than a possibility-filled encounter with new places. When seen as a product that can be critiqued in the same manner as running shoes or dish detergent, travel becomes subject to insipid disappointments that say less about the places we visit than the expectations we've attached to them. To be sure, travel has become an industry that is subject to market forces, but—by its very definition—a journey is not something that can be standardized for our convenience.

Indeed, as much as tourism marketers and influencers offer us Platonic fantasies of timeless beauty and empty beaches, the world itself is subject to traffic jams and construction noise, beggars and bar touts, rolling blackouts and daylong rainstorms. Realizing that engaged journeys are mixed up with discomforts and imperfections can be a first step in leaving yourself open to experiences that go beyond what was advertised.

NO LIST OF TRAVEL RECOMMENDATIONS IS EVER AUTHORITATIVE

What does culture want? To make infinity comprehensible. . . .
How does one attempt to grasp the incomprehensible? Through
lists, through catalogs, through collections in museums and
through encyclopedias and dictionaries.
                                   —Umberto Eco, *The Infinity of Lists* (2009)

Years ago, while writing a deadline-driven column for Yahoo
Travel, I dashed off a half-baked article outlining my ten favorite
places to visit in the United States. Though the article wasn't particularly well-written, it went viral by simple virtue of the fact that it took
the form of a top-ten list. Since my recommendations were, by the
very premise of the article, pegged to my own life, I featured the Flint
Hills of Kansas (my home state) alongside California's Big Sur coast
and the historic jazz neighborhoods of New Orleans.

In the wake of my column, the article's online comments flooded
with enraged Mainers and Texans and Oregonians, who insisted that
the inclusion of Kansas over their own states' sites proved Yahoo was
an irredeemably corrupt media organization. Meanwhile, regional
newspapers like the *Kansas City Star* published exultant articles celebrating the idea that Kansas's Flint Hills had been deemed a top-ten
attraction by "the national Web site and search engine Yahoo!"

Though at the time I was bewildered that my own opinions would
be conflated with the entire Yahoo web portal, I have since come to
realize that any enumerated list of recommendations carries an implied authority that invariably outstrips its real-world intentions. Psy-
chologically, lists are comforting, since they narrow down choices and
make seemingly infinite options easier to grasp and remember—but
they also invariably evoke the subjective biases and personal idiosyncrasies of the list maker.

This in mind, treat any seemingly authoritative rundown of travel
recommendations as a purely conceptual starting point—a flawed
pretext for creating your own, more meaningful list of travel favorites.

February 9

THE POINT OF A "BUCKET LIST" IS SIMPLY TO GET OUT THE FRONT DOOR

The whole idea of a bucket list is to give yourself a framework for giving yourself the best possible life you can think of.
—*Bucket List* screenwriter Justin Zackham, in a 2019 interview

Though it feels like the term *bucket list* has been around for ages, it actually dates back no further than the 2007 movie of the same name, which starred Morgan Freeman and Jack Nicholson as terminally ill hospital patients seeking out a handful of long-dreamed-of life experiences before they died. Travel figures prominently in *The Bucket List,* as the movie follows the protagonists to places like Egypt's Great Pyramid and India's Taj Mahal.

In the years since the movie came out, the term *bucket list* has come to represent less an existential imperative than a more generalized list of things you want to do within a certain time frame. What's more, in the movie, the iconic travel sights of Egypt and India mainly serve as visual backdrops for the movie's plot. In real life, the Egyptian and Indian cultures that lie beyond Giza and Agra offer far more rewards than what can be found at famous monuments.

In saying this, I don't mean to knock the idea of the bucket list. In the case of travel, however, the list of attractions that takes you to distant places is usually less important than what you find when you get there. The reality of these places contains far more possibility than you could have imagined while you were sketching out the list at home.

Use a bucket list to get yourself out the front door, but allow yourself to see the list's specifics as a mere starting point for a much richer journey.

MUCH TRAVEL WRITING DRAWS ON THE TROPES OF ADVERTISING

Nowhere else in nonfiction [outside of travel writing] do writers use such syrupy words and groaning platitudes. . . . These are subjective concepts in the eye of the beholder. One man's romantic sunrise is another man's hangover.
—William Zinsser, *On Writing Well* (1976)

When the travel industry boomed in the years after World War II, newspapers across America created Sunday "travel sections" to provide readers with information about vacation possibilities. This proved profitable, since newspapers could build these sections around travel industry advertising. Over time, however, tourism marketers realized that subsidizing travel writers' trips was cheaper and more effective than buying advertisements. "From the beginning, publications didn't question the idea of getting free trips," wrote journalist Elizabeth Becker. "The editors told themselves it was the only way they could afford to cover the travel world. And the public relations professionals were thrilled, knowing that a handsome write-up in a magazine was far more credible than an advertisement."

One side effect was that by the late twentieth century, the language of commercial travel writing had become uncomfortably mixed up with that of advertising. In his writing-craft primer *On Writing Well,* William Zinsser coined the term "travelese" to describe the trite language of travel-feature articles. "It is a style of soft words which under hard examination mean nothing," he noted. "It is a world where . . . buildings boast, ruins beckon, and the very chimney tops sing their immemorial song of welcome. The clichés bloom with fertility."

As traditional travel media increasingly competes for our attention with the idealizations and half-truths of social media, it's useful to recognize the marketing-driven tropes of "travelese"—and keep in mind that the language of advertising only goes so far in preparing you for what you'll really find on the road.

AVOID MAKING TRAVEL CHOICES
BASED ON WHAT IS "TRENDY"

Today, the traveler has become passive . . . because travel dif-
fers very little from going to a movie or turning the pages of a
magazine. . . . Such people never really leave their beaten paths
of impercipience, nor do they ever arrive at any new place.
—Marshall McLuhan, *Understanding Media* (1964)

Of the many ways travel media has come to depict distant places, one of the more absurd is the notion that destinations can become "trendy." Using the same kind of "top-ten" and "can't miss" language used to describe beauty products or TV shows, magazines and websites imply that choosing where to travel is as much a fashion undertaking as it is a geographic one. The more this happens, the more destinations are forced to market themselves as more "hip" than their competitors.

A central problem here (in addition to the causal loop wherein destinations deemed fashionable attract a disproportionate number of tourists fixated on fashion) is that the methodologies used in declaring a place trendy invariably betray baked-in media prejudices. In his 2018 book *Rediscovering Travel,* journalist Seth Kugel observed that travel media tends to promote the same kinds of boutique hotels, microbreweries, and gentrified beachfronts one might find in the hipster-oriented districts of one's own city. "[Why] fly fourteen hours from New York to Johannesburg to see a South African version of Brooklyn?" he wrote. "To me, the only reason to know what destinations are 'hot' is to avoid them."

Fortunately, one need not focus one's journey using the same logic people use to visit nightclubs or buy Halloween costumes. Trends can certainly be a consideration in choosing where to go, but the most rewarding journeys follow a subtler, more self-directed sense for which places might be worth seeking out.

RESEARCH THE JOURNEY ON GLOBES AND PAPER MAPS

That is the charm of a map. It represents the other side of the horizon, where everything is possible.
—Rosita Forbes, *From Red Sea to Blue Nile* (1925)

In the fifteenth century, the hottest objects on offer in Europe's underground economy were navigation charts. "In the time of Ferdinand and Isabella and other maritime monarchs, maps were top-secret, much like electronic discoveries are today," wrote Marshall McLuhan in his 1964 book *Understanding Media*. "When the captains returned from their voyages, every effort was made by the officers of the crown to obtain both originals and copies of the maps made during the voyage. The result was a lucrative black-market trade, and secret maps were widely sold."

The contraband in question tended to be routes and waypoints meant to be utilized by people traveling through the same landscapes and seascapes. As cartography evolved in the years that followed, standardized maps like the 1569 Mercator Projection allowed travelers to conceive of the world not in terms of specific itineraries so much as a broad overview of options. In time, the practical task of planning a journey became inseparable from daydreaming about what lay in the blank spaces beside and beyond one's intended destination.

Though GPS technologies have returned us to a more subjective manner of plotting our journeys, it is useful to balance digital precision with the more abstract sense of possibility that flows from thumbing atlases and spinning globes. Instead of zooming in and out to calculate projected transit times and restaurant options on an interactive screen, paper maps enable us to revel in vaguely imagined futures—to see the world as an intoxicating menu of options, and to dream of what might happen if we visit those as-yet-unseen blank spaces.

GUIDEBOOKS ARE AN OUTMODED (BUT STILL USEFUL) RESOURCE

> A good guidebook makes you want to keep reading and discover its serendipitous rewards, just as a good city makes you want to keep wandering its streets.
>
> —Doug Mack, "Go Your Own Way" (2013)

Franz Kafka might be best remembered for his 1915 novella about a man who gets transformed into a giant cockroach, but before the Bohemian author became renowned for his fiction, his core ambition was to write a series of guides to European destinations. According to biographer Reiner Stach, Kafka was frustrated by mainstream travel books, which focused on hotel and restaurant listings, and he wanted to create budget-minded guides that listed things like affordable tram routes and free concerts. "Kafka was convinced that a travel guide that supplied reliable recommendations would instantly beat out the competition," Stach wrote.

Though Kafka's travel book idea never made it past the proposal phase, the fact that he saw it as a moneymaking venture reveals that guidebooks had become central to the way people traveled in his era. More than a century later, paper books have been largely displaced by crowdsourced travel apps and online recommendations—but this doesn't mean traditional guidebooks can't be a great place to start as you research your travels.

American author Doug Mack, whose 2012 book *Europe on Five Wrong Turns a Day* documented his attempt to explore the continent using a fifty-year-old Frommer's guide, found that paper guidebooks still stand out in the way they contextualize their travel tips and offer the kind of counterintuitive advice you might not realize you needed. "The key is their fine-tuned curation, that binds the information into more than a scattered array of anonymous opinions and unverified facts," Mack wrote. "You don't get that on Yelp, on TripAdvisor, or on Google."

READ BOOKS WRITTEN BY PEOPLE WHO LIVE IN THE PLACES YOU VISIT

Why am I finding lists called "Books to Read Before Your African Safari" that don't include a single African author? Use travel . . . to be part of the solution.

—Faith Adiele, in a 2019 interview

Though I've always been attuned to the fact that reading prepares a person for travel, my approach to this process has evolved over the years. When I first started taking long-term journeys, I tended to stick to travel guidebooks and online resources—though in time I found that narrative travel memoirs deepened my emotional and intellectual understanding of the journey ahead. It wasn't until I traveled to India in my late twenties, however, that I realized reading the perspectives of Western travelers would offer only a partial perspective on the places I was visiting. In seeking out novels by Indian-born writers, such as Arundhati Roy, Salman Rushdie, Pankaj Mishra, Anita Desai, and Amitav Ghosh, I developed a more intuitive sense for the culture I was about to encounter.

As you prepare for the road, seek to diversify guidebook information and travel memoirs with books written by people from the places you're visiting. Most countries' iconic novels are well known (in Chile, it's Isabel Allende's *The House of the Spirits;* in Nigeria, Chinua Achebe's *Things Fall Apart;* in Iceland, Halldór Laxness's *Independent People*), and you can use these books as a springboard to discover others. If you enjoyed Jack Kerouac's *On the Road* in advance of a USA journey, for instance, try Tim Z. Hernandez's *Mañana Means Heaven*, which is told from the perspective of Kerouac's "Mexican Girl."

In reading a diverse array of books by local novelists, you won't just sharpen your sense for a culture—you'll cultivate empathy for the people you'll meet there.

TOURIST LOW SEASON HAS COUNTERINTUITIVE REWARDS

The nomadic life makes you sensitive to the seasons: you rely on them, even become part of the season itself.
—Nicolas Bouvier, *The Way of the World* (1963)

By all conventional wisdom, my visit to Bagan was poorly timed. Whereas savvy travelers journeyed to Myanmar's iconic Buddhist ruins in the dry season, I'd elected to go there during the sweltering summer monsoon. Numerous Southeast Asia travel veterans warned me that I'd get soaked during my June visit, and they were right: For three days, I bicycled through the sprawling complex of eleventh-century temples and pagodas in an unrelenting drizzle.

Yet while those same travel veterans had warned of Bagan's aggressive souvenir vendors and tourist-clotted photo vistas, I discovered I had the thousand-year-old archaeological site largely to myself. Local villagers invited me into their houses for tea, saffron-robed monks flagged me down to practice their English, and I wandered the ancient temple complex for hours without seeing other tourists. On my last night there, I treated my new Burmese friends to the least expensive beer (a brimming pitcher of Myanmar Lager for the equivalent of 40¢) I've found anywhere in the world. Rain-soaked as it was, my Bagan sojourn was also delightful.

As it happens, every region of the world has seasons that are less popular with visitors (summer in the Middle East, winter in Europe, wet season in the tropics), and this can be a counterintuitively rewarding time to visit. For those willing to deal with imperfect weather, tourist low season invariably means that lodging is cheaper, beaches less crowded, museums more peaceful, locals more welcoming. In traveling to places at a time of year when most tourists would prefer not to, you increase your odds of seeing those places as they see themselves.

SAVING MONEY ON THE ROAD
IS A MATTER OF ATTITUDE

To travel cheaply, in any form at all, weakens the power of money to trick you into phony realities that profit only the Travel Industry.

—Ed Buryn, *Vagabonding in the USA* (1980)

In his book *Libyan Sands,* English explorer Ralph Bagnold posited that being able to travel long-term was less a matter of wealth than of attitude. "There are two kinds of travelers," he wrote, "the Comfortable Voyager, round whom a cloud of voracious expenses hums all the time, and the man who shifts for himself and enjoys little discomforts as a change from life's routine. Both may enjoy themselves, but the latter sees more of the country and its people, and has the added pleasure of going where lack of comfort excludes the former."

Nearly a century later, Bagnold's observation still holds true, particularly since so much of what tourists pay for on the road (particularly what they pay for in advance) involves amenities and efficiencies that can insulate them from the very cultures they're trying to experience. Indeed, for all the presumed perks offered by luxury hotels and tourist-district restaurants, sleeping in locally owned guesthouses and dining on street food is not just cheaper—it's far more likely to embed travelers in the daily life of their destination.

On the road, rich journeys don't flow from extravagant budgets; they are found in forgoing the minor comforts and conveniences we've been convinced we want, and using what money we have to embrace what a place offers us.

CHEAPER DESTINATIONS ENABLE
LONGER JOURNEYS

----

*"I can't afford to travel" is a false statement if you currently have
a nice place to live, and a car. You're already spending more
than budget travelers just to maintain your routine life at home.*
—Tim Leffel, *The World's Cheapest Destinations* (2002)

When I took a vagabonding journey across Asia, Europe, and North Africa in my late twenties, I improvised my route along a budget travel principle that went back at least to the Hippie Trail of the 1970s: If your budget is limited, you'll get more days out of your dollars in cheaper countries. This in mind, I sipped cups of tea and rode trains in India rather than England; I wandered avenues and explored ancient monuments in Cairo rather than Rome; I visited temples and sampled cuisine in Thailand rather than Japan.

Around the time I was doing this, American travel writer Tim Leffel distilled this time-honored backpacker tactic into a guidebook entitled *The World's Cheapest Destinations*. "The way to really travel well without spending your life savings is to go to where your first-world dollars are worth a fortune," he wrote. "You're going to be living on fewer dollars per day if you're traveling in Southeast Asia or South America or the Middle East than you will if you're just paying your rent and buying your groceries at home."

In favorably comparing the cost of traveling in less expensive countries to the cost of living at home, Leffel was underscoring the fact that long-term journeys aren't something you purchase so much as they are something you give to yourself. "Calculate what you spend on a daily basis at home for all your living expenses," he noted. "Cut that number in half, and you'll have a daily budget that can take you around the world indefinitely."

DON'T LET YOUR TRAVEL EXPECTATIONS CONSTRAIN WHAT IS POSSIBLE

In the nineteenth century [guidebooks began to make] it easy
for the less intrepid to plan in advance, to know where they
might stay, what to see, what to expect. The information acted
as insulation against the threat of too much raw reality.
—James Hamilton-Paterson, "The End of Travel" (2006)

Of the many things Mark Twain lampooned in his 1869 book *The Innocents Abroad,* he found particular relish in skewering the way his fellow tourists used their guidebooks. "I can almost tell, in set phrase, what they will say when they see Nazareth, Jericho, and Jerusalem—*because I have the books they will 'smouch' their ideas from,*" he wrote. "Guidebook authors write pictures and frame rhapsodies, and lesser men follow and see with the author's eyes instead of their own, and speak with his tongue."

Twain was traveling at a moment in history when the popularity of guidebook brands like Murray and Baedeker reflected the rise of leisure travel among the middle classes. A few decades earlier, in *Views A-Foot,* Bayard Taylor had been perplexed to witness Murray-guidebook-clutching tourists "read about the very town they were passing, scarcely lifting their eyes to the real scenes" as they cruised down the Rhine; a few decades later, a scene in E. M. Forster's *A Room with a View* hinged on the protagonist's sense of helplessness as she wandered around Florence without her Baedeker.

Easy as it is to make fun of these tourists' overreliance on guidebooks, they were, in fact, among the earliest members of the travel milieu we still inhabit. Despite our technological sophistication, we too can find ourselves overly dependent on what it is we think we're supposed to do in the places we visit—and every engaged journey reveals realities that no guidebook or list of recommendations can predict.

February 19

THE BEST PARTS OF TRAVEL CAN'T BE PACKAGED IN ADVANCE

Epcot Center features pavilions built by various foreign nations, where you can experience a realistic simulation of what life in these nations would be like if they consisted almost entirely of restaurants and souvenir stores.

—Dave Barry, *Dave Barry's Only Travel Guide You'll Ever Need* (1991)

The first time Disneyland ever closed its gates early came on August 6, 1970, when three hundred members of an anti-authoritarian collective known as the Yippies infiltrated the Anaheim theme park, claiming Tom Sawyer Island as their own sovereign territory and threatening to "barbecue Porky Pig" (who, it is worth noting, is not a Disney character). Though the Yippies had a broad range of motives for this act of absurdist political theater, the group chose Disneyland because they felt the park symbolized the conformist blandness of American corporate life.

Around the same time, the term *Disneyfication* was coined by sociologists to describe the process by which places are stripped of their original character and sanitized to appear simpler, safer, and more predictable. As the French philosopher Jean Baudrillard wrote in his 1981 book *Simulacra and Simulation,* Disneyland has become "hyper-real" by its very commitment to artificiality. "Disneyland is presented as imaginary in order to make us believe that the rest is real, when in fact all of Los Angeles and the America surrounding it are no longer real," he quipped.

Though I have pleasant memories of visiting Disneyland when I was younger, I can see how its long lines and totalizing fantasy environment are a ready metaphor for the limits of consumer travel. Knowing that Disneyland has perfected the art of creating a standardized "attraction," we are thus free to seek the truer essence of travel—its surprises and serendipities and quiet marvels—in places that aren't packaged for our amusement.

JOURNEYS OUTGROW THE MOTIVES
THAT INSPIRED THEM

Traveling outgrows its motives. It soon proves sufficient in itself. You think you are making a trip, but soon it is making you—or unmaking you.

—Nicolas Bouvier, *The Way of the World* (1963)

Geoff Dyer's 1998 novel *Paris Trance* depicts the sojourn of a twenty-six-year-old Englishman named Luke, who travels to France with the intention of writing a book about what he finds there. Luke makes little progress on his novel once he arrives in Paris, yet his experiences in the city soon outstrip his motives for going there. "The book had assumed the status of a passport or travel visa," Dyer noted. "Something which, by enabling him to leave one country and pass into another, had served its purpose, and could be, if not discarded, then stored away and ignored."

As was the case with Luke's would-be novel, our specific motivations to travel someplace often serve as a psychological passport—a formalized pretext to leave a familiar place and seek out distant horizons. Some of us travel seeking adventure sports, or exotic culinary experiences, or the chance to study a new language. Others seek travel as a more general escape from the dull routines of home, or an encounter with a more enlightened vision of the world, or as a way to embrace life before it passes us by. As often as not, we travel to honor an urge we can't quite explain, making the journey itself a way to better clarify why we've taken the journey.

Whatever the motivation, most journeys outgrow the motives (or the ambiguities) that inspired them. "When you don't know what to do, you travel," Jedidiah Jenkins wrote in his 2018 book *To Shake the Sleeping Self.* "You go out and see. You have to rattle the bed, shake yourself out."

EACH DAY ON THE ROAD WILL MAKE YOU A SAVVIER TRAVELER

I do not want to know where this journey ends. Otherwise, why call this action "journey"?
—Matsuo Basho, "Record of a Travel-Worn Satchel" (1688)

I frequently tell people not to get too caught up in the hyper-specifics of planning a journey, since each new day on the road will make you savvier about what to do (and where to go) next. But it wasn't until *Far Out Podcast* co-host Julie-Roxane Krikorian inadvertently coined a new phrase while riffing on this idea in the middle of our 2020 interview that I came to appreciate the advice in a whole new way.

"Why would I limit my ten-year plan to what my mediocre now-brain can imagine, when I can just let things happen and let the intelligence of life guide me?" she said. "I will know much more in five years than I do now, so I don't want to box myself into a bunch of plans that won't fit who I will become."

I have since appropriated Julie-Roxane's phrase "mediocre now-brain" when I explain to people why, for all the joy that comes in planning your dream trip, you should accept that your future self will grow wiser and more capable as each new day of the journey plays out. In accepting that your "mediocre now-brain" has little idea what specific wonders and challenges and life-changing epiphanies are in store, you better equip yourself to simply follow your curiosity and passions and discover amazing new things as you go.

February 22

WHILE YOU'RE STILL HOME,
SEEK THE GLOBAL

The spirit with which the journey is carried out transforms the near into a distant unknown, into a wonderland.
—Bernd Stiegler, *Traveling in Place* (2013)

When my sister Kristin got a job teaching English in the central Kansas town of Lindsborg, she was charmed by the town's Swedish heritage. *Dala*-horse statues lined the streets, *köttbullar* and *ärtsoppa* featured on menus in local restaurants, and a biennial Hyllningsfest celebrated the town's historical relationship to Sweden. Lindsborg, my sister discovered, was not just generically Swedish—its settlers had come from a specific rural area in the Norway-adjacent province of Värmland.

Noting that present-day immigrants to central Kansas hailed from Mexico, Kristin asked around and found out that most of them came from a specific part of the state of Zacatecas. Intrigued, she bought tickets on a local minibus service that Mexican migrants used to commute home, and brought her husband and sons on an inexpensive cross-border vacation to the city of Fresnillo. In getting to know more about one corner of north-central Mexico, my sister's family thus got to know more about their own corner of north-central Kansas.

The twenty-first-century world has, in fact, become so globalized that—regardless of where you live—it's possible to get a taste of the greater world in your own home community. Even if your own global travels are still months or years away, you can get a feel for distant lands by eating at an Ethiopian or Argentine restaurant across town, visiting a nearby Bulgarian Orthodox Church or Vietnamese Cao Dai temple, or testing your wicket skills at a Pakistani-immigrant cricket scrimmage in a local park. In seeing how your own hometown connects to the greater world, you thus sharpen your own instincts for journeys to come.

ROAD TRIPS ARE PRACTICE FOR
THE GREATER JOURNEY

I remember the first road trip I took as a boy. . . . It's a cherished memory, and even at the time my experience was consistent with a sense that I was going to have to go on some sort of journey in order to find out who I was.

—Barack Obama, in a 2021 podcast

State Line Road is a fairly unremarkable north-south thorough-fare that stretches twelve miles across metropolitan Kansas City, but when I first learned of it on a family road trip at age five, I thought it was the most exotic place on Earth. One side of the street, my father pointed out, belonged to our home state of Kansas, while the other belonged to Missouri—and the people who lived on the Missouri side of the road had different political leaders and phone-number prefixes than we did. Fetching barbecue supplies from stores along State Line Road might involve leaving and reentering Kansas a half dozen times—a concept that baffled my young mind.

While that formative road trip had transported me just three hours up Interstate 35 from my Wichita hometown, it captured my geographical imagination in a way that still resonates. Long before I owned a passport, my earliest journeys involved riding across the Great Plains with family, and these trips, brief as they were, sharpened my appetite for travel.

Road trips are a distinctively North American vernacular (people in other places might find a regional travel equivalent in train or ferry excursions), but getting away from your hometown in any form for a few hours or days is an indispensable travel exercise. In allowing yourself to be openhearted, improvisational, and curious about everything you encounter as the road trip plays out, you are putting yourself into the mindset of more far-flung journeys.

WALKING AT HOME PUTS YOU INTO THE MINDSET OF TRAVEL

- -

> Walking, as they say, "empties the mind." In another way, walking fills the mind with a different sense of purpose. Not connected with ideas or doctrines, not in the sense of a head full of phrases, quotations, theories: but full of the world's presence.
> —Frederic Gros, *A Philosophy of Walking* (2015)

The concept of *solvitur ambulando*—Latin for "it is solved by walking"—goes back to fourth-century B.C.E. Greek philosopher Diogenes, who, when confronted with one of Zeno's paradoxes about the unreality of motion, responded by getting up and walking away. At the time Diogenes's point was that practical application counts for more than theoretical arguments, though in the ensuing centuries *solvitur ambulando* has come to imply that going for a walk is a more effective way of unraveling intellectual and emotional problems than simply sitting and pondering them.

This in mind, *solvitur ambulando* can be an effective technique in preparing for a journey. It's one thing to read books or go online and sketch out travel plans; it's another task (and perhaps an equally essential one) to set aside travel research and walk yourself into a clearer understanding of the upcoming journey by having a brief, close-to-home one.

In seeking to experience a familiar environment at a walking pace, you aren't just slowing down and savoring that place in a new way; you're opening yourself up to ways of knowing and feeling that you can't encounter while cooped up at home. Instead of filling your mind with new information, a walk clears it out and opens it to innovative ways of thinking; instead of focusing your attention on concrete plans, a walk allows you to more vividly dream of wide-open possibilities.

February 25

RESIST THE URGE TO PLAN TOO MUCH OF THE JOURNEY IN ADVANCE

> Traveling with no itinerary, no plan, you take life as it comes, moment by moment. Every joy, every sorrow, every surprise. You go where the wind blows.
> —Eddy L. Harris, *Native Stranger* (1992)

One of the temptations novice travelers face in the Information Age is the compulsion to plan out every aspect of the journey in advance. This arises in part because the travel industry has conditioned us to be leery of spontaneity, but also because there's something soothing about researching each aspect of the trip before it happens. A worthy argument could in fact be made for detailing an itinerary in advance—but only if it's created with the understanding that it can be ignored whenever the unplanned textures of the journey itself begin to guide the travel experience.

Some of the most useful preparation doesn't involve a specific sense for lodging and tourist attractions so much as a generalized understanding of the customs, manners, cultural norms, and linguistic idiosyncrasies of the places you'll be visiting. Leaving a journey open to chance need not mean being reckless so much as receptive to the impromptu challenges and delights a journey offers. Explore possibilities, in other words, but don't plan out every possibility.

"Ordinary travelers through life try to control everything, in order to protect their delusions from the nasty shocks of reality," Ed Buryn wrote in *Vagabonding in the USA*. "Vagabonds know better, and book the details of their trip with an agent called Chance. Giving up control of your life frees you from the illusion that you *can* control it, and this freedom in turn connects you into its unlimited potential."

LONG-TERM JOURNEYS NEED NOT BE EXPENSIVE

Staying abroad beyond the temporary [vacation] period that is usually the norm in Western society has become an established tourism alternative akin to the Grand Tour of yesteryear.

—Klaus Westerhausen, *Beyond the Beach* (2002)

Part of the reason long-term travel has, over the years, come to be seen as an expensive indulgence is that modern tourism has inherited many of the assumptions of the aristocratic Grand Tours of previous centuries. When the English Romantic poet Lord Byron traveled to Switzerland in 1816, for instance, he brought along a guide, a valet, a personal physician, and a sparring partner, and he made his way through the Alps in a giant coach that featured dining quarters, a sleeping chamber, and a perambulating menagerie including dogs, a peacock, and a monkey.

Though it would be faintly ridiculous to set out on a journey laden with such ostentation these days, the travel industry has perpetuated the notion that journeys revolve around aspirational luxury and recreating all the smallest comforts of home. Yet while travel has often been a pretext to assert social standing and celebrate conspicuous consumption, its truest rewards don't cost much. Finding ways to move beyond two-week vacation cycles and embrace journeys that stretch on for months (or years) is less a matter of deep financial resources than the willingness to slow down and stay flexible, to cut out tourism-industry intermediaries and travel within local economies, to "see" less and experience more.

MOST OF THE THINGS WE PACK FOR A JOURNEY ARE NOT NECESSARY

The pleasure of travel increases in direct proportion to the decrease of baggage.
—Richard Halliburton, *The Royal Road to Romance* (1925)

Late in the summer of 2010, I embarked on a journey that took me around the world—traveling through twelve countries on five continents over the course of six weeks—with no luggage or bags of any kind. Stowing a single change of clothing and a few small utility items (toothbrush, deodorant, smartphone, passport, emergency cash) in various vest and pants pockets, I designed the journey to be an intentional experiment in minimalist travel. Once I got into a travel rhythm, the baggage-free aspect of the trip was simple. Two-a-day showers kept me as clean as I'd ever been on the road, and daily clothes-washings (of my socks, underwear, and T-shirt) kept my wardrobe looking and smelling great.

I wrote and co-produced a real-time video series as my travel-minimalism experience played out—and one of the initial narrative challenges was the fact that traveling with no luggage wasn't as difficult as I thought it might be. Thus, instead of dramatizing the hardships of traveling with no luggage, my videos depicted the simple joys of taking a journey (touring Paris in a Citroën, wandering the markets of Morocco, going on safari in South Africa, taking a train from Thailand to Malaysia, zip-lining through a New Zealand forest) with nothing to pack, nothing to lose, and nothing to slow me down.

What I learned in the process is that each day of travel is a gift in and of itself—and most of what we pack for a journey (entertainment gadgets, spare toiletries, "just-in-case" clothing items) has little bearing on the travel experiences we remember best.

February 28

THE BEST METRIC FOR BETTER TRAVEL IS AN INTERNAL ONE

Tourists are reproached for being satisfied with superficial experiences of other peoples and other places. . . . [Yet] all tourists
desire deeper involvement with society and culture to some degree; it is a basic component of their motivation to travel.
—Dean MacCannell, *The Tourist: A New Theory of the Leisure Class*
(1976)

In my 2003 book *Vagabonding* I invoked a number of writers—Pico
Iyer, Freya Stark, G. K. Chesterton—in an attempt to illustrate why
the snobbish dichotomy that separates travelers from tourists is a
meaningless one. "In reality, travel is not a social contest," I wrote,
"and vagabonding has never represented a caste on the tourist/traveler
hierarchy." This point seems to have been well taken, though over the
years I have lost track of how many readers have nonetheless stated—
both online and in person—that *Vagabonding*'s core philosophy is
about "how to be a traveler instead of a tourist."

I'm not the only person who's dealt with this seeming contra-
diction. TV host Anthony Bourdain had little patience for tourist/
traveler hair-splitting, yet magazine advertisements for his 2005
Travel Channel show *No Reservations* carried the chirpy tagline "Be
a Traveler, Not a Tourist." Similarly, travel writer Daisann McLane,
who asserted in interviews that we all travel as tourists, wrote a
monthly column that *National Geographic Traveler* published with
the subheading "How to Be a Traveler, Not a Tourist."

Indeed, while it's easy to intellectualize how (as guests in distant
places) we're all essentially tourists, the travel milieu seems to require
a status-driven rhetoric that separates good travelers from not-so-
good ones. If in doubt, the most reliable metric for becoming a better
traveler is not the one you use to compare yourself with your fellow
wanderers, but the quieter one you apply to yourself.

February 29

IT IS PERFECTLY NORMAL TO FEEL ANXIETY BEFORE A BIG JOURNEY

There is an uncertainty about travel that affects even seasoned travelers. . . . To travel is to make yourself vulnerable—leaving, with your papers and plastic, the high-tech security of your home and wandering sumptuously among imperfect strangers.
—Thomas Swick, *The Joys of Travel* (2016)

In the spring of 1480, a Dominican friar named Felix Fabri, inspired by a "fever of longing" to see distant places, set off on a pilgrimage to Jerusalem from the German city of Ulm. Fabri had scarcely made it beyond the gates of his own city, however, before he was gripped with something resembling a panic attack. "I felt a loathing for travel," he wrote later, "and the pilgrimage, which had appeared so sweet and virtuous, now seemed wearisome, bitter, useless, empty, and sinful. I was angry with myself for having undertaken it. Ulm appeared to me pleasanter than Jerusalem."

In particular, the young monk was terrified at the prospect of traveling by sea once he reached Venice, and the only thing that kept him from quitting the journey altogether was a dull sense of pride. "Had I not been ashamed, I would have returned to Ulm," he confessed, "and I should have had the greatest delight in doing so." As it turned out, Friar Fabri overcame his anxiety and completed his passage to Jerusalem—a journey he found so inspiring that he repeated the trip three years later.

Though present-day travels are not nearly so dangerous as those faced by medieval pilgrims, it's not uncommon for would-be wanderers to feel anxiety about a trip that has yet to begin. Yet, in an information-drenched society that tempts us to choose unhappiness over uncertainty, it is helpful to remember that one of the key gifts of travel has always been uncertainty itself.

March/April

GETTING STARTED ON THE ROAD

JOURNEYS TEND TO BEGIN WITH AN INEFFABLE SENSE OF JOY

Of the gladdest moments in human life is the departure upon a distant journey into unknown lands. Shaking off the fetters of habit, the leaden weight of routine, the cloak of many cares and the slavery of home, man feels once more happy.

—Richard Francis Burton, *Zanzibar* (1872)

When I embarked on my first North American vagabonding journey at age twenty-three, I felt an odd sense of déjà vu as I rolled down the windows of my Volkswagen Vanagon and savored the first minutes of what would eventually become an eight-month journey around the United States and Canada. In time I came to realize that feeling the wind on my face as I sped down that Oregon highway evoked the exact same sense of possibility I'd felt when I'd rolled down the car windows en route to Colorado for the first time at age six.

Since then, I've discovered that the earliest moments of all my best journeys—smelling Bangkok's tropical air at age twenty-eight, hearing the polyglot chatter of the London Tube at age thirty-nine, feeling the baby-powder softness of Namibia's desert sands at age forty-six— have been in conversation with each other. In these moments, my whole being vibrates with a heightened sense of receptivity to the as-yet-unseen experiences that await.

This sense of joy that accompanies the early moments of my journeys is so intrinsic and ineffable that I can scarcely describe it in words—though I usually fall back on Walt Whitman's ecstatic declarations from "Song of the Open Road":

Henceforth I ask not good-fortune, I myself am good-fortune.
. . . From this hour I ordain myself loos'd of limits and imaginary
*   lines,*
Going where I list, my own master total and absolute.

AIR TRAVEL IS A PREAMBLE
TO THE REAL JOURNEY

To fly is the opposite of traveling: you cross a gap in space, you vanish into the void, you accept not being in any place for a duration that is itself a kind of void in time; then you reappear, in a place and in a moment with no relation to the where and the when in which you vanished.

—Italo Calvino, *If on a Winter's Night a Traveler* (1979)

It has now become so normal to begin your journey by stepping onto an airplane that it's easy to forget how miraculous the act of traveling through the air really is. One century ago, planes were still a novelty, and it was unthinkable to cross an ocean by air. In 1929, the inaugural New York–Los Angeles air route involved so many stops it took forty-eight hours to complete. One decade later, the earliest transpacific flight itineraries cost $1,710—roughly equal to the annual income of the average American worker at the time.

The Jet Age brought a semblance of glamour to air travel in the 1960s, but by the end of the century commercial jets had become so common and affordable as to be faintly irritating. "Air travel is annoying, and a cause of anxiety," wrote Paul Theroux in 2001. "It is like being at the dentist's, even to the chairs."

Indeed, what was once seen as a miracle has now become something of a necessary evil—a kind of fast-forward button across the world map, wherein you kill time by reading books and listening to music and (if you're lucky) getting some sleep before the real journey begins.

Still, the flight to your true destination is worth savoring: It's a chance to begin a mental transition, to imagine the wonders that await as the familiar world grows smaller and fades from view down below.

MANY JOURNEYS BEGIN WITH A SENSE OF UTTER DISORIENTATION

I like going places where I don't speak the language, don't know my way around, and don't have any delusions that I'm in control. Disoriented, even frightened, I feel alive, awake in ways I never am at home.

—Michael Mewshaw, "Travel and the Literature of Travel" (2004)

When Sofia Coppola's *Lost in Translation* first hit cinemas in 2003, some reviewers complained that its protagonists—an aging movie star played by Bill Murray, and a young university graduate played by Scarlett Johansson—were utterly ignorant about the Japanese culture they encountered in Tokyo. What these critics didn't apprehend was that the movie is not a tale of savvy travelers discovering the truths of a city; it is a story about two accidental tourists using the strangeness of a new place as an unwitting pretext to examine their own lives.

When Murray's and Johansson's characters leave the sterile cocoon of their Shinjuku hotel rooms and make tentative forays into Tokyo (to a shrine, a subway, a game room, a karaoke lounge, a hospital), the viewer encounters Japan as they do—as outsiders, enjoying the simple moments of confusion, connection, and joy in a place that feels utterly foreign. Coppola doesn't provide subtitles for the Japanese dialogue—nor does she indulge in cheap cross-cultural epiphanies—and in this way she draws us into the characters' culture-shocked disorientation as they make their private discoveries amid the neon sprawl of Tokyo.

Though the protagonists of *Lost in Translation* are essentially seeing Tokyo as jet-lagged business tourists, their experience of Japan will feel familiar to anyone who has tried to navigate an unfamiliar culture for the first time. Though with experience we become more seasoned as travelers, most journeys begin in this intimidating, intoxicating haze of disorientation.

THERE IS NO SUBSTITUTE FOR SMELLING A PLACE

I find the first few moments in a new country or city strange and disorienting. Things look and sound and smell different, humans dress different, sometimes even the dogs bark different.
—Seth Kugel, *Rediscovering Travel* (2018)

In the early to mid-1800s, panorama paintings—which gave viewers the illusion of being surrounded by a high-fidelity, 360-degree view of exotic environments—became so popular that some commentators thought they would replace the need to travel. "Panoramas are among the happiest contrivances for saving time and expense," one British magazine reported in 1824. "Throwing out the innumerable miseries of travel, a journey that cost two hundred pounds half a century ago now costs a shilling."

Though panoramas proved popular for much of the nineteenth century ("I floated along under the spell of enchantment," Henry David Thoreau marveled after beholding a Rhine panorama in Boston in 1851), they never did replace the popular desire to embark on real journeys. And while newer generations of critics have posited that corporeal travel will become obsolete with each subsequent development of virtual-reality technology—first photography, then cinema, then video games, then computer-generated imagery—people's desire to wander through the organic world remains as strong as ever.

This is because, for all of the simulations and entertainments that endeavor to re-create the experience of real-world places, no technology can replace the sensation of actually being there. Indeed, while panoramas once did a decent job of evoking vistas (and still can, where they've been preserved, in places like Wroclaw and The Hague)—and while virtual-reality devices now mimic the audiovisual textures one can encounter in faraway places—there is no substitute for showing up, breathing in, and smelling those places in person.

TRAVEL CAN RETURN YOU TO A KIND OF CHILDHOOD

One travels to learn once more how to marvel at life in the way a child does.

—Ella Maillart, *The Cruel Way* (1947)

In taking us to unfamiliar places and cultures, new journeys have a way of transporting us to an earlier time of life—specifically childhood, that time when so much of life remained a bright-edged mystery, and we weren't fully attuned to the rules and schedules and expectations of the adult world. Surrounded by languages and routines we cannot fully understand, we have to relearn how to ask for food, read simple instructions, and cross the street without endangering ourselves.

At times the heightened vulnerability of being in a foreign place can bring out our worst childish instincts as travelers, such as the coddling we expect at luxury hotels, or the tantrums we throw when we feel we've been cheated by street vendors or taxi drivers. But at its best, this vulnerability allows us to embrace our ignorance, interact with our surroundings as optimistic beginners, and celebrate small accomplishments—finding the right bus, ordering a dish that proves delicious, making an unexpected friend—as giddy travel triumphs.

"If every journey makes us wiser about the world, it also returns us to a sort of childhood," Pico Iyer wrote in his 1988 book *Video Night in Kathmandu*. "In alien parts, we speak more simply, unencumbered by the histories that we carry around at home, and look more excitedly, with eyes of wonder."

March 6

STAY VULNERABLE TO THE UNCERTAINTY
OF LIFE ON THE ROAD

> In the beginner's mind there are many possibilities. In the expert's mind there are few.
> —Shunryu Suzuki, *Zen Mind, Beginner's Mind* (1970)

In his 2003 book *Deep Survival,* author Laurence Gonzales noted that children under the age of six tend to have better wilderness-survival aptitude than adults, for the simple reason that they instinctively pay attention to (and rely on) their immediate surroundings rather than falling back on abstract stratagems and mental maps. "We like to think that education and experience make us more competent, more capable," Gonzales wrote. "Yet the opposite might sometimes be true in life-or-death situations. . . . I couldn't help thinking of the Zen concept of the 'beginner's mind,' the mind that remains open and ready despite years of training."

Though our travels rarely become a matter of life or death, embracing the "beginner's mind" is a useful strategy for the disorientation that comes at the outset of a journey. Back home, many aspects of daily life have become so familiar that we no longer pay attention to them; on the road, we see the world with new eyes, undimmed by routines and familiarities. Cut off from our usual media diversions, we pay fuller attention to our immediate environment; unsure of where we'll find our next meal, we eat our food with awareness and gratitude; uncertain of what exactly is happening in a given moment, we embrace the joy that comes with learning and discovery.

Freed of expectations—and without any illusions of expertise—we are thus more fully immersed in the novelty and mystery of everything we see, hear, and smell. In staying open to all that we don't know, we learn to accept each day's new uncertainties as an ongoing gift of travel.

A SIMPLE SENSE OF NOVELTY ATTUNES US TO NEW PLACES

> As it always is with leaving home, it is the details that displace us. . . . Sirens, passing in the street, are a note lower. So is the dial tone on our red plastic telephone. . . . The bathroom faucets read C and F, and the C is for calda, not cold but hot.
>
> —Anthony Doerr, *Four Seasons in Rome* (2008)

In Quentin Tarantino's 1994 film *Pulp Fiction*, a hitman named Vincent asserts that his most evocative memory from an Amsterdam sojourn wasn't the legalized hash bars, but the slight cultural differences. "You can walk into a movie theater in Amsterdam and buy a beer," he marvels to his partner Jules. "And I don't mean just like in no paper cup, I'm talking about a glass of beer. And in Paris, you can buy a beer at McDonald's."

A few years after I saw this scene in an American movie theater, I felt a similar sense of novelty when I traveled to the Philippines. It was my first-ever visit to a tropical country, and the scent of the air there—a hard-to-pin-down mix of floral fragrance and organic rot and the faint ping of spice—was unlike anything I'd ever smelled before. I commuted on "jeepneys"—jam-packed, dirt-cheap freelance buses that had been painted as brightly as psychedelic comic books. When I bought a soda in the street, the vendor emptied the bottle into a plastic sandwich bag, popped in a straw, and passed me the bubbly sack of liquid.

Taking notice of such details in a new place isn't just a charm that accompanies the early days of a journey; it is a way of attuning you to an ever-broadening sense of experiential possibility as the journey deepens in new ways.

A JOURNEY FREES YOU FROM THE CONSTRAINTS OF HOME

The history of pilgrimage brings out multiple, mixed motives. . . .
Sincere devotion mingled with simple wanderlust, or the urge to
escape one's sodden, smelly cottage after a long winter.
—Elizabeth A. Bohls, *Travel Writing 1700–1830* (2005)

One of the more peculiar sins in medieval Christendom was *curiositas,* which St. Augustine defined as "the lust for experience and for knowledge." As the rite of pilgrimage to places like Rome and Jerusalem became popular during the Middle Ages, church leaders fretted that *curiositas* might distract pilgrims from the task of religious piety. In the minds of many parish priests, a key danger of pilgrimage was that travel could be mind-expanding and pleasurable, and hence at odds with the prim prescriptions and hierarchies that underpinned their authority.

Indeed, for all of the religious ideals that motivated pilgrimage, sometimes the most tangible spiritual reward of travel was the chance to leave behind stifling routines (and nosy neighbors), experience firsthand the risks and rewards of new landscapes, and gradually grow in one's understanding of the world. Some pilgrims used their newfound freedom to engage in sexual escapades and drunken indulgence, but for the most part they thrilled in the simple joys of new foods, new sights, new people, new pastimes, and new perspectives on what their lives could be.

"When pilgrims begin to walk several things usually begin to happen to their perceptions of the world which continue over the course of the journey," wrote Nancy Frey in her 1998 book *Pilgrim Stories.* "They develop a changing sense of time, a heightening of the senses, and a new awareness of their bodies and the landscape." In this way, a mindful journey allows us to experiment with new ways of seeing and being, far from the constraints and prejudices of our home communities, in a way that enhances our whole being.

THE GOLDEN AGE OF TRAVEL IS ALWAYS RIGHT NOW

As long as people have been traveling, it seems, they have been . . . looking back nostalgically to an earlier time when favorite destinations were less crowded, when one could truly be a "traveler" rather than a "tourist."

—Lynne Withey, *Grand Tours and Cook's Tours* (1997)

When I set off on a two-year Asia vagabonding trip at age twenty-eight, I noticed that a lot of the backpackers I met—cool indie travelers from places like Denmark and Tasmania and Oregon—were fixated on the notion of what travel must have been like in the 1970s. As enjoyable as Asia was in real time, there was this sense that we had missed out on a purer era of travel some two decades before.

A couple of years later, a *New York Times* article seemed to confirm those backpackers' suspicions. "The world of travel has been tamed," it read. "Internet cafes and long-distance telephone connections have brought almost every outpost closer to home. All roads have been traveled and the words 'remote' and 'exotic' have all but lost their meaning."

Having just wandered the obscure corners of Asia, Europe, and North Africa, however, I couldn't help but take issue with the *Times*'s prim conclusions. While the world of travel might have indeed appeared tame in the eyes of some office-bound newspaper reporter, I felt like the past two years of my life were proof that travel still had the power to plumb new horizons and change one's life for the better.

I have since resolved never to assume that the "golden age" of travel expired sometime in the not-too-distant past. For me—and for anyone with the audacity to realize it as such—the golden age of travel will always be right now.

THE "BEATEN PATH" IS BEATEN FOR GOOD REASONS

> There are infinite ways to cross a landscape; the options are
> overwhelming, and pitfalls abound. The function of a path is to
> reduce this teeming chaos into an intelligible line.
>
> —Robert Moor, *On Trails* (2016)

In the 1980s, a German urban design professor named Klaus Humpert became so intrigued with a series of dirt-path shortcuts that branched off from the paved walkways of his university's campus that he had groundskeepers completely re-sod the central quad. To Humpert's fascination, the dirt paths soon reappeared in the exact same places as the old ones. These improvised walkways—created not by the university's professional design planners, but by the real-life needs of the students who used the campus—came to be known as "desire paths."

Travelers often declare an inclination to get "off the beaten path," but the fact is that tourism's beaten paths usually correspond with the explicit desires of previous generations of travelers. In his book *On Trails,* author Robert Moor explored the dynamism of the world's established byways, which, he noted, have been created "to guide our journeys, transmit messages, refine chaos, and preserve wisdom." If most of our journeys tend to begin on the well-trodden routes of the tourist trail, it's because these routes have always given travelers an engaging frame of reference from which to begin experiencing new places.

Moor added that the concept of a "path" is a common metaphor in most all spiritual traditions—as a symbol that guides belief, yes, but also as an analogy that underpins how wisdom is not just learned by following a path, but *earned* through actively seeking one's own path. In walking where others have gone before us, we are thus better prepared to forge our own way.

BEGIN YOUR JOURNEY IN A TRAVELER SCENE (THEN MOVE ON)

> Traveler centers act like magnets in a stream of charged parti-
> cles, and represent a vital element in travelers' destination
> choices once they have arrived.
>
> —Klaus Westerhausen, *Beyond the Beach* (2002)

At the outset of my first vagabonding trip across Asia, I began my journey by flying into Bangkok and checking in to a $4 guest-house on Khao San Road, the city's famous backpacker ghetto. There, alongside young travelers from places like Norway and Brazil and New Zealand, I could reserve a discount bus to Phuket or Chiang Mai, buy bootleg VHS tapes of recent Hollywood movies, or get a tribal tattoo. Street carts served muesli, fruit shakes, and banana pancakes; storefront businesses offered laundry services, Balinese masks, novelty T-shirts, kickboxing lessons, Bob Marley CDs, and shiatsu massage.

In short, I hadn't really arrived in Thailand so much as a pragmatic duty-free zone that catered to people passing through. I found it easy to meet people there—not just international backpackers, but curious young Thais, who themselves found the place foreign and exotic. Within a couple of days of wandering Khao San Road and talking to travelers who had more road experience than I did, I had a few dozen enthusiastic recommendations about where to travel next.

Khao San Road proved to be a great resource. For all the research I had done in advance of my Asia travels, talking to people who'd already been traveling in Asia made the task seem less daunting. Similar vagabonding scenes exist all over the world. Provided you eventually find ways to get away from traveler cliques and make your own discoveries in a place, they make as good a place as any to begin a journey.

IT'S OKAY TO FEEL OVERWHELMED BY THE TASK OF SIGHTSEEING

Florence is nothing better than a vast museum full of foreign tourists, and each nationality brings with it its own manners and customs.

—Stendhal, *Rome, Naples, Florence* (1817)

When a thirty-four-year-old aspiring novelist from France named Marie-Henri Beyle traveled across Italy in 1817, he found himself increasingly despondent at visiting the tombs of Machiavelli and Galileo and walking through churches filled with Michelangelos. In Florence, the sight of so much art in one place led to something resembling a panic attack. "As I emerged from the porch of Santa Croce, I was seized with a fierce palpitation of the heart," he wrote. "I walked in constant fear of falling to the ground."

More than a century later, the Italian psychiatrist Graziella Magherini noticed similar symptoms among tourists who checked themselves into Florence's Santa Maria Nuova hospital. Overwhelmed by the rich variety of art displayed at places like the Uffizi Gallery, sightseers reported feeling anxiety, rapid heartbeat, paranoia, and a rising sense of panic at so much human genius and mortality gathered in one location. Using Beyle's pen name to describe the psychosomatic condition, Magherini dubbed it "Stendhal Syndrome."

Though it is rare to literally suffer from Stendhal Syndrome during a journey, it's not uncommon to feel overwhelmed by the density of art in Italy's churches and galleries, or the sprawl of architecture around Cambodia's Angkor Wat, or the teeming wildlife at Tanzania's Ngorongoro Crater. Often this feeling is a blend of delight and disorientation at finally witnessing in person the splendor of something you previously only knew from books and online images. If in doubt, don't try to see too much at once: Pace yourself, savor each moment, and focus on the simplest details of the wonder that surrounds you.

SEEING SIGHTS ISN'T THE SAME THING AS EXPERIENCING A CULTURE

The illusion of speed is the belief that it saves time. It looks simple at first sight: finish something in two hours instead of three, gain an hour. . . . But haste and speed accelerate time, which passes more quickly, and two hours of hurry shorten a day.

—Frederic Gros, *A Philosophy of Walking* (2015)

I've been teaching a creative writing workshop in Paris each summer since the mid-2000s, and over the years I've hosted dozens of American friends in the city. Though my guests always enjoy themselves, I've found that first-time visitors in particular suffer anxiety when they dine at the storied brasseries and cafés of the French capital. Eager to get out and see the sights of the city, they become exasperated at how unhurried the waitstaff is in taking their order, in bringing out their food, and in presenting them with their bill. This lunchtime procedure, which can be accomplished in well under thirty minutes in American establishments, can stretch across hours in a place like Paris.

I'll admit I also felt irritation at the unconcerned tempo of French dining my first few summers in Paris. What I eventually came to learn was that the leisurely pace of brasseries and cafés was a far more genuine evocation of Paris than any combination of monument tours and museum exhibits. In France, a lunch that stretched out across three hours didn't compromise one's ability to experience the city; it *was* the experience of the city.

Often in our travels, the best way to appreciate a place isn't to hurry off on an itemized sightseeing agenda, but to first slow down—to sit still for a few hours, and let the place reveal itself through its own rhythms and rituals.

THE TRAVEL INDUSTRY IS HERE TO HELP (FEEL FREE TO IGNORE IT)

> The travel industry has developed cheaper, mass-produced products to be as tempting as possible to consumers, sometimes disregarding what is good for them.
> —Seth Kugel, *Rediscovering Travel* (2018)

Two thousand years ago, there were no passenger ships, so people who needed to travel bought passage on merchant vessels. As part of the bargain, these travelers were expected to bring their own supplies and help out with onboard tasks. Improved roads existed to expedite government business, inns doubled as brothels, and few people traveled for travel's sake. Travel was thus perceived to be as difficult and utilitarian as the services and technologies that enabled it.

This didn't change significantly until the nineteenth century, when an emergent middle class created a self-contained travel industry focused on leisure, and people in industrialized nations came to see travel as a lifestyle option rather than a privilege. The more travel was seen as a consumer act, the more it was expected to deliver a standardized consumer product. Yet, as Seth Kugel pointed out in *Rediscovering Travel,* the notion that "everything will be conveniently packaged, familiar, and controlled, aside from a carefully monitored IV drip of novelty and exoticism" is at odds with the spontaneous discoveries that had always made travel worthwhile.

Though it's a relief that world travelers are no longer required to sleep in brothels and hitch rides on merchant ships, it's good to remember that the modern travel industry is designed to deliver efficiencies rather than epiphanies, certainties rather than serendipities. Use it as a tool that helps convey you around the world, but endeavor to break out of its market-researched assumptions of what it thinks you might want, and develop your own instincts for how your journey will take shape.

THE BEST ASPECTS OF TRAVEL CAN'T BE CONVEYED BY RANKINGS

> When I envisioned roaming France with a Michelin guide, my mind focused on starred restaurants and Romanesque churches rather than the French themselves.
>
> —Taras Grescoe, *The End of Elsewhere* (2003)

One of the more peculiar functions of travel guidebooks over the years was the way they were used in military campaigns during World War II. When Hitler ordered the invasion of Norway in 1940, for instance, his commanding general planned the attack using maps from a Baedeker guidebook he'd purchased at a stationery store. When Allied forces clashed with Nazi units in Normandy in 1944, American officers used Michelin's *Red Guide France* to help them navigate tanks through medieval villages.

The most infamous use of guidebooks in the war was Germany's 1942 "Baedeker Blitz," when the Luftwaffe sought to bomb every English site that had garnered a three-star rating in the eponymous travel guidebook to Britain. Baedeker had pioneered its star-based ranking system a century earlier as a way to help steer time-strapped middle-class travelers to what its writers had determined were the best cultural and historical attractions (and, later, hotels and restaurants) on offer at a destination. To this day, most travel resources, online and off, employ similar ranking systems to indicate which sites are most worthy of a traveler's attention.

Much like the Baedeker Blitz proved to be a failed strategy for the Nazi military (damaging such non-strategic settlements as Exeter, Bath, and York without dampening England's will to fight), planning travel around lists of starred attractions is a dubious way to approach a journey. If in doubt, use travel rankings as a way of orienting yourself in an unfamiliar place, then seek out more personally resonant attractions when you get there.

DON'T SET LIMITS ON WHAT THERE IS TO SEE

You know, I have seen many things in this museum, but I still have not seen everything in the whole wide world. Where did they put everything else?

—Grover the Muppet, *Grover and the Everything in the Whole Wide World Museum* (1974)

Back when I was first learning to read, one of my favorite children's books was a Sesame Street storybook entitled *Grover and the Everything in the Whole Wide World Museum*. The story follows Grover, an upbeat furry blue monster, as he explores the halls of a museum that purports to display everything in the world.

Grover's excitement grows as he wanders through the various rooms of the museum, including the Small Hall (which includes things such as apple seeds, grains of salt, and freckles), the Carrot Room, and the All the Vegetables in the Whole Wide World (Except Carrots) Room.

The more Grover explores the museum, however, the more perplexed he becomes at the fact that he has yet to see everything in the world. Just as he is beginning to get frustrated, Grover comes upon a door that reads: EVERYTHING ELSE. When he opens this door (which happens to be the museum's exit), Grover is thrilled to discover that the *world itself* is a museum of beautiful and amazing objects.

While I'm fond of visiting museums as I travel, it's worth noting that museums are popular with travelers because their exhibits offer a concentrated dose of culture for people without a lot of time to linger in a new place. Even as we enjoy museums, it's good to consider Grover's discovery that the truest exhibits of a culture lie beyond the museum's exit—that the entire world can be a museum if we can just slow down and pay attention.

THE ESSENCE OF TRAVEL CAN BE FOUND IN THE SIMPLEST OF MOMENTS

I think the real miracle is not to walk either on water or in thin air, but to walk on earth. Every day we are engaged in a miracle which we don't even recognize: a blue sky, white clouds, green leaves, the black, curious eyes of a child—our own two eyes. All is a miracle.

—Thich Nhat Hanh, *The Miracle of Mindfulness* (1975)

In December 1933, an English student named Patrick Leigh Fermor set off on a fourteen-hundred-mile hike across Europe. His memoir of the journey, *A Time of Gifts,* radiates with the unadorned joy of a young wanderer making friends, learning phrases of new languages, and eating basic meals of bread and cheese as snow melts off his boots in travelers' inns.

As he recounted settling in to sleep under the stars one night on the banks of the Hungarian Danube, Leigh Fermor reflected on the simple pleasure of being there. "I lay deep in one of those protracted moments of rapture that scatter this journey like asterisks," he wrote. "Why should the thought that nobody knew where I was, as though I were in flight from bloodhounds or from worshipping corybants bent on dismemberment, generate such a feeling of triumph? It always did."

Reading *A Time of Gifts,* I was reminded of my own young travel-journal reflections. Perhaps aware of the naivety of my ecstasies, many early journal entries poked fun at their own enthusiasm. "Travel lends itself to 'stoner' thoughts," reads a notation from my journey across North America at age twenty-three. "Sunsets are awesome, man, and they happen EVERY DAY. You just have to SHOW UP!"

Though in time the vivid density of experiences on a journey becomes the "new normal," it's important to never let go of the simple excitement that comes with savoring small moments on the road.

DON'T LET TRAVEL GOALS CONSTRAIN TRAVEL POSSIBILITIES

I travel not to go anywhere, but to go. I travel for travel's sake. The great affair is to move.

—Robert Louis Stevenson, *Travels with a Donkey in the Cévennes* (1879)

On the fiftieth anniversary of Sherpa Tenzing Norgay's pioneering climb of Mount Everest, his son, Jamling, complained that summiting the mountain had turned into an experiential trophy for thrill-seeking amateurs who hadn't accumulated meaningful mountaineering experiences elsewhere. "There are people going up there who have no idea how to put on crampons," he said in a 2003 interview. "They are climbing because they're able to pay someone $65,000 to do the work for them. They don't know anything about the mountain; they just know it's the highest one in the world."

Norgay was critiquing the modern tendency to set goals based on arbitrary superlatives rather than nuanced longing and inquiry. As it happens, the Buddhist cultures that thrive in the Everest region honor the concept of *apranihita* (Sanskrit for "aimlessness"), which asserts that externally oriented ambitions have a way of pulling one out of the joy to be found in the present moment. In seeking to adjust our existence to serve our goals, we neglect to adjust our goals to serve our existence.

As your travels begin, remember that your pre-trip goals will only constrain the journey if you aren't willing to reinvent them as you learn and discover new things along the way. Reaching the summit of a well-known mountain might earn you bragging rights, but reserving the right to steer your route into more ambiguous landscapes is what makes a journey personally rewarding.

CULTURE SHOCK IS REAL (AND USEFUL)

- -

Culture shock is a good thing: It's the growing-pains of a broad-ening perspective. You get to realize that we are not the norm.
—Rick Steves, "Why We Travel" (2020)

When I moved to South Korea to teach English in my mid-twenties, it was the first time I'd ever truly been away from the United States. As thrilled as I was to be learning new skills and meeting new people, I found that my early weeks in Korea were offset by a persistent sense of self-consciousness and anxiety. Though I wasn't fully aware of it at the time, I was in fact experiencing "culture shock"—a common psychological response to the loss of familiar systems of relationships and social interactions when you leave your home culture for a new one.

Culture shock was first defined in the 1950s by Canadian anthropologist Kalervo Oberg, who noted that the unspoken rules that govern how people interact with one another within a given society can be the source of frustration to newly arrived outsiders. "Once you realize that your trouble is due to your own lack of understanding . . . rather than the hostility of an alien environment," Oberg noted, you can gain a more objective understanding of your own culture-driven instincts, and adapt accordingly.

For travelers, culture shock is invariably a positive development—a sign that you have broken out of the cocoon of your own societal comfort zone and begun to grow beyond preconceived notions of how things should be. In doing so, you don't just come to terms with the subtleties and intricacies of your host culture; you begin to see your own culture (and its basic assumptions) in a new way, and to grow into a more fully formed citizen of the world.

FIND WAYS TO BE FASCINATED WITH WHEREVER YOU ARE

Anything that is remarked, even little flowers or leaves picked up off the ground and shown a child, even a shoeshine or a gravel pit, anything is potentially an attraction. It simply awaits one person to take the trouble to point out to another as something noteworthy, as worth seeing.

—Dean MacCannell, *The Tourist: A New Theory of the Leisure Class* (1976)

There is a certain tautology in speaking of "tourist attractions," since, by simple definition, they are places that attract tourists. In the ancient world, this meant otherwise unremarkable landscapes associated with mythology, such as the road near Sparta where Penelope was thought to have made up her mind to marry Odysseus, or the overlook in Salamis where an aging Telamon was said to have watched his sons sail off to Troy. Part of what made these places worth seeing was, for ancient Roman tourists, the fact that other Roman tourists went there.

"Other people give atmosphere or a sense of carnival to a place," wrote scholar John Urry in a 1996 book called *The Sociology of Tourism*. "They indicate that this is *the* place to be and that one should not be elsewhere." Indeed, from the macabre "morgue tours" of the 1870s to the camera-ready "Instagram walls" of the 2020s, part of what attracts people to tourist attractions is the fact that other tourists have deemed these places worthy of seeing.

Often, trying to figure out why so many people keep coming to a given tourist attraction (Rome's Spanish Steps, for instance, or the Dubai Marina) can be part of the charm of being there. If in doubt, figure out ways to become fascinated by the subtlest, most quotidian aspects of a new place, regardless of whether or not it has been certified by the presence of other tourists.

TRAVELING WITH CHILDREN CAN BE A DELIGHTFUL CONSTRAINT

- -

Alone a youth runs fast, with an elder slow, but together they go far.

—Kenyan Luo proverb

The imaginative and openhearted spirit of vagabonding need not be compromised when one has children in tow—a fact I was reminded of when I visited Paris's Père Lachaise Cemetery with my fourteen-year-old nephew Cedar some years ago. Whereas the adult guests I'd taken there on prior visits were interested in the tombs of famous writers like Oscar Wilde and Molière, or musicians like Edith Piaf and Jim Morrison, Cedar had no idea who those people were. Cheerfully uncertain of what he was looking for, he walked through Paris's sprawling City of the Dead attuned to whatever captured his imagination.

In this way, the curious abundance of freshly laid bouquets attracted him to the grave of Frank Alamo, who (we learned later) was a 1960s Beatles-style French *yé-yé* pop singer who'd recently passed away. Cedar also lingered at the massive nineteenth-century tomb of Elizaveta Demidoff to marvel at its bas-relief carvings of weasels and hammers—a detail that made sense when we learned she'd been a Russian baroness, heir to a fortune built on fur and iron. In experiencing Père Lachaise guided by the curiosity of my adolescent nephew, I was able to see beyond my guidebook-driven expectations of what the place had to offer.

To be sure, traveling with kids—particularly younger ones, who need more structure and assistance than your average travel companion—is more schedule-driven and detail-oriented than traveling in the company of adults. Yet the inherent constraints of family travel don't merely compel you to embrace kid-friendly pursuits: They allow you to see the world through younger sets of eyes.

TRAVEL THRIVES IN A WEB OF HOSPITALITY AND GRATITUDE

We think of monks as being remote from the world, but Saint Benedict, writing in the sixth century, notes that a monastery is never without guests, and admonishes monks to "receive all guests as Christ."

—Kathleen Norris, *Dakota* (1993)

One of the greatest travel chroniclers of antiquity was Egeria, a Galician nun who traveled to Jerusalem and Egypt in the fourth century. Unlike the high-profile men who recounted medieval pilgrimages to the Holy Land, Egeria didn't bother with theological pontification or rundowns of daily distances traveled. Instead, in writing to her sister nuns back home, she exuded a simple joy at the hospitality she found as she went from place to place on her spiritual journey.

In recounting a visit to the Desert of Paran (said to have been the location of the Israelites' wanderings recounted in the book of Exodus), Egeria's narrative exudes humble gratitude at the generosity of the monks who hosted her there. "Although I deserved it not," she wrote, "I cannot sufficiently thank those holy men who deigned with willing mind to receive my littleness in their cells and to guide me through all the places I was seeking."

By accommodating travelers like Egeria, medieval Christian monks presaged the sprawling web of global hospitality that welcomes modern travelers. Guest-host relationships have become more transactional than they were in Egeria's day, but her example is a reminder to practice gratitude toward the people who, having acknowledged our humanity, welcome us as guests in their land.

THRIFT HAS ALWAYS INFLUENCED WHERE (AND HOW) PEOPLE GO

> [American writers] were attracted [to Paris] by the absence of Prohibition and Puritanism . . . but they were attracted even more by the rate of exchange, which, Hemingway recalls, was so enticing that in the 20's "two people could live comfortably and well in Europe on five dollars a day and could travel."
>
> —Paul Fussell, *Abroad* (1980)

In the 1974 debut issue of the counterculture magazine *High Times,* a review for a book called *Head East: Travel Cheap! 50¢–$2 a Day* marveled at how inexpensive food and lodging could be in countries like Turkey, Afghanistan, and India. "You can live on two dollars a day or less throughout the East," it noted, "residing in relative comfort and eating well. If you have as much as $100 a month you can afford *la grande tour*."

While shoestring-budget travel was being touted as an intriguing alternative to commercial tourism in hippie-era America, it certainly wasn't new. In fact, the modern strategy of saving money on the road by forgoing popular tourist destinations (and avoiding all but the cheapest food, transport, and lodging) probably goes back to the 1840s, when an aspiring poet from Pennsylvania named Bayard Taylor wandered Europe for two years for less than $500 by sleeping in hostels built for itinerant merchants, subsisting on bread and cheese, and walking everywhere. "Had I possessed more I should have spent more," Taylor wrote in his 1846 travel memoir, *Views Afoot.* "The only value of my experience is to prove that those of scanty means need not be debarred from enjoying the pleasures and the advantages of travel."

Nearly two centuries later, this sentiment still holds true—and, thanks to the ubiquity of budget guidebooks and crowdsourced online resources, the shoestring-budget approach to travel is as safe and accessible as ever.

INTERNATIONAL BORDERS ARE
A SLIPPERY CONCEPT

The border remains a fluid, mutating, stubbornly troubling . . .
region. Perhaps it's not a region at all. Maybe it's just an idea
nobody can agree on.

—Luis Alberto Urrea, *The Devil's Highway* (2004)

One of the more curious places I've encountered in my travels is the town of Baarle on the Belgian-Dutch border, which—for abstruse historical reasons—is administratively divided into a Belgian half (Baarle-Hertog) and a Dutch half (Baarle-Nassau). In addition to the fact that each portion of the town has its own mayor and police force, parts of Baarle-Hertog exist as small enclaves within Baarle-Nassau—and some of those Baarle-Hertog enclaves contain counter-enclaves belonging to Baarle-Nassau. Thus, the notion of "international" in Baarle is a concept that cuts through individual houses, restaurants, and retail shops.

As it happens, Baarle isn't even unique (Cooch Behar in the Indian state of West Bengal includes 106 enclaves within Bangladesh), and one need not even cross physical frontiers to appreciate how arbitrary international borders can be.

The whole notion of national borders is, in fact, a slippery concept—more a matter of governmental protocol and administrative procedure than an expression of the human cultures that live along those borders. "Borders are fascinating, shapeshifting things, sometimes flimsy, often formidable, always changing," wrote Kate Harris in her 2018 book *Lands of Lost Borders*. "And they're not even 'things,' really, so much as ideas and abstractions that sometimes find physical expression."

LIGHTER LUGGAGE MAKES FOR FREER EXPERIENCES

When we pack too well, we are telling the world that it isn't good enough on its own, that it makes us uncomfortable and scared. We don't know if we can depend on anything or anyone, and we've decided it's better not to take the chance.
—Stefany Anne Goldberg, "You Can Take It with You" (2012)

When the American travel writer Mary Morris spent her junior year of university studying in Paris in 1968, she steeled herself for the uncertainty of the sojourn by packing way too much gear. "Among my material excesses," she recalled later, "were assorted electrical appliances I'd never use, high heels that made no sense on cobblestone streets, weighty guidebooks I abandoned in trains, and all those innumerable items called 'accessories,' as if they were accomplices in crime."

Morris's compulsion to overpack was a normal one. At home we surround ourselves with our possessions as a kind of comfort ritual, but on the road those seeming comforts only serve to weigh us down. It's not until we find ways to let go of excess gear that we begin to engage the journey in a reimagined way.

For Morris, this happened quite literally, one decade after her time in Paris, when an airline lost her luggage during a trip to Mexico. At first she obsessed about the items she was missing, but she eventually saw the airline's mistake as a blessing. "I settled into the freedom that lightness brings," she wrote. "Unencumbered, I moved for several days from place to place. When my bags were finally located, I wondered why I thought I'd needed all that stuff in the first place."

March 26

OVERSEAS DANGERS ARE
OVEREXAGGERATED (AND EASY TO AVOID)

I've been to damn near 100 countries and I've almost been killed
three times. All three times in the United States.
—Henry Rollins, *Travel Slideshow* (2018)

In the 1960s, when American pundits and government officials were worried about depictions of crime and aggression on television, media researcher George Gerbner coined the term "mean world syndrome" to describe a condition wherein mass-media audiences perceive the world to be more dangerous than it really is. "Fearful people are more easily manipulated," Gerbner reported. "They may accept simplistic ideas that promise to relieve their insecurities."

While Gerbner's research found that the United States was exponentially less dangerous in real life than it appears on television, decades of subsequent research have shown that Americans are even less likely to encounter violent crime traveling overseas. Even as global terrorism featured in mass-media headlines in the 2000s and 2010s, for example, per capita homicide rates for Americans traveling abroad remained twenty times lower than for Americans at home. Statistically, the most dangerous activities for travelers of any nationality from year to year have not been headline-grabbing events like terrorism or violent crime, but avoidable things like riding rental motorcycles without a helmet, swimming in unfamiliar waters, and failing to take proper health precautions against well-identified maladies.

Most any part of the world can be home to conventional dangers and high-risk areas, but these can be identified and largely avoided with a bit of cursory guidebook or online research. Even then, most warnings tend to address worst-case scenarios, and simple common sense is your best defense wherever in the world you choose to wander.

FOR A SAFER JOURNEY, DON'T BRING EXPENSIVE THINGS

In regions where there are highwaymen, facetiously termed "road agents" by the Californians, carry as little money as possible and leave your gold watch behind. . . . When you have no alternative but to hand over your valuables, do so with alacrity, and lead your assailants to think it the happiest moment of your life.

—Thomas W. Knox, *How to Travel* (1881)

Travel writers often get approached to test out all manner of accessories designed for the journey. Clothing, backpacks, and boots are common items, though over the years I've been offered dozens of products designed to keep a traveler's valuables safe: luggage locks, money belts, neck pouches, leg pouches, pack-safes, pulsating alarms that can be wedged under hotel room doors. "It's really not that dangerous out there," *San Francisco Chronicle* travel editor John Flinn observed in a 2006 essay lampooning these kinds of gadgets. "Foil thieves by carrying only a small amount of cash and one credit card. You can stash it in your sock, even without a hidden security pouch. Leave the expensive jewelry at home."

The more one travels, in fact, the less it feels necessary to pack expensive items in the first place. Author Paul Theroux, who after writing dozens of bestsellers over the years could easily choose to travel with ostentation, has packed fewer items as he's gotten older. "In faded clothes, with a twenty-dollar wristwatch and cheap sunglasses, carrying a small, plastic twenty-dollar cell phone, how could I be worth mugging?" he wrote in his 2013 travel book *The Last Train to Zona Verde*.

Indeed, in an age when bank cards have eliminated the need to carry large amounts of cash, and travel documents like tickets and permits can be stowed on a digitally backed-up smartphone, the simplest way to protect yourself against theft on the road is to not carry much worth stealing.

GETTING SICK ON THE ROAD IS COMMON (AND LARGELY AVOIDABLE)

> To talk of diseases is a sort of Arabian Nights entertainment.
> —William Ostler, *Aequanimitas* (1889)

Global travel literature has, over the centuries, been curiously fixated on the way illness can affect the journey. When the French philosopher Michel de Montaigne visited Rome in 1581, for instance, his companion noted that the water there "caused him three stools in a single evening." Two centuries earlier, Moroccan explorer Ibn Battuta detailed a diarrhea attack that gripped him south of Baghdad, grimly noting, "I had to be dismounted from the camel many times a day." More than a millennium before that, the Roman poet Horace, stuck overnight in a grungy Appian Way post station, wrote "because of the drinking water, which was horrible, I declare my belly a public enemy."

If the experience of illness has been so well documented in travel literature, it's likely because unfamiliar settings have a way of attuning us to the maladies we suffer on our journeys. Diarrhea in particular figures so prominently in travel lore that it has become something of a badge of honor for indie travelers seeking to prove that they've pushed their comfort zone. It can also mostly be avoided, provided one takes care to drink plenty of purified water, dine on properly cooked food in clean eateries, ritually wash one's hands before meals, and pay attention to local health warnings.

Even when you do get sick on the road—and anyone who travels in earnest can fall ill from time to time—dealing with it is a simple matter of taking practical, no-nonsense measures to treat the ailment, and maintaining a positive attitude. Any mindful experience of sickness can, after all, create a sharpened appreciation for days that have been blessed with good health.

GOING SOLO OPENS UP NEW POSSIBILITIES IN A PLACE

> When you're not sitting across from someone, you're sitting across from the world.
>
> —Stephanie Rosenbloom, *Alone Time* (2018)

In the 2004 interview anthology *A Sense of Place,* travel writer Jonathan Raban noted that for all the advantages of journeying with a friend or loved one, going solo is his preferred method of travel. "Traveling with a companion, you are too much of a self-contained world for the rest of the world to be able to penetrate," he said. "Whereas traveling alone, everything happens. Traveling alone puts you in this position where you will do almost anything to make contact with other people. Half the point of traveling alone is that you get so lonely you need to talk to other people."

Even when solitary travel doesn't yield new social interactions, the very act of encountering a place without a companion has a way of deepening the experiences one finds there. In her book *Alone Time,* journalist Stephanie Rosenbloom cites a vast array of research that underpins how going solo can enhance the travel experience: in museums, solo travelers make a stronger psychological connection to the art; in restaurants, eating alone allows one to take things slow and savor each aspect of the meal; on the street, walking alone stimulates new modes of thought and deepens one's connection to new environments.

Ultimately, traveling solo is less about risking loneliness than embracing solitude—which is a more dynamic way of being alone. Even when going on a journey with a companion, occasionally splitting up to explore a place in independent solitude is a great way to find new experiential possibilities there.

ATTUNE YOURSELF TO THE TELLING DETAILS OF A NEW PLACE

When you go to a Cuban marketplace, your first instinct is to catalog everything you see, especially the stuff that's typical of a third-world marketplace. But Hemingway's advice is to find the one thing that isn't typical.

—George Saunders, in a 2007 interview

Author Ernest Hemingway developed his concise, unadorned writing style while working as a young reporter for the *Kansas City Star*. Constrained by word counts, he learned to evoke the mood of places not by summarizing everything he saw, but by focusing on "telling details." Later, as a novelist, Hemingway still attuned himself to illuminating idiosyncrasies rather than obvious stereotypes. Evoking the dynamism of a Havana market wasn't a matter of comprehensively cataloging the merchants, he told a 1958 interviewer, but of noting how the vendors of fighting cocks would shove the roosters' entire heads into their own mouths and blow, making the suddenly angry animals appear fiercer than had they just been sitting in a cage.

As travelers, it is in seeking "telling details" that we are able to see cultural realities that go beyond postcard expectations. I loved Rio de Janeiro's beaches the first time I went there in 2004, for instance, but it was the city's department-store mannequins—far curvier than the underfed-looking mannequins on display in North American stores at the time—that revealed as much about Brazilian beauty ideals as did its bikini scene. Similarly, the curious abundance of nouveau riche Chinese women I saw posing for bridal photos at Seljalandsfoss waterfall in 2017 revealed something true about the rising global status of both China and Iceland.

Indeed, what at first seems strange about a place we visit is often a revelatory window into its culture.

ON THE ROAD, TIME SPOOLS OUT IN A SLOWER, RICHER WAY

- -

I travel so as to recover a whole, undamaged world on which time has no hold. . . . Two days in a new country are worth thirty lived in familiar surroundings—thirty days worn and shorted, spoiled and damaged by habit.
—Eugene Ionesco, *Journal en Miettes* (1993)

In his 1990 travel memoir *Shopping for Buddhas,* Jeff Greenwald observed that time felt different in Kathmandu than it did back home in California. "One day can seem like a week; a week, like months," he wrote. "Mornings stretch out and crack their spines with the yogic impassivity of house cats. There is time enough to do everything—write a letter, eat breakfast, read the paper, visit a shrine or two, listen to the birds, bicycle downtown, change money, buy postcards, shop for Buddhas—and arrive home in time for lunch."

Though aspects of the enlivened way Greenwald was experiencing time were specific to Nepal, the act of traveling through any unfamiliar culture has, through its very novelty, a way of making each day feel slower and stranger and more intense. At home, we have the compulsion to manage time rather than inhabit it—to cut it down into standardized, consumable chunks that make our days more efficient. On the road, freed of those micromanaged routines, we embrace time in a richer way.

In a sense, travel becomes, to quote French ethnologist Michel Leiris, "a symbolic way to stop growing old, to deny time by crossing space." In denying time, travelers receive its passing in an awakened manner. As Paul Theroux put it in his 2008 book *Ghost Train to the Eastern Star:* "The best of travel seems to exist outside of time, as though the years of travel are not deducted from your life."

DON'T LIMIT WHAT IS POSSIBLE TO DO AS A TRAVELER

Most travelers, . . . even those who would scorn to think of themselves as tourists, actually move about within predetermined, quite limited circuits and itineraries.

—Elizabeth A. Bohls, *Travel Writing 1700–1830* (2005)

As the Continental Grand Tour developed as a kind of peripatetic finishing school for British aristocrats in the seventeenth and eighteenth centuries, young travelers were expected to abide by specific routines as they went from place to place. When English traveler Thomas Coryat went to Germany in 1608, for instance, he visited fifteen cities in less than three weeks, climbing each town's highest steeple for an initial overview, then systematically seeking out local courts, libraries, treasuries, warehouses, museums, and theaters—tallying statistics and copying inscriptions into his notebook as he went.

Coryat had been subjected to these travel protocols in part to structure his learning, but also because England's aristocratic class feared that its young were liable to have too much fun if they followed their own instincts in foreign places. In 1731, an editorial in London's *Gentleman's Magazine* argued that Grand Tour itineraries had become inadequately structured. "The rational design of traveling is to become acquainted with the languages, customs, manners, laws and interests of foreign nations," it read. "Instead, [our young] are immersed in all manner of lewdness and debauchery, and have brought home dancing, gaming, and masquerades."

Though we modern travelers aren't required to check off a systematic list of activities, we still tend to constrain the journey by falling back on accepted routines. But in spite of the trendy attractions, social-media-certified photo vistas, and sightseeing routes that tell us what we're supposed to see and do in a place, don't let other people's priorities constrain the spontaneous possibilities that you find along the way.

GENERATIONS OF PAST TRAVELERS
HELP GUIDE OUR JOURNEYS

Pausanias's ancient guidebook will be studied so long as Greece shall continue to awaken the interest of mankind.
—James Frazier, *Pausanias, and Other Greek Sketches* (1900)

The oldest bit of tourist literature to have survived from the ancient era is Pausanias's second-century *Description of Greece*, an encyclopedic work that encompassed ten papyrus scrolls. This travel compendium listed cities and rivers, described markets and courts, and warned against the aggressive professional tour guides who lurked around monuments in places like Corinth. Utilitarian information, such as where to eat or find accommodation, was nonexistent, though the history, architecture, and mythology of Greece were outlined in obsessive detail. To this day, one can use Pausanias's descriptions to orient oneself in excavated sections of Delphi and Olympia.

While Pausanias is thus celebrated as the originator of the guidebook, travelers have always called on the experience and wisdom of wanderers who went before them, hearkening back to the indigenous North Americans who used navigation songs to chart the waters of the Pacific Northwest fifteen thousand years ago, or the indigenous Australians who shared mythological and geographical information using an oral tradition known as "songlines" as far back as 40,000 B.C.E.

Hence, while travel apps that rely on user-generated data, satellite-driven geopositioning systems, and crowdsourced social media advice feel like cutting-edge resources, they are in fact the latest manifestation of the ways travelers have always aggregated existing intelligence to make their way around the world.

CROSSING LAND BORDERS IS A MIND-BENDING TRAVEL RITE

The border means more than a customs house, a passport officer, a man with a gun. Over there everything is going to be different; life is never going to be quite the same again after your passport has been stamped.

—Graham Greene, *The Lawless Roads* (1937)

One of my more peculiar experiences amid a Syria sojourn in the spring of 2000 came in the border town of Qamishli, where a Kurdish smuggler offered to drive me to Erbil in his Ford Escort. "Erbil is Kurdish, just like Qamishli is," he'd quipped when I told him I wasn't allowed to cross into Iraq. "Travel there, and you'll see that the line between Syria and Iraq exists only in the minds of bureaucrats."

Though I never mustered the nerve to go to Erbil that day, the newly abstract notion of what separated Syria from Iraq reminded me of previous experiences along the Montana-Alberta frontier in North America, the village of Panmunjom in the Korean DMZ, and the curious railroad bureaucracy involved in going from Chinese Inner Mongolia to Mongolia proper. In each case, the border felt far more conceptual than cultural or geographical. As British wanderer Robert Byron wrote of Central Asia in the 1930s: "There is something absurd about a land frontier."

Yet as abstract as land borders can feel, it is rare to cross one without experiencing an innate sense of excitement (or mild disappointment, when no border stations exist to certify the transit—as happened when I first commuted from Germany to Luxembourg). As you cross the hypothetical line that separates entities with different capital cities, different holidays, and different statues of different heroes, you feel the intoxicating promise of new sights, new people, and new possibilities.

LUXURIOUS LODGING CAN BE A MIXED BLESSING

A hotel can be so much like home that it becomes a barrier to understanding the outside world and its discomforts.
—Paul Theroux, *The Last Train to Zona Verde* (2013)

In the 1989 Jim Jarmusch film *Mystery Train,* a Japanese hipster named Jun takes photos of nothing apart from hotel rooms as he and his girlfriend, Mitzuko, journey across the United States. "Jun, why do you only take pictures of the rooms we stay in and never what we see outside while we travel?" Mitzuko asks him during a stop in Memphis. "Those other things are in my memory," Jun replies. "The hotel rooms I'll forget."

If Jun found hotel rooms difficult to remember, it's because they have, over the years, evolved to become placeless. For most of human history, travelers sought out private hospitality or roadside inns as they went from place to place, and there was no such thing as a hermetic night's sleep. Even when grand hotels with indoor plumbing were established in major world cities in the nineteenth century, posh travelers shared centralized bathrooms and relaxed together in communal lobbies. It wasn't until the twentieth century that hotel rooms were designed as self-contained, temperature-controlled pods that mimicked the comforts and anonymity of home.

Though many hotels now boast of being destinations in themselves—offering a variety of dining, recreation, spa, shopping, and nightlife options under one roof—they invariably have a way of trapping you into a pleasant, sterilized home bubble that is only vaguely connected to the world beyond the hotel's walls. This can be comfortable for vacations and business trips, but engaged journeys work best (and cost less) when they are based out of humbler guesthouses and home stays—places that aren't cut off from the cultures you've come to experience.

April 5

BEACHES OFFER YOU PERMISSION
TO PUT YOUR LIFE ON HOLD

Beaches are giant blank spaces, washed clean every day, onto which all sorts of hopes are projected.
—Charles Leadbeater, "Beach Party" (2004)

Though beach outings have become synonymous with travel to warm places, the first popular seaside resorts developed in chilly England in the nineteenth century. Before that era, some aristocrats built vacation villas in European coastal enclaves, but beaches in general—those detritus-specked strips of sand that lined the edge of vast, oceanic wildernesses—were considered to be the domain of smugglers and fishermen. This began to change as the rise of railroads brought holiday-makers to affordable seaside resort towns like Blackpool, and swimming and sunbathing caught on as leisure activities for common Brits.

As beaches began to be associated with freedom and recreation, the British model of seaside holidays began to take hold in other parts of the world, first in places like the French Riviera (which boasted laxer attitudes toward nakedness), and later along the warm waterfronts of Australasia, Africa, and the Americas. Beaches became so synonymous with health, pleasure, and laid-back social codes that by the late twentieth century city-states like Monaco and Singapore were building artificial beaches to attract more visitors, and landlocked municipalities (including my Kansas hometown, twelve hundred miles from the nearest ocean) began to develop water parks and wave pools.

While twenty-first-century travelers hardly need encouragement to seek out exotic seashores, it's useful to remember that beaches' appeal as recreational Arcadias grew out of their proximity to fear-inspiring wildernesses—and that apprehending our smallness amid the waves and the water is part of the point as we put our lives on hold for a few days and relax (or hike, or paddle) into a more open-ended way of being in the world.

OVERLAND TRAVEL HAS EXPERIENTIAL (AND ETHICAL) REWARDS

Take a look at your itinerary—if it involves a domestic flight, think again. Get out an atlas, look at what is in between. Break the trip up. Slow down, see more.
—Stuart McDonald, "Take the Train, Not the Plane" (2021)

The most strident reader response I received during my years as a travel columnist came in 2007, when I wrote an essay entitled "The Death of the Mile-High Club." Within hours of this satirical article appearing online, my inbox filled with emails from chagrined readers asserting that having sex on airplanes (the act that certifies membership in the Mile-High Club) was still a thing. But my point hadn't been that sex on planes had ceased to occur; it was that the act no longer carried its original aura of Jet Age glamour. In an era of cheap airfares, long security lines, and cramped seating schemes, having sex on a commercial flight felt as tacky and quotidian as having sex in a Walmart.

Sexual aesthetics aside, the normalization of jet travel can turn travel into a game of city-to-city hopscotch, erasing the more immersive physical and cultural experience of moving through the landscape overland. While many journeys begin with a long-haul flight to a distant part of the world, booking a series of short-hop domestic flights after you've arrived in your destination is a sure way to compromise your experience of that place (and escalate the environmental impact of your journey).

As cheap and convenient as air travel has become, don't seek highlight-reel efficiency at the expense of the slower rewards that come with an overland journey. Indeed, it is through the experience of trains and buses, bicycles and ferries, hikes and horseback treks that the truer textures of a place reveal themselves.

YOU DON'T NEED TO BE FLUENT IN LANGUAGES TO TRAVEL

> You can go to the market and feel awkward because you don't speak the language, or you can go to a market and remind yourself you're not a tourist: you're one in a thousand-year-long line of hungry travelers. Hold your ground. You're part of the scene.
> —Rick Steves, "Europe Through an Open Door" (2004)

Of all the travel instincts I've developed over the years, few compare to the skills I picked up as an English-conversation teacher in South Korea. This experience made me a better listener—attuning my ear to how often language-learners stress the wrong syllables (rather than mistranslate their words). It also made me more aware of the ways other languages' consonants, vowels, and diphthongs don't have an identical English equivalent. Perhaps most significantly, it taught me that speaking slowly and simply and clearly is better than speaking loudly when one aims to be understood.

Since English is the world's most common second language, Anglophone travelers can thus increase their chances of understanding (and being understood) by being aware of the linguistic idiosyncrasies of neophyte speakers. But in situations where even ultra-simplified "Tarzan English" makes little headway, generations of travelers have learned to fine-tune their nonverbal communication skills.

"Our basic needs—sleeping, eating, drinking—can always be indicated by signs or globally understood noises," Irish travel writer Dervla Murphy noted in a 2011 essay. "Even on the emotional level, the language barrier is quite porous. People's features, particularly their eyes, are wonderfully eloquent."

Of all the nonverbal cues at your disposal as a traveler, it can't hurt to lead with a smile—a universally understood sign of good faith everywhere in the world.

April 8

TOURIST CROWDS ARE A TIME-HONORED PART OF THE TRAVEL SPECTACLE

We wish, often vehemently, that every ugly tourist would stay at home in his living room by his wretched fire, and leave such noble places to their emptiness—or at least, to us.
—Simon Winchester's introduction to *Small World* (1995)

Of all the photo books commemorating the act of travel, perhaps the most idiosyncratic—and bluntly honest—is *Small World*, British documentary photographer Martin Parr's collection of travel images featuring rain-dampened group tourists hunched in Hawaiian sightseeing boats, camcorder-clutching retirees riding donkeys on the Turkish coast, and majestic Swiss Alpine vistas foregrounded with tacky souvenir stands.

These images are amusing to flip through, in part because they highlight the mundane realities tourists try their best to ignore at otherwise magnificent attractions, and in part because we all invariably become a part of this absurd pageant in our own travels. Though the photos in *Small World* are now more than a quarter century old, they are instantly identifiable to anyone who has scrolled through a stream of gorgeously filtered social media travel images and wryly speculated on what was happening just outside the camera's field of vision.

If in doubt, consider the more banal aspects of the tourist experience—slow-moving lines outside of Mexico's Teotihuacán, screaming groups of schoolchildren on the National Mall in Washington, idling tour buses disgorging jet-lagged Europeans near Uluru in the Australian outback—to be just another fascinating texture of the travel experience. You are, after all, by the very act of being there, a part of the spectacle.

THE VAGABOND'S WAY – 103

PHOTOGRAPHS ARE A WAY OF CERTIFYING THE JOURNEY

> To me, photography is the simultaneous recognition, in a fraction of a second, of the significance of an event.
> —Henri Cartier-Bresson, *The Decisive Moment* (1952)

In the early 2000s, the monks at a Buddhist monastery near Surat Thani, Thailand, discovered a persistent problem whenever they opened their ten-day silent meditation retreats to Western travelers. For the most part, the travelers proved earnest in embracing the physical and mental challenges of meditative silence, but they had the vexing habit of sneaking cameras into the monastery. Eventually the monks circumvented this problem by offering each traveler a formal photo ceremony on the first day of the retreat. As it turned out, the Westerners had simply wanted to certify that they were spending time sequestered in such an exotic place, and getting a portrait with the orange-robed monks at the outset allowed them to be more focused in the meditation sessions that followed.

In her 1977 book *On Photography,* critic Susan Sontag noted that "needing to have reality confirmed and experience enhanced by photographs is an aesthetic consumerism to which everyone is now addicted." When we travel, she added, cameras don't just document what we see and do; they become a tool that helps us navigate the experience. "Travel becomes a strategy for accumulating photographs," Sontag wrote. "The very activity of taking pictures is soothing, and assuages general feelings of disorientation that are likely to be exacerbated by travel."

Yet even as taking pictures can be something of a passive ritual on a journey, travel photographs need not be seen as a mere frivolity. As we stumble into new experiences on the road, taking photos can be a way of orienting ourselves—of marking off a moment, and expressing curiosity about what we don't fully understand.

MUSEUMS CAN BE LIKE GOING ON A FIRST DATE WITH A PLACE

> A country's past culture as a whole, whenever it is formed from museum visits, is inevitably factitious. It has been put together for your convenience, instruction, amusement, and delight.
> —Daniel Boorstin, *The Image* (1962)

One charm of visiting a country's national museum, be it the Egyptian Museum, the British Museum, or Taipei's National Palace Museum, is that it can be like going on an extended first date with someone who is trying to impress you: You get a lot of firsthand access to fascinating stories, but it's best to be skeptical about the details. For example, the National Archives oversees America's presidential libraries, yet Richard Nixon's glosses over the 1972 Watergate break-in, Bill Clinton's describes his 1998 impeachment as "the politics of persecution," and George W. Bush's interactive "Decision Points Theater" mainly exists to justify his 2003 Iraq invasion.

Museums have always reflected the idealized narratives of the people who've established them. One of the first museums in world history was organized in the sixth century B.C.E. by Babylonian ruler Nebuchadnezzar the Great, whose collection of excavated statues and temple inscriptions was an attempt to present his own kingdom as the successor to the once-formidable Sumerian and Akkadian and Assyrian empires. Self-advertisement of greatness continues to be a central mission of state museums, though exhibits tend to shift with cultural mores. The statue of Hercules that first appeared at London's Great Exhibition in 1851, for instance, had its genitals sawn off in 1883, replaced with a carved fig leaf for nearly a century, then reattached in 1977.

Indeed, part of the charm of visiting countries' official museums comes in the revealing tension between how the nation presents itself in its formal galleries and how it reveals itself outside those galleries.

SOME TRAVEL SIGHTS ARE AKIN TO CELEBRITIES

Tourist attractions are success stories—people go to see them because their fame precedes their original historical value. Their importance within their social context has been lost in the void of their popular fame.

—Francesco Bonami, "The Authentic and the Universal" (2005)

One of the more curious aspects of the Louvre in Paris is the way so many of the museum's visitors (as many as 80 percent of its seven million annual guests, according to some surveys) consistently seek out one painting amid its thirty-five thousand works of art. Indeed, the *Mona Lisa* has become so associated with the genius of Leonardo da Vinci—and so emblematic of what one is supposed to seek out in art museums—that the Louvre has posted signs directing impatient tourists to its gallery. Viewing the painting there, amid hordes of camera-clutching rubberneckers, can feel akin to paparazzi clustering around celebrities at film premieres.

Historian Daniel Boorstin's 1962 book *The Image* is best known for defining a celebrity as "a person who is known for his well-knownness"—and he frequently extended this metaphor to include the things we seek as travelers. "All over the world now we find these 'attractions,'" he wrote, "of little significance for the inward life of a people, but wonderfully salable as tourist commodity."

Just as movie stars have quotidian lives (and the *Mona Lisa* was not commissioned to hang in a tourist-clotted museum), the well-knownness of what we seek at tourist attractions is invariably the least meaningful aspect of what we encounter there. As might be the case with encountering a real-life celebrity, finding imaginative ways to be in conversation with these places counts for more than snapping photos and moving on.

HARBORING DISDAIN FOR TOURISTS DOESN'T MEAN YOU AREN'T ONE

Despite the suffering he undergoes, the anti-tourist is not to be confused with the traveler: his motive is not inquiry but self-protection and vanity.

—Paul Fussell, *Abroad* (1980)

In promoting his 2006 travel book *The Lost Cosmonaut,* Scottish author Daniel Kalder came up with a thirteen-point "Anti-Tourist" manifesto, suggesting that the best places to visit are areas other people take pains to avoid. This in mind, the anti-tourist makes a point to eschew comfort, stay in crappy hotels, travel at the wrong time of the year, and favor "disorientation over enlightenment." Though Kalder's manifesto was a largely tongue-in-cheek gesture that highlighted his decision to visit under-touristed corners of former Soviet republics, it evokes the time-honored tourist ritual of taking great pains to not be mistaken for a tourist.

In his 1980 book *Abroad,* cultural historian Paul Fussell poked fun at anti-tourists, noting that they attempt to conceal their tourist status by not carrying a camera, avoiding the standard sights, eating weird local food, donning native fashions, and sitting in cafés regarding other tourists with contempt. For Fussell, the anti-tourist pose is not an act of resistance to mass-tourism so much as it is an expression of it. "The anti-tourist deludes only himself," he wrote. "We are all tourists now, and there is no escape."

While the attitude of "anti-tourism" can (in Kalder's sense of the term) help steer our travels into "new zones of experience," it does not (in Fussell's sense of the term) absolve us from the fact that we—as strangers in strange lands—also qualify as tourists. Experienced travelers remain humble about their inevitable tourist status, even as they find counterintuitive new ways to wander away from the tourist trail.

TOURIST DESTINATIONS BEND TO TOURIST EXPECTATIONS

The successful urban tourist space is one which offers excitement, spectacle and stimulation at the same time as safety, security and familiarity. . . . The paradox is that at some point this process may make the area less attractive to precisely those people it is trying to attract.

—Duncan Tyler and Yvonne Guerrier, *Managing Tourism in Cities* (1998)

Many years ago, I traveled to the Indian pilgrimage town of Pushkar, which at the time had become popular with backpackers. From the moment I arrived in Pushkar, something irritated me about the little holy town. As I walked along the shores of the local lake, a number of long-bearded, monk-like Hindu sadhus approached me and suggested I take their photo for the "bargain price" of 15 rupees; Brahmin priests kept hustling up and offering to take me through a *puja* ceremony for just 50 rupees.

Prior to Pushkar, no Indian had ever implied that there was a cash value to *puja* (a Hindu ablution ritual), and most of the sadhus I'd seen were more interested in piety and asceticism than photo opportunities. The longer I stayed in Pushkar, the more I realized that the town's idiosyncrasies had less to do with its significance to Hindu pilgrims than its popularity among Western backpackers. Though Pushkar wasn't a tourist town in the resort-hotel and souvenir-boutique sense of the word, it had developed a makeshift economy in the kind of photogenic, stereotypical Hindu "authenticity" travelers were looking for.

Often, the cultural "annoyances" we experience as travelers are less an organic expression of a culture than a utilitarian reaction to the desires of travelers who came before us. In seeking to experience these places, we often end up witnessing the curious ways they've come to accommodate what outsiders (like us) had hoped they might experience there.

WE LONG TO SEE PLACES
THAT NEVER EXISTED

Idealizing more primitive ways of life is a fixed mental tendency, a psychological constant, if you will, inseparable from the rise of civilization itself.

—Roger Sandall, "10,000 Years of Nostalgia" (2005)

From early in his career, Spokane–Coeur d'Alene novelist Sherman Alexie was puzzled by Germans' outsized interest in Native American communities and culture. "I gave a poetry reading in Berlin about seven years ago, and about two hundred people showed up," he marveled in a 2009 essay. "There were a dozen old German guys wearing full eagle feather headdresses. It was crazy." As it turned out, modern German *Indianertümelei* (Indian enthusiasm) dates back to the pulp fictions of a nineteenth-century Saxon named Karl May, whose tales of a wise Apache chief named Winnetou had been inspired by reading American cowboy novels. In idealizing May's vision of Wild West Indian life, generations of Germans had come to long for a place that had never really existed.

Similarly, the Namibian Kalahari outpost of Tsumkwe began to attract scores of Western tourists in the late twentieth century after a number of films—most notably the 1980 movie *The Gods Must Be Crazy*—depicted !Kung San as gentle hunter-gatherers. As it turned out, the notion that !Kung San were non-hierarchical souls living in perfect harmony with nature was based on a discredited 1950s anthropological study that had more to do with American postwar fantasies than with day-to-day life in the Kalahari.

Often, the reveries that we harbor about other places—particularly places in which we perceive people as living simple, traditional lives— have more to do with our own fantasies than with daily life in those places. Visiting these places is not just a chance to interact with the cultures that inspired these fantasies; it is a chance to exchange our fanciful reveries for the subtler realities we find there.

April 15

A KIND OF DISAPPOINTMENT IS AN INEVITABLE PART OF TRAVEL

We never experience the world exactly as it is. We bring our expectations to a moment, and then we see that through varying lenses of hope, grief, and disappointment—especially the despair that descends when something doesn't live up to the idea we have constructed.

—Maggie Downs, *Braver than You Think* (2020)

In 1986, a psychiatrist working at the Sainte-Anne Hospital Center in France coined the term "Paris Syndrome" to describe a condition that had been afflicting visitors to the city. Numerous first-time tourists—in particular those from Japan and other East Asian countries—were said to have experienced shortness of breath, rapid heartbeat, and hallucinations when they visited such sites as the Notre-Dame Cathedral, the Louvre, and the Eiffel Tower.

Doctors initially assumed that these symptoms derived from the excitement of finally seeing iconic landmarks that had previously only been dreamed about, but Paris Syndrome was ultimately determined to be an acute form of *disappointment*. Conditioned by movies and magazines to believe that Paris was a paragon of high culture and beautiful people, some visitors to the city fell into anxious despair at the spectacle of overcrowded tourist queues, surly shopkeepers, and urine-scented alleyways.

Paris Syndrome continues to afflict a few dozen visitors each year and is in fact an extreme version of what most of us feel when our long-held dreams crash up against the occasional letdowns of the travel experience itself. In such situations, the best response is to take those less-than-romantic realities—the overlong queues and unpleasant odors and rude locals—as a part of the inherent complexity (and inevitable mix of joy and disappointment) that comes with keeping yourself open to the promise of a new place.

FOOD IS ONE OF THE BEST WINDOWS INTO A LOCAL CULTURE

Food is everything we are. It's an extension of nationalist feeling, ethnic feeling, your personal history, your province, your region, your tribe, your grandma. It's inseparable from the get-go.
—Anthony Bourdain, in a 2010 interview

When I first visited Madrid, I was a few hours into a night of eating and drinking with my host, Miguel, when I asked him when we were going to stop in at a place that served tapas. His reply underscored how, for the cross-cultural traveler, no encounter with food is purely about the food itself.

Tapas, Miguel explained, might be best understood as a verb as much as a noun—a word that applies less to specific menu items than a way of structuring an evening out on the town. Since dinner often starts at 10 P.M. or later in Spain, tapas dishes are meant to assuage the appetite and counterbalance the effects of alcohol while socializing in the early evening. In this sense, he said, we'd been engaging in tapas ever since he'd served me wine and olives in his apartment hours ear-lier.

Just as the tapas ritual underpins the unhurried, socially minded charm of life in Spain, food and drink anywhere can be a window into the culture that prepares it. In Ethiopia, where meals are shared from a single plate (and the ritual of *gursha* involves popping the tastiest morsels directly into each other's mouths), meals are as group-oriented and openhearted as the people you meet there; in China, ritually swilling the liquor *baijiu* at meals underscores the cultural importance of both camaraderie and formal respect.

On the road, these sorts of cuisine rituals aren't just appetizing—they are among the most pleasurable cultural discoveries a journey can provide.

April 17

LOOKING FOR LOCAL CROWDS BEATS "CROWDSOURCING"

By shaping the menus we pick from, technology hijacks the way we perceive our choices and replaces them with new ones.
—Tristan Harris, "Technology Is Hijacking Your Mind" (2016)

Some years ago, while visiting the Indonesian city of Bukittinggi, I decided to seek out *rendang,* a local delicacy consisting of slow-cooked meat caramelized in coconut milk and spices. Using the Wi-Fi connection in my guesthouse, I found a TripAdvisor review with a header along the lines of: "Best *rendang* in Bukittinggi!!!" The place was just a five-minute walk from where I was staying, so I decided to go.

As it happened, the TripAdvisor-approved *rendang* restaurant was empty when I arrived. The owner opened the kitchen for me, apologetically explaining that she usually catered to the tourist bus trade, and she hadn't expected the buses to arrive until later that evening. Her *rendang* tasted okay, if a bit dry. When I left, I was still her only customer.

On the walk home I noticed something I'd overlooked on the way to the TripAdvisor-sanctioned restaurant: The street that led back to my guesthouse was lined with food tents packed with local diners. Somehow, I had completely overlooked a local street-food scene that had attracted throngs of Bukittinggi natives at the very hour my internet-approved restaurant sat empty. Had I simply used my eyes and my nose (rather than an online review), I no doubt would have had a more enjoyable meal.

This experience thus taught me a simple but elegant travel lesson: If you're going to crowdsource an eating recommendation, the virtual advice of bygone travelers counts far less than the presence of a real-life crowd.

BARGAINING AND HAGGLING HUMANIZES TRANSACTIONS

> If the African, Indian, Arab, South American, or Mediterranean seller wants to sell a product, and the tourist wants to buy it, why not set a fair price and let the sale proceed? Because the sale is only one part of the interaction. . . . The buyer and seller reaffirm that they're dealing with—and that they are—humans, not machines.
>
> —Deborah Tannen, *That's Not What I Meant!* (1990)

In his 1968 travelogue *The Voices of Marrakesh,* Vienna-based author Elias Canetti expressed astonishment at how malleable the prices could be in a Moroccan souk. "The price that is named first is an unfathomable riddle," he wrote. "No one knows in advance what it will be, not even the merchant. . . . Each one relates to a different situation, a different customer, a different time of day, a different day of the week."

Though bargaining to arrive at a price while shopping is often seen as an Eastern practice ("Only God can fix prices," asserts a saying from the Islamic hadith), set prices didn't arrive in the West until the nineteenth century, when mail-order catalogs and high-traffic urban department stores made haggling impractical. Before that time, prices varied according to the needs, social position, and bargaining ability of each customer, and—even in the United States—not wanting to haggle was seen as naive and churlish.

For Western travelers who've done no bargaining beyond the detached abstraction of online auctions, haggling for items in the crowded marketplace of a distant country might seem intimidating. It need not be. In practice, bargaining to arrive at a mutually agreed-upon price can be a cheerful (and tactically stimulating) form of face-to-face social capital—an intricate trust relationship that can offer travelers a window into local ways of life, even as it humanizes both parties to each other.

April 19

SCAM ARTISTS ARE AN INEVITABLE PART OF THE TRAVEL ECONOMY

If you don't occasionally get scammed on your travels, you aren't pushing yourself. . . . Most scam artists are trying to wring a few bucks out of a tourist to feed his family.
—Matt Kepnes, *Ten Years a Nomad* (2019)

When American novelist John Dos Passos traveled from Baghdad to Damascus by camel caravan in 1922, he encountered a curious scam as he made his way through the region's tribal areas. Every fifty or so miles, he had to ransom his baggage to tribal leaders, who claimed they would defend him against rival Arab tribes. Then, crossing into those rival tribes' territories, he was asked to pay a similar protection racket to defend himself from the tribes he'd just visited. Though the shakedown Dos Passos encountered might sound like an enterprise directed at credulous non-Muslim travelers, it was identical to a scam Persian poet Nasir Khusraw reported east of Mecca amid his Islamic pilgrimage nine centuries earlier.

Indeed, travel scams have likely existed for as long as people have journeyed to new places—in part because travelers tend to be ignorant of local norms, dependent on the assistance of others, and relatively easy to deceive. In my own experience I've encountered a dizzying array of would-be travel rackets—from bogus moneychangers and fake tour guides, to card-game confidence tricks and gem shop resale schemes, to orchestrated fistfights designed to distract attention and enable pickpockets.

If in doubt, be suspicious of any encounter that would feel weird or unsafe if it were happening back home—especially in areas popular with tourists (where scam artists tend to congregate). And even if you occasionally fall prey to a scam, think of it as a kind of traveler's tax—an irritating, mostly harmless expense that comes with experiencing new places.

DON'T LET THE THINGS YOU PACK
DETRACT FROM THE JOURNEY

Jesus told the twelve disciples: "Take nothing for the journey—no
staff, no bag, no bread, no money, no extra shirt."
— The Gospel of Luke (c. 90 C.E.)

At the height of the Roman Empire nearly twenty centuries ago, aristocratic tourists took great pride in traveling around the Mediterranean seaboard with all the comforts of home. Some noblemen equipped their coaches with crystal goblets and dice tables, others traveled with their favorite works of art; the ultra-rich invested in *carrucae dormitoriae*—sleeping carriages outfitted with rotating seats and goosedown cushions. Naturally, such luxuries required a retinue of servants to carry equipment and prepare food, which meant that ancient luxury travel was a painfully slow and predictable affair.

A contemporary skeptic of these Roman tourists was a Berber Christian named Minucius Felix, who pointed out that ostentatious packing lists only served to detract from the spiritual essence of a journey. "The wayfarer's step is jauntier the lighter he travels," Minucius noted. "In this journey of life, a man is happier who lightens his needs by poverty and does not groan under the burden of riches."

Though modern tourists are not likely to travel with servants and dice tables, stuffing one's luggage with the arbitrary comforts of home is still one of the surest ways to make a journey more cumbersome and less serendipitous. As the Thai Buddhist monk Ajahn Buddhadasa observed in an interview just before his death in 1993, travel can be a life-altering endeavor for the very reason that it introduces you to places where nothing belongs to you. "When you're at home, surrounded by your possessions, you're weighed down," he said. "Away from home, you come to understand how unimportant those possessions really are."

SAVING MONEY IS A MATTER OF FORGOING SMALL CONVENIENCES

You want to save money? Then just spend less, and care less.
—Matt Gross, *The Turk Who Loved Apples* (2013)

The worst bathroom facilities I've encountered on recent journeys were all clustered in central Sumatra. At Lake Toba, my guesthouse toilet didn't flush, which meant I had to brandish a plastic scoop (the same one I used to "shower") to splash water into the bowl after I used it. The toilet in my Harau Valley cottage was little more than a hole in the floor, and while the communal bathroom at Rimba had a proper commode, its shower didn't have hot water, and I had to hike there each morning from my beach hut.

As it happened, that part of Sumatra offered me one of the most affordable and rewarding travel experiences I've had anywhere. The guesthouse at Lake Toba cost me $11.75 a night, and was close enough to the gorgeous volcanic caldera that I could dive into its deep-blue waters from the rail of my balcony. The Harau Valley cottage—which cost me $8.50 a night, breakfast included—sat over a lotus pond, and its porch hammock had a view of a cascading waterfall one hundred meters away. My $18-a-night lodging at Rimba featured three full meals a day at the eco-lodge, and my beach hut sat fifty meters from a reef full of butterflyfish and sea turtles.

I could gripe more about other aspects of traveling in central Sumatra (the highways, for example, were honeycombed with potholes and washouts), but these challenges were minor compared to the stupendous natural beauty I found there. On the road, saving money is often a matter of altering your expectations—of forgoing a few conveniences and embracing the richness of the journey itself.

April 22

IF IN DOUBT, WALK UNTIL YOUR DAY BECOMES INTERESTING

There's no need for an itinerary. Walk, and the day arranges itself. . . . From the sidewalk, the best of the city can be had for free.

—Stephanie Rosenbloom, *Alone Time* (2018)

In her 1930 essay "Street Haunting," English writer Virginia Woolf posited that the most important tool for seeking experience on the streets of a city was a pencil. "When the desire comes upon us to go street rambling, the pencil does for a pretext," she wrote, "and getting up, we say: 'Really I must buy a pencil,' as if under cover of this excuse we could indulge safely in the greatest pleasure of town life—rambling the streets of London."

For Woolf, the conviction to go out and buy a pencil was less about the pencil than the conviction to go out—that is, to wander out into the streets and open herself up to new experiences. This is an activity travelers engage in all the time by accident: Leaving a Cesky Krumlov hostel in search of laundry detergent, one winds up stumbling into a Czech beer festival; wandering out of a Jodhpur guesthouse looking for a pharmacy, one winds up getting invited to a Hindu wedding; meandering the streets of Perth seeking dinner at day's end, one winds up stopping to absorb the splendor as orange-purple sunlight flares over the Indian Ocean.

Pencil notwithstanding, Woolf's ritual evokes one of the best fall-back strategies you can develop as a traveler: *If in doubt, walk until your day becomes interesting.* That is, instead of worrying about lists of goals and attractions at a given place, find a neighborhood that intrigues you and keep all your senses open as you wander through it. In this way, your instincts become your guidebook, and possibility becomes your map.

SOMETIMES THE BEST WAY TO FIND A PLACE IS TO GET LOST

In the middle of the forest there's an unexpected clearing that can only be found by those who have gotten lost.
—Tomas Tranströmer, "Gläntan" (1980)

One of the counterintuitive life enhancements Henry David Thoreau explored in the pages of *Walden* was his nonchalant willingness to occasionally lose his way in the woods. "It is a surprising and memorable, as well as valuable experience, to be lost," he wrote. "Not till we are lost, in other words not till we have lost the world, do we begin to find ourselves, and realize where we are and the infinite extent of our relations."

Indeed, the willingness to get lost (and found again) has always been a ritual that various global cultures have employed in the service of creativity and revelation. "The most ubiquitous vehicle of ritual lostness—the most basic embodiment of disorientation—is the labyrinth," wrote Will Hunt in his 2019 book *Underground*. "We find labyrinthine structures in every corner of the world, . . . [and they are] devised to engineer a concentrated experience of disorientation. . . . In this state, we are primed to undergo a transformation."

Though it's possible for travelers to visit classic labyrinth remnants in places like Knossos in Crete or the Old Summer Palace in Beijing, the willingness to lose one's way, and embrace the unexpected encounters and unplanned discoveries that result, can be as simple as leaving your GPS smartphone at the guesthouse and improvising your way around a new environment. Practiced with awareness—and a commonsense nod to safety—getting lost can be the surest way, as a traveler, to find what you didn't know you were looking for.

SLOW JOURNEYS MAKE FOR MORE ENGAGED CONNECTIONS

I don't want to hurry it. When you want to hurry something, that means you no longer care about it and want to get on to other things.

—Robert M. Pirsig, *Zen and the Art of Motorcycle Maintenance* (1974)

Of the many reasons industrial-fortune heir Michael Rockefeller was killed (and possibly eaten) in the Indonesian province of Papua in 1961, a key one may have been his unwillingness to slow down as he traveled the region seeking Asmat tribal art. "Michael was working with a bottomless supply of money," journalist Carl Hoffman noted in his 2014 book *Savage Harvest*. "Had Michael had less money, he would have had to move more slowly, would have had to settle in villages for longer, to trade, to make connections, to become known. Instead, he averaged a day or two in every village; he arrived, bought, and moved on." As Rockefeller rushed from place to place collecting art, he became something of a specter to his Asmat hosts, who wound up killing him, Hoffman surmised, out of confusion over an unrelated clash with Dutch colonial officials five years earlier.

Though Michael Rockefeller's fate is an extreme example of what happens when you prioritize abstract travel goals over the nuances of what you discover en route, it can serve as a metaphor for the perils of racing to fulfill any arbitrary set of goals on the road. A cursory, list-driven quest—be it seeking out Asmat art items, UNESCO World Heritage sites, or new pages of passport stamps—tends to compromise an engaged experience of the very communities that exist along the route of that quest. If in doubt, alter your goals as the journey plays out, seeking meaningful connections in a single place before hurrying along to the next one.

TRAVEL GIVES YOU THE PRETEXT
TO BE A BEGINNER AGAIN

To me, there's nothing more humbling than a new culture high-
lighting my own inexperience, naïveté, and sense of entitlement.
But this side of travel can actually be (painfully) wonderful—if
we recognize it and *use* it constructively.
—Lavinia Spalding, *Writing Away* (2009)

Back in the mid-2000s, I decided that learning how to dance
would give my travels through Latin America a heightened sense
of purpose. Starting with a monthlong attempt to learn merengue in
the Dominican Republic, I later spent a month attempting salsa in
Cuba, and another studying samba in Brazil. Each new dance had its
own set of complexities, but some challenges were consistent from
country to country. Men were always expected to be the lead partner,
for example, which meant that learning the *vueltas* was easier for my
female classmates (who, understandably, preferred practicing these
moves with partners more seasoned than I).

As much as anything, however, practicing these dances made me
come to terms with being a beginner again: It made me admit my vast
ignorance, and endure the small humiliations that came with trying
to learn something new. Confronted with my own ineptitude on the
dance floor, I had no choice but to swallow my pride and try to improve. In doing this, I engaged with my host cultures in a more vulnerable way.

Though most any aspect of traveling to a new place can render us
beginners, attempting to learn a specific skill imbues you with a
heightened sense of attention to those places. "Learning a craft . . . can
help remediate narcissism by rebalancing our relationship to ourselves," philosophy professor Alexander Stern wrote in a 2021 *Aeon*
essay. "In the process of submitting to discipline and focusing our attention on a craft, we find ourselves neither omnipotent nor helpless,
but somewhere in between."

IT'S OKAY TO CHANGE YOUR TRAVEL GOALS MID-JOURNEY

Even when the outcome isn't what we hoped it would be, making the effort to experience something new can still be good for us. It can help us think of ourselves as the kind of people who are capable of taking action.

—Stephanie Rosenbloom, *Alone Time* (2018)

Amid my attempts to learn how to dance in Latin America in the mid-2000s, I befriended a group of recent university graduates in Havana. Brilliant, beautiful, and effortlessly hip, my Cuban friends were ambivalent about salsa dancing (which to them was as quaint and uninspiring as the Electric Slide might have seemed to me). They were far more passionate about the Asturian bagpipes, which had first been introduced to the island from northern Spain in the nineteenth century. After a few weeks of wandering Havana's Malecón with my Cuban friends, my salsa skills were still sorely lacking, but I had learned how to play a decent bagpipe rendition of "Don't Get Married in Oviedo."

In retrospect, it might have made sense to return to Cuba and master the *gaita asturiana,* but the travel writer part of me thought I should stick to my original mission and seek Latin dances elsewhere. Even more significantly, I should have paid keener attention to what really inspired me on the road: The Spanish bagpipes (and the young Cubans who played them) had sparked my imagination in ways salsa hadn't.

Initial goals notwithstanding, it's important to give yourself permission to find and follow new passions on the road. "[We are] a moving edge between what we know about ourselves and what we are about to become," wrote David Whyte in his 2014 book *Consolations.* "What we are about to become . . . always trumps what we think we are already."

WHAT SEEMS ODD ABOUT OTHER CULTURES CAN REVEAL YOUR OWN

> Food can be defined as an objectively edible substance, that is, one that is capable of nourishing the body, but edible substances must be culturally defined as food before they will be eaten.
> —Ina Corinne Brown, *Understanding Other Cultures* (1963)

One memorable footnote to my mid-2000s Havana sojourn came a few years later, when I met up with my Cuban bagpiper friends at a Celtic music festival in Canada. Away from Cuba for the first time, they enjoyed the standard sights of Nova Scotia (things like whale-watching and colorful fall foliage), but they also thrilled at quotidian experiences not possible under communist restrictions in Cuba. Young Americans who shared their hipster-musician temperament would not have regarded big-box retail stores as travel attractions, for instance, but my friends marveled at seeing more consumer options in a single Halifax Walmart than they might have found in a decade of navigating Cuba's dysfunctional black-market economy.

Viewing Canada through my Cuban friends' eyes didn't just expand my notion of what might be considered exotic in Nova Scotia; it also made me question my own culture-bound assumptions. Having grown up savoring Doritos, I was startled to discover that the Cubans found them disgusting ("How is this even considered food?" one of them grumbled). Indeed, even as they enthused at consumer options not available in their own country, my friends were astonished that American consumers would voluntarily eat mass-produced triangular corn chips dusted with maltodextrin, disodium phosphate, and Yellow #5.

In this way, something so basic as going shopping or eating food in an unfamiliar place (or seeing people from that place eat or shop in your culture) doesn't just allow you to note what is unusual about other cultures; it helps you appreciate what is idiosyncratic about your own.

WHAT SEEMS CULTURALLY "INAUTHENTIC" CAN BE REVEALING

Pardon him, Theodotus: he is a barbarian, and thinks that the customs of his tribe and island are the laws of nature.
—George Bernard Shaw, *Caesar and Cleopatra* (1898)

The first time I visited Cairo, I felt faintly self-conscious one evening when—having sampled such local fast-food dishes as shawarma and *kushari* the previous few days—I walked to the McDonald's restaurant near Tahrir Square and ordered a Big Mac. To be honest, I wasn't really there for the food.

Indeed, over the years, McDonald's has become something of an ecumenical hangout for travelers—less for its menu than for its reliable air-conditioning and clean restrooms. This was certainly the case for me in Cairo, though the longer I lingered there, the more I realized it had a different clientele than American franchises. At least half of the customers, I noticed, were well-dressed young Egyptians and their chaperones out on chaste first dates. What felt familiar to me was, for the Cairenes at the McDonald's, urbane and culinarily exotic.

I have since come to regard McDonald's franchises as a kind of measuring stick for cultural nuance as I travel from place to place. In China, where familial identity is a core virtue, Ronald McDonald has a wife, Aunt McDonald. In India, where Hindu and Muslim taboos forbid beef and pork, a McDonald's serves chicken "Maharaja Macs" rather than Big Macs. And, as any *Pulp Fiction* fan will know, one can order a beer with *le Big Mac* at a McDonald's in Paris.

My point here isn't to advocate for eating at McDonald's so much as to point out that any seemingly standardized global enterprise—fast food included—can be surprisingly revelatory of the local culture as you travel from place to place.

KEEP THE TRUE HARDSHIPS OF TRAVEL IN PERSPECTIVE

If you must suffer, then plan your suffering carefully—as you choose your dreams.

—Edward Abbey, *A Voice Crying in the Wilderness* (1989)

When sailors on British explorer James Cook's ship *Endeavour* were suffering from a dysentery outbreak off the coast of Java in 1771, Cook noted in his journal that sickness itself was often less dangerous than anxiety about worst-case scenarios. "Such are the dispositions of men in general in these Voyages that they are seldom content with the Hardships and Dangers which will naturally occur," he wrote, "but they must add others which hardly ever had existence but in their imaginations by magnifying the most Trifling accidents and circumstances to the greatest Hardships and unsurmountable dangers."

Though the hardships we modern travelers encounter rarely compare with those of Cook's *Endeavour*, we are also at risk of letting worst-case scenarios compromise our real-time experience and enjoyment of the journey. One strategy for lessening apprehension of the unknown is "negative visualization," a modern twist on the ancient Stoic exercise of meditating on adverse outcomes as a way of training oneself not to worry about them. Imagining worst-case scenarios thus becomes a bulwark against (rather than an embrace of) anxiety, and an exercise in gratitude for the realities of the true situation one is dealing with.

Ultimately, making the most of life on the road doesn't come in trying to avoid real or imagined difficulties, but in maintaining a realistic perspective on the difficulties that do arise in the course of a journey. "Be master of your petty annoyances and conserve your energies for the big, worthwhile things," goes a saying attributed to British Canadian poet Robert W. Service. "It isn't the mountain ahead that wears you out—it's the grain of sand in your shoe."

KEEPING A JOURNAL HELPS YOU MAKE SENSE OF THE JOURNEY

Keep a notebook. Travel with it, eat with it, sleep with it. Slap into it every stray thought that flutters up into your brain. Cheap paper is less perishable than gray matter, and lead pencil markings endure longer than memory.

—Jack London, "Getting into Print" (1903)

Keeping a handwritten journal as you travel can prove to be one of the most rewarding daily rituals of a journey—in part because it amounts to more than the specific thoughts and observations you record on the page. In her 2009 book *Writing Away*, author Lavinia Spalding noted that a journal can be a powerful tool for self-understanding while you make sense of new places. "It can become a haven, a sacred oasis to come home to when travel has thrown you off-kilter," she wrote, "a personal traveling shrine, where you commune with only you."

Whereas the public task of sharing travel observations on social media has popularly usurped the rite of keeping a private travel journal, recording your thoughts on paper for the exclusive audience of yourself is a far more reflective and enduring way to document the journey. Social media posts tend to evoke a cocksure, performative sense for what happens on the road, while a journal allows you to be vulnerable and reflective—to make sense of anxiety and uncertainty and loneliness, as well as joy and triumph.

In this way, a travel journal can end up becoming both an insightful chronicle of the journey and an ever-expanding testament to what you've learned along the way. "In the end, your travelogue will help you remember more than what you did and saw," Spalding wrote. "It will help you remember how you became the person you are today."

EMBRACING THE DAY-TO-DAY RHYTHMS OF THE JOURNEY

FIND WAYS TO LET FAMOUS SIGHTS
CATCH YOU OFF GUARD

> The tourist who arrives at the Leaning Tower of Pisa, or the Grand Canyon of Arizona, can now merely check his reactions to something with which he has long been familiar, and take his own pictures of the same.
>
> —Marshall McLuhan, *Understanding Media* (1964)

In his 1897 book *Following the Equator*, Mark Twain complained that visiting India's Taj Mahal came with too many superlative expectations. "I had read a great deal too much about it," he wrote. "I saw it in the daytime, I saw it in the moonlight . . . [and I knew] that of its kind it was the wonder of the world. . . . And yet, it was not *my* Taj. *My* Taj had been built by excitable literary people; it was solidly lodged in my head, and I could not blast it out."

Philosopher Robert M. Pirsig made a similar observation when viewing Oregon's Crater Lake alongside tourists snapping pictures of it. "The quality of the lake is smothered by the fact that it's so pointed to," he wrote in his 1974 book *Zen and the Art of Motorcycle Maintenance*. "You point to something as having Quality and the Quality tends to go away." Indeed, the famous places we seek as travelers get so tied up in their aura that what we experience there can get mixed up with what we had hoped to experience there.

An anecdote attributed to Twain asserts that a play becomes more interesting when a stray cat wanders onstage, since the cat is not bound by the same dramatic rules as the actors. This in mind, one way of making famous landmarks more comprehensible is to look for the "cat"—that is, the surprises, good and bad, that go beyond what you are expected to encounter there, details that open you up to the raw imperfections of the encounter itself.

WHAT A PLACE OFFERS IS RICHER THAN WHAT BROUGHT YOU THERE

[Ma] turns to me and says, "You give [tourists] history, temples, pagodas, traditional dance, floating markets, seafood curry, tapioca desserts, silk-weaving cooperatives, but all they really want is to ride [elephants] . . . and to lie there half-dead getting skin cancer on the beach."

—Rattawut Lapcharoensap, *Sightseeing* (2005)

In the mid-2010s, the appearance of French lavender fields in the Asian TV drama *Dreams Behind a Crystal Curtain* attracted tens of thousands of Chinese tourists to Alpes-de-Haute-Provence each summer. Though local officials welcomed the economic boost, they had trouble figuring out what, apart from taking selfies in the lavender fields, these new visitors wanted. "They take pictures, cut a few lavender stems, and leave for other parts of France," one perplexed farmer told *Der Spiegel*. Provençal villagers eventually opened Asian noodle shops and offered lavender-oil hotel massages in an attempt to convince Chinese tourists to stay for more than a few hours.

Though it's tempting to poke fun at anyone who would race through a culturally rich part of the world in search of a few cursory snapshots, seeking out the most obvious, predetermined aspects of a place is not an impulse unique to Chinese tourists. The first time I went to New Orleans, for instance, I spent the bulk of my time there wandering around the French Quarter drinking Hurricanes, since I thought that's what revelers did during Mardi Gras. It wasn't until I returned a decade later and strayed beyond the Quarter into the Marigny and Tremé (and areas well beyond these sightseeing-map neighborhoods) that I began to properly experience the city.

"Meaningful experiences don't typically happen in tourist zones and backpacker hot spots," wrote Lavinia Spalding in her 2009 book *Writing Away*. "They're found in barbershops, classrooms, markets, hospitals, playgrounds, remote villages, and hole-in-the-wall kitchens. You'll find them by taking risks and getting involved."

EMBRACE THE KINDNESS OF STRANGERS

> I saw a crocodile in this part of the Niger, close to the bank; it looked like a small boat. One day I went down to the river to satisfy a need, and lo, one of the natives came and stood between me and the river. I was amazed at such a lack of manners on his part, and spoke of it to someone. He answered, "His purpose in doing that was solely to protect you from the crocodile. By placing himself between you and it."
>
> —Ibn Battuta, *The Travels* (1355)

Marco Polo is remembered as the most prolific traveler of the late Middle Ages, but his journey was actually eclipsed by a Berber-Moroccan traveler named Ibn Battuta, who first departed his home at age twenty-one, in 1325, roughly one year after Polo died. Battuta's intention at the time was to perform the Muslim pilgrimage to Mecca, but—seized by wanderlust—he wound up traveling seventy-five thousand miles across Asia and Africa over the course of the next thirty years.

Amid his ongoing adventures, Battuta took pains to point out the kindness of the strangers he met—from the Algerians who comforted him when he was lonely in North Africa, to the Iraqis who tended to him when he suffered diarrhea near the Euphrates, to the Sri Lankan Buddhists who went out of their way to give hospitality to Muslims.

Centuries later, Battuta's experiences feel most relatable to me when I recall the kindnesses offered to me by strangers in my own travels. As Paul Theroux pointed out in *Ghost Train to the Eastern Star,* "Most travel, and certainly the rewarding kind, involves depending on the kindness of strangers—putting yourself into the hands of people you don't know, and trusting them with your life."

EVERYDAY RITUALS REVEAL A PLACE IN A WAY "SIGHTS" DON'T

The invariable mark of wisdom is to see the miraculous in the common.

—Ralph Waldo Emerson, *Nature* (1836)

O f the many things I experienced on a 2010 visit to Cairo (including riding horses near the Great Pyramid of Giza, and getting invited to a Ramadan *iftar* banquet), one of the most memorable was the shave I got at a back-alley barbershop on Zamalek Island in the Nile.

There, under Egyptian soap operas flickering on the wall-mounted television, a hip young barber named Ihab gave me the most meticulous and detail-intensive shave of my life. In what I later determined was a twenty-one-step process, Ihab massaged my beard with lotion, shaved it with a straight razor, treated my face with a series of menthol sprays and hot towels and iced towels, shaved my face again, applied aftershave, trimmed my scalp hair with shears, singed away stray ear hairs with a cigarette lighter, massaged my scalp, proffered me a can of Pepsi, and cheerfully demanded *baksheesh* (which I gladly paid him). Hence, for about $6, I didn't just get to experience the kind of barbershop shave that hasn't existed in my own country for half a century; I got a unique window into the meticulousness of Arab masculinity in an affluent corner of Cairo.

In this way, partaking in the quotidian rituals we've become inured to at home—shaving, watching TV, shopping for groceries, waiting for transit buses, standing in line for concerts—can be as revelatory to experiencing a place as any of its formal sights. "The happy surprise of traveling is that the familiar can come to seem wondrously exotic," Pico Iyer noted in *Video Night in Kathmandu*. "Abroad, we are not ourselves, and as the normal and the novel are transposed, the very things that we might shun at home are touched with the glamour of the exotic."

SWAP YOUR HOME MEDIA HABITS
FOR LOCAL OUTLETS

> While traveling, read the local news. Scan the *Times of India* in Mumbai. Listen to expat radio on Spain's Costa del Sol.... Imagine how the American approach to vexing societal problems might work in other places—and (more importantly) vice versa.
>
> —Rick Steves, "Tips for Traveling as a Political Act" (2015)

Before the days of formal journalism, travelers were an essential conduit for spreading news. Knowing that they could repay local hospitality by sharing what they'd seen and heard in other regions, wanderers made a point of collecting news and vetting rumors as they went from place to place.

Though newspapers and electronic media have absolved travelers from carrying information to new places, seeking local news is still a way of creating a more intimate relationship with the places one visits. When I started vagabonding across Asia in the late 1990s, seeking out the local English-language newspaper—the *Korea Herald,* the *Bangkok Post,* the *Hindustan Times*—was a reliable way to keep up with local issues. Often, reading these newspapers helped me learn of events and festivals I might never have known about otherwise. While the rise of digital media means it's rarer to find English broadsheets locally, it has made it easier than ever to read them online, even as we prepare for new journeys.

As it happens, digital access also has a way of tempting us to stay tethered to our homebound media habits while traveling through exotic new places—of falling back on outlets like the *New York Times* or CNN when one could be following local news (and podcasts, and social media personalities) in Malawi or Paraguay or Lithuania. If in doubt, find ways to diversify your media habits with news reports from the places your journey takes you.

TOURIST ZONES HAVE THEIR OWN UNIQUE ENERGY

Tourism tends to separate us from the inhabitants of the countries we've come to visit. They remain shadowy, occasional figures. . . . The real focus is always elsewhere, on the culture and the monuments, the natural spectacles and the food.

—Alain de Botton, *How to Travel* (2019)

In his 2021 book *The World in a Selfie,* Italian theorist Marco D'Eramo expressed frustration at how tourist popularity had transformed parts of Paris and Rome into places that belonged as much to visitors as to the people who lived there. "Hospitality workers are usually the people tourists most frequently come into contact with, and in some cases, the only people they come into contact with," he wrote. The tourist trade, he added sourly, fills entire neighborhoods "with museums and sandwich bars, antique ruins and luxury boutiques . . . 'entertainment districts' where no one actually enjoys themselves."

D'Eramo was describing what might be called "tourist zones"— places that, by catering to the needs of visitors, become a bit less like the place that first attracted those visitors. As the presence of itinerant outsiders affects these areas (which can exist as readily in Maui or Bali as Paris and Rome), local residences become home-share rentals, hardware stores become souvenir boutiques, and residential laborers become service-industry commuters.

Though tourist zones need not be seen as undesirable places, it's useful to keep in mind that they don't fully belong to the cultures that host them. Here, you are more liable to befriend fellow tourists than local residents, less liable to encounter serendipities and surprises, and more likely to overpay for food and accommodation.

Tourist zones make great places to begin journeys, but the most memorable travel experiences lie beyond their borders, in places that haven't been transformed for your convenience.

HISTORY, AS PACKAGED TO TRAVELERS, TENDS TO BE FICTIONAL

Monuments exist to remind history what to think.
—Carlos Monsiváis, *Historia, ¿Para Qué?* (1980)

Of my many travel journal entries amid a North American vagabonding trip at age twenty-three, one of the more irreverent came after I wearied of all the monuments I saw at a Civil War battlefield in Mississippi. "The shrines at Vicksburg are so vast and detailed as to be ridiculous," I wrote. "There are an absurd number of statues, all of them identically sullen and dignified. Graffiti on the cannons ('I love Lenny') feels like the truest, most legitimately human thing I've seen here."

Though I wrote that in a moment of touristic exasperation, monuments everywhere can obfuscate history as much as they illuminate it. In his 2019 book *Here Lies America,* Jason Cochran noted that American Civil War monuments in particular—most of which were constructed amid Jim Crow–era efforts to perpetuate racial inequities several decades after the conflict—tend to serve contemporary ideologies rather than historical memory. "History, it is said, is written by the winners," Cochran wrote. "This actually isn't true. History is written by the people most eager to write it. . . . Can you name a single notable work from the era celebrating the smashing of African-American chains? Other countries, including Brazil, Guyana, Haiti, Mexico, Cuba, and others, have monuments to the quashing of slavery. America has mostly paternalistic statues of white soldiers."

Though the United States has no monopoly on overblown statuary (Central Asian dictators in particular have a knack for building tributes to themselves), its monuments stand as an example of how historical shrines anywhere tend to be a form of historical fiction. If in doubt, daily street life is a truer signifier of a place's legacy than the monuments that have been erected in that place.

CHEAP JOURNEYS ARE SUSTAINABLE JOURNEYS (TO A POINT)

- -

> If you've got a class of tourist that stays longer, spends more, creates employment in local communities and has less environmental impact, why are they being ignored? My theory is the word "backpacker" has become a bit of a pejorative.
>
> —Stuart McDonald, "On Backpackers" (2021)

In the last half of the twentieth century, shoestring-budget backpackers prided themselves on being the most ethical and environmentally sustainable members of the global travel community. Even as government tourist authorities courted high-end, short-term boutique "ecotourists," backpackers invariably traveled overland, ate locally grown food, shared rooms at home stays, and—in staying longer and patronizing mom-and-pop businesses—fed more money into the local economy, even as they left a smaller carbon footprint than they did in their daily lives back home.

As it turned out, this all was less a result of high-minded idealism than a compulsion to save money. When the early 2000s saw a boom in budget air carriers, backpackers proved to be among their most faithful customers. Whereas an affordable Bangkok-to-Bali or London-to-Crete sojourn used to require a time-intensive series of local buses, ferries, and overnight hostel stays, a cheap Jetstar or EasyJet flight meant indie travelers could now make the transit for less than it cost to island-hop. Asia's overland "Banana Pancake Trail" began to fade, as did Europe's hitchhiking circuit. As this happened, less money went into local economies, and more carbon-dioxide emissions went into the troposphere.

Traveling cheap remains a reliable way to minimize one's environmental impact, but saving money is no longer an automatic way to make a journey more sustainable. Ethical travel now involves intentional choices—a willingness to slow down, to "see" less and experience more, to be less fixated on getting to destinations and more mindful about the journey itself.

FIND WAYS TO ENGAGE WITH PEOPLE ON A PERSONAL LEVEL

> When I travel, I hit the streets every day with no real plan be-
> sides walking and seeing what happens. People come up and
> ask, "My friend, what are you doing here?" My icebreaker is,
> "I'm here to meet you."
>
> —Henry Rollins, in a 2011 interview

As would-be travel gurus go, Henry Rollins has a decidedly un-
conventional road pedigree. A young punk rock aficionado,
Rollins was working at a Washington, D.C., ice cream store in 1981
when the seminal California hardcore band Black Flag recruited him
as their new lead singer. For the next five years, Rollins lived a life of
almost constant travel, as Black Flag performed at grotty punk clubs
all over North America and Europe. After Black Flag disbanded, he
went on to travel solo to dozens of countries around the world.

In time, Rollins collected his far-flung travel photos and stories
into a spoken-word tour called the *Henry Rollins Travel Slideshow*,
which is where I first learned of his strategy for breaking the ice with
people in faraway countries. "I'm here to meet you," he says when
people ask him what brought him to their corner of the world—an
invariably disarming sentiment that I have since stolen and used to
great effect in my own travels.

The only wrinkle here is that many of the people we meet in our
travels work in the "service matrix" of folks who interact with travelers as bartenders, hotel managers, or trekking guides. These are all
legitimate enough encounters, but interacting with local folks in a
more meaningful way is often a matter of wandering away from the
service matrix and being disarmingly open to meeting the people
who take a genuine interest in you.

THE "TRADITIONAL CULTURE" WE SEE AS TRAVELERS IS OFTEN STAGED

[Tourists'] limited knowledge of the culture and life of the indigenous people tends to narrow their conception of the "typical" to the stereotypical. . . . Locals often stage themselves in response to perceived touristic demands for authenticity.
—Erik Cohen, "Stranger-Local Interaction in Photography" (1992)

Though Robert J. Flaherty's 1922 feature *Nanook of the North* is considered a pioneering documentary film, its depiction of indigenous life in the Canadian Arctic was often staged by the filmmaker. The movie shows Inuk people hunting walruses with harpoons, for example, yet Nanook and his kinsmen typically hunted with rifles. When a white trader displays a gramophone, Nanook pretends to not know what it is (at one point putting the phonograph disk into his mouth and biting it), even though he was already familiar with the technology. The Arctic world of Nanook (whose less alliterative real name was Allakariallak; Nanook is Inuktitut for "polar bear") was thus depicted not as it was, but as the filmmaker imagined it might have been a century or so earlier.

Anthropologists use the term "staged authenticity" to describe how indigenous people perform their culture to fit the expectations of tradition-obsessed outsiders—and this is as intrinsic to travel as it is to filmmaking. Hawaii's tourist-friendly hula, for example, originated as a sacred dance performed for the indigenous chiefly class, whereas the traditional-looking Balinese frog dance was created specifically for tourists in the 1960s. The distinction between traditions and modern adaptations can be complicated (as evidenced by the fact that the frog dance was reappropriated for Balinese weddings), though as travelers we tend to fixate on the most colorful and traditional-looking aspects of a culture—not realizing we're seeking out visions that have more to do with our own fantasies than with the nuanced ways people have come to live their lives.

THE JOURNEY OFFERS A NATURAL BOND WITH OTHER TRAVELERS

The primal character of the pilgrimage [is] a coming together of normally separate groups to celebrate a common bond.
—Eric J. Leed, *The Mind of the Traveler* (1991)

Central to the medieval rite of pilgrimage was the notion that all pilgrims were united by the shared effort of the journey. Geoffrey Chaucer's fourteenth-century story collection *The Canterbury Tales*, for example, depicted people from a wide variety of social backgrounds (a miller, a prioress, a doctor, a beggar, various artisans, an estate agent, a pardoner) socializing as peers on the Canterbury pilgrimage. Around the same time, Muslims chronicling the hajj to Mecca included poets and princesses, scholars and slaves, traders and fugitives. Christian pilgrims walking the road to Rome or Jerusalem traded their workaday clothes for coarse russet tunics and broad-brimmed hats; Muslims completing the hajj collectively changed into seamless white garments known as *ihram* clothing. The goal in both traditions was to eliminate all social distinctions and travel not as representatives of a nation or a social class, but as human equals, united by their common journey in the eyes of God and humans.

As modern wanderers, we don't typically travel with the same orthodox intentions as medieval pilgrims, but we do share the bonds of motion and possibility with the other travelers we encounter. On the road, we find ourselves alongside wanderers who have sloughed off the routines and hierarchies of home, seeking to embrace the world in a more openhearted, open-ended way. Even when not headed in the same direction, travelers share the journey in a way that makes them more receptive to camaraderie and empathy in each other's presence.

THE SIMPLEST TRAVEL INTERACTIONS CAN BE THE RICHEST ONES

> When I meet people, I just think of myself as another human being, I don't think about being a Buddhist, a Tibetan or the Dalai Lama—just a human being. I find it's easier to make friends that way.
>
> —The Fourteenth Dalai Lama, on Twitter (2021)

In the mid-1980s, a young American named Barry embarked on his first solo journey across Europe. Without much of a travel budget, he slept in hostels and *pensiones* and survived on baguettes and cheese. In recounting those early travels, his favorite memories tended to be the simplest ones. "On the bus from Madrid to Barcelona I met a fellow traveler who couldn't speak English," he recalled. "My Spanish wasn't very good. I shared some bread and he shared some wine. By the time we pulled into Barcelona, at dawn, we were friends."

Decades later, when Barry (who now went by his birth name, Barack) had finished two terms as president of the United States, he still regarded his youthful European sojourn as an essential chapter in his own self-discovery. "Those kinds of trips become a part of you as a young person trying to discover what your place in the world is," he said. "There is something spectacular about seeing a new place, being exposed to new ideas and experiencing a new culture. Traveling makes you grow."

Even international policymaking, Obama added, can benefit from the intimate understandings that travel provides. "Part of diplomacy is letting other people know that you recognize and appreciate their cultures, their stories, their history, their memories," he said. "When people feel as if they're known and understood and seen, they're more open to your perspectives as well. That's true in individuals and in nations."

GLOBAL POP CULTURE INTRODUCES US BEFORE WE MEET

> The European tends to . . . [cling] to such information as is afforded by radio, press, and film, to anecdotes considered to be illustrative of American life, and to the myth that we have ourselves perpetuated.
>
> —James Baldwin, *Notes of a Native Son* (1955)

Pico Iyer's 1988 essay collection *Video Night in Kathmandu* will always be among my favorite travel books, since it so accurately evoked the Asia I encountered as a novice traveler one decade after it was written. Whereas other Asia memoirs viewed places like Japan and India through the lens of hermetic traditions, Iyer's book acknowledged that the Japanese loved and played their own brand of baseball, and Indians loved and filmed their own variation of Hollywood movies.

Iyer was the first writer to explicitly illustrate the way globalized pop culture was reinventing how people viewed themselves in the context of a greater world—though hints of this could be seen in travel anecdotes from earlier books, such as Malcolm X's 1965 *Autobiography,* when the American activist used the Louisville-born boxer Muhammad Ali as a pretext to bond with his fellow pilgrims in Saudi Arabia. "All of the Muslims listening lighted up like a Christmas tree [when I mentioned him]," he recalled. "Apparently every man, woman, and child in the Muslim world had heard how Sonny Liston had been beaten in Goliath-David fashion by Muhammad Ali . . . and Allah had given him his victory."

One of the charms of traveling in our global mass-media era is that popular culture has already introduced so many of us to each other. While this doesn't mean that a Korean will necessarily love K-pop (or a Jamaican reggae, or a Fijian rugby, or a Thai Muay Thai), it does give us a human starting point as we reach out to one another across cultural lines.

THE WORLD IS CELEBRATING
(AND YOU'RE INVITED)

- -

In the art of the festival, life is experienced as enjoyment of the passage of time. But this enjoyment of passage is itself a passing enjoyment.

—Guy-Ernest Debord, *The Society of the Spectacle* (1967)

One of the more charming details in Ibn Jubayr's twelfth-century *Travels* is the Andalusian geographer's attempt at Muslim restraint while detailing a Christian wedding celebration in the Lebanese port city of Tyre. Ibn Jubayr marveled at details from the bridal processional that would never have featured at a more conservative Islamic celebration. "The bride, pearls flowing down the top of her breast, came forward with a languid air, like the floating of a cloud," he wrote. "It was only by chance that we were privileged to witness this spectacle, and we ask Allah to preserve us from the danger of being tempted by it!"

Ibn Jubayr's willingness to relax religious decorum in the interest of celebrating a special occasion echoes the Christian rite of Carnival, which occurs just prior to Easter season each year. Celebrated as Carnaval in Rio de Janeiro and Mardi Gras in New Orleans, both perennial draws for travelers, Carnival is a time when people hide their identities behind masks, ignore traditional rules and hierarchies, and unite across racial and socioeconomic lines to eat too much, drink too much, and dance together in parades and street parties.

Most every culture has its iconic festivals—such as Holi in India, Day of the Dead in Mexico, Oktoberfest in Bavaria, and Songkran in Thailand—but community and even family celebrations abound in all parts of the world at all times of the year. Keeping an eye out for such festivities (and being respectful when invited to join in) can lead to some of the best experiences a journey can offer.

DON'T RESTRICT YOUR COMPANY
TO FELLOW TRAVELERS

Wherever man wanders, he still remains tethered by the chain that links him to his own kind.

—Alexander Kinglake, *Eothen* (1844)

At the outset of E. M. Forster's 1908 novel *A Room with a View,* one of the many disappointments Miss Lucy Honeychurch encounters upon her arrival in Florence (including the fact that her room has no view of the Arno River) is that her *pensione* is filled with English people. "It might be London," she complains to her chaperone. Though the novel's characters give lip service to seeing the "true Italy," their time in Florence is spent mainly in the company of other English people. Italians occasionally show up in *A Room with a View,* but its English characters tend to dine with other English travelers, swap sightseeing tips with other English travelers, and gossip with other English travelers about their fellow English travelers.

While Forster's decision to set his novel in Italy was a sly way of satirizing the mores and manners of Edwardian England, there was nothing unusual about its characters' tendency to stick with their own. Travelers have always sought the comfort of the familiar, from medieval Islamic travelers like Ibn Battuta and Nasir Khusraw (who for all their far-flung journeys tended to seek out regions where some form of Arabic was understood) to the young backpackers who cluster on the international hostel circuits of today.

This need not be a bad thing—some of my own favorite travel experiences have come in the company of my own compatriots—but restricting your social circle to fellow travelers is a sure way to limit possibilities in parts of the world where the biggest gift of showing up is the chance to meet the people who live there.

DON'T ASK A LOCAL PERSON WHERE TO EAT; ASK WHERE *HE* OR *SHE* EATS

In this part of the world one is always at the mercy of the Far Eastern peoples' broadmindedness and ingenuity in matters of food. . . . A moody Vietnamese waiter now arrived with a . . . [dish] for Europeans, described as a Chateaubriand maison, a huge slab of bluish-gray meat, undoubtedly cut from the haunches of some rare, ass-like animal that had been shot in the local forest.

—Norman Lewis, *A Dragon Apparent* (1951)

At the outset of my first vagabonding sojourn through Asia, an American friend offered me seemingly sage advice for finding food. "Don't ask other travelers to recommend places to eat," he said. "Ask local people where to eat."

In principle this strategy should have worked, but at times it yielded strange results. In Phnom Penh, a sweet grandmother recommended an expat bar that served lukewarm pizza; in Chiang Mai, three different locals sent me to three different banana-pancake stands (all of them crowded with European backpackers); in Pushkar, a friendly Indian sent me to a restaurant that "specialized" in Mexican, Chinese, Italian, Greek, and Israeli food.

In time I came to realize that these folks were simply trying to be helpful: Seeing a foreign-looking person, they assumed he wanted foreign food. Moreover, part of the reason pizza and falafel were on offer in parts of Asia that boasted spectacular local cuisine was that travelers have always had a weakness for the familiar. As an Istanbul café owner quipped in *Magic Bus*, Rory MacLean's narrative history of 1960s youth travel, "the hippies didn't want Turkish coffee; they wanted macaroni and ice cream."

I have since learned to ask local folks not where I should eat, but where *they* would eat. It seems like a minor distinction, but it yields exponentially more satisfying results.

LOCAL PEOPLE DON'T CARE IF YOU'RE A TRAVELER OR A TOURIST

> The distinction between tourism and travel is a Western myth of identity and should be analyzed as such. . . . From the native perspective, a self-declared traveler is simply another variety of foreign visitor (i.e., tourist).
>
> —Edward M. Bruner, "Transformation of Self in Tourism" (1991)

In his 2015 surf travel memoir *Barbarian Days*, William Finnegan pondered what local villagers must have made of the bedraggled backpackers who visited the Sumatran island of Nias in the 1970s. "Here was a large, awkward member of the global ruling elite who had probably spent more in an air-travel day than anyone on Nias could make in a year of hard work," he wrote, "all for the pleasure of leaving an unimaginably rich, clean place for this desperately poor, unhealthy place." Whereas the backpackers took great efforts to distinguish themselves from commercial tourists, Finnegan added, locals saw them as just another group of well-heeled outsiders who, frustratingly, were less inclined to spend money there.

Anthropologist Erve Chambers recounted a similar situation in the Australian outback, where local Aborigines tended to prefer mass tourists to self-styled "travelers" for the simple reason that tourists spent more money and asked fewer intrusive questions. "What makes sense to us on the basis of our own preferences . . . might not make the same sense to those who are visited by tourists," Chambers wrote in *Native Tours*. "It can be disarming to discover that some tourist 'hosts' might be more content to just have the tourists' money and be rid of them."

Though host communities don't always see travelers in raw pecuniary terms, it's useful to remember that simple generosity—including, but not limited to, the willingness to spend money locally—is more meaningful to the people we visit than the self-satisfied labels we apply to ourselves as wanderers.

SAVOR THE SUBTLE DIFFERENCES IN OTHER CULTURES

There was a time when traveling brought the traveler into contact with civilizations which were radically different from his own and impressed him in the first place by their strangeness. During the last few centuries such instances have become increasingly rare.

—Claude Lévi-Strauss, *Tristes Tropiques* (1955)

Though the term *orientalism* has come to imply a willful misapprehension of unfamiliar cultures, it entered the French language in 1830 as a catchall phrase for any intellectual interest in Eastern cultures and customs. By the mid-nineteenth century, pretentious European aristocrats were so given to collecting and showcasing *chinoiserie* furnishings and *turquerie* fashions that the novelist Gustave Flaubert sardonically quipped that an *orientaliste* was merely "someone who travels a lot."

A few centuries earlier, in his 1580 essay "On Cannibals," Michel de Montaigne pointed out that the surest way to misunderstand the distant tribes of the Amazon was to obsess about their rumored cannibalism rather than to observe the way they engaged in everyday activities—dancing, marriage, house construction, religious worship—that had a French equivalent. "There is nothing barbarous and savage in this nation, by anything that I can gather," he wrote, "except that everyone gives the title of barbarism to things that are not done the same way in his own country."

In truth, the most rewarding aspect of experiencing another culture is the subtle variations in such universal human customs as clothing design, cooking, and composing music. Indeed, as globalization puts various corners of the world into more active dialogue with one another, the most meaningful task for the traveler may well be to look past what feels "exotic" and learn to savor subtle differences in the things we already have in common.

OVER-IDEALIZING PLACES CAN BE A WAY OF NOT SEEING THEM

If the old form of travel writing said, "Look at these laughable people different from ourselves," the new one advises, "We should listen to and learn from the greatness of these people so other than ourselves." In both cases the final emphasis is on "ourselves."

—Pico Iyer, "Nowhere Need Be Foreign" (2009)

One of the more curious footnotes to Napoleon Bonaparte's rise as a French general was the inspiration he found in traveling through Egypt on a 1798 military expedition. "I found myself freed from the obstacles of an irksome civilization," he recalled later. "I saw myself founding a religion, riding an elephant, marching into Asia . . . a turban on my head."

Going to an unfamiliar culture and viewing it through the lens of one's own idealized fantasies is not unique to would-be European emperors. First-century Roman historian Tacitus enthused about Germanic tribes in a way that didn't accord with their reality; seventh-century Chinese traveler Yijing described the feats of Indian Brahmans with questionable credulity; and eleventh-century Persian poet Nasir Khusraw's own reaction to being in Egypt was nearly as fantastical (if less baldly narcissistic) as Napoleon's.

All these travelers were experiencing xenophilia—an inversion of xenophobia—which causes a person to fixate on quixotically romantic visions of foreign cultures. "The yearned-for community is symbolic, not actual," Australian academic Roger Sandall wrote in his 2001 book *The Culture Cult*. "Its undivided natural wholeness is something imagined rather than observed."

Optimism about other cultures—and who we might become when we encounter them—is part of what inspires us to travel to distant places. But once we arrive, it's important to balance admiration with clear-eyed realism, lest our ideals become a way of not actually seeing those places.

STAY OPEN TO WHAT A PLACE OFFERS
YOU IN THE MOMENT

- -

You know what drives me crazy? All these people talking about how great technology is, how it saves all this time. What good is saved time if nobody uses it?
    —Ethan Hawke as Jesse, in *Before Sunrise* (1995)

When I first watched Richard Linklater's travel romance *Before Sunrise*, I felt faint anxiety over the fact that its protagonists, Julie Delpy's Céline and Ethan Hawke's Jesse, don't have a plan when they spontaneously disembark a Eurail train to explore Vienna together.

Since I had yet to travel internationally at the time, my naive anxiety lay less in the characters' hypothetical itinerary than in their conviction that soul-enriching things might happen if they wandered the city at random. I envied Jesse's comfort with the uncertainty ("No projections," he says, "let's just make tonight great"); had I been in his place at that age, I'd have been so nervous in the presence of Céline that I would have jammed the evening with tourist activities.

Céline and Jesse do visit a few tourist sights, but their understated vulnerability to incidental experiences in Vienna underscores their vulnerability to each other. Twenty-five years after *Before Sunrise* debuted, Hawke noted that his daughter envied the way travelers of Jesse and Céline's generation hadn't been beholden to such seeming conveniences as smartphones. "There's something about always being digitally present that allows you to be less [emotionally] present," he said. "Part of what Jesse and Céline try to do in that movie is to be fully present with each other."

In an age when it's easier than ever to plan the experience of a new place in advance, some of the richest rewards of travel still come in staying vulnerable to what you discover as you wander through that place in real time.

IF IN DOUBT, TRAVEL THROUGH THE LENS OF YOUR OBSESSIONS

I often port a skill I practice domestically to other countries. Instant social life and camaraderie. It need not be a sport—it could be hiking, chess, or almost anything that gives you a chance to interact with people.

—Tim Ferriss, "Filling the Void" (2011)

Though visiting distant lands ideally involves trying new things rather than seeking what you already know, I've always been inspired by people who are able to incorporate their core obsessions into the way they travel. I have been particularly impressed by how skateboarders can experience unfamiliar cities in unique ways—and make lots of local friends—by grinding curbs and popping ollies with local skaters in the public spaces of Melbourne and Guangzhou and Brasilia.

During my journey through Sumatra a few years ago, sharing an ecolodge with French birders helped me understand how what seemed like unvariegated jungle was alive with hornbills and skinks. And taking the Siberut island ferry with surfers from Estonia and Alaska helped me appreciate how having a concrete mission in a place is a great pretext to learn languages, meet people, and veer away from standard sightseeing activities.

William Finnegan's *Barbarian Days* has been celebrated as a travel book, but it was ultimately less about travel itself than using the love of surfing to explore places like Hawaii, Fiji, Tonga, South Africa, and Mexico. My favorite section of the book comes when Finnegan and a friend wander a part of Western Samoa looking for surf breaks. "Within weeks, it felt like we had been knocking around the South Pacific for half our lives," he wrote. "We traveled by local bus and truck and ferry, by canoe and freighter and open boat, by small plane and yacht and taxi, on horseback. We walked. We hitchhiked. We paddled. We swam. We walked some more. . . . Fishermen helped us. Villagers took us in."

ANYTHING ABOUT A PLACE CAN
BE WORTHY OF ATTENTION

Early tourism took in hospitals, prisons, businesses, schools; lumbering, sawmills, and factories were not yet anathema to the well-bred tourist. People were more likely to be curious about all aspects of life in a place.

—Lucy R. Lippard, *On the Beaten Track* (2000)

In a satirical 1967 *Artforum* essay entitled "The Monuments of Passaic," artist Robert Smithson described traveling through a semi-industrial New Jersey suburb as if it were full of tourist attractions. Identifying "monuments" in things like parking garages and sewage pipes, Smithson's excursion was in part a critique of the utilitarian blandness of the suburbs, but it was also an inquiry into the notion that new and under-construction edifices (what he called "ruins in reverse") might be as worthy of attention as the monuments of Rome.

Sardonic though Smithson's essay was, it recalled a prior era of popular tourism, when travelers actively sought out places like slaughterhouses and insane asylums. Thomas Cook of England is remembered for his nineteenth-century group tours of continental Europe, for example, but some of his earliest group excursions visited prisons (and witnessed criminal executions) not far from London. In 1870, one of the biggest draws in Paris was, according to the *Illustrated London News*, "the gigantic collecting-sewer beneath the city"—a site so popular with tourists that pickpockets were said to do good business there.

Though the tourist popularity of sewers and prisons was emblematic of an era when most any new aspect of rapidly modernizing cities was deemed worthy of attention, it's still worth seeking out the quotidian monuments of unfamiliar places. In learning to regard any urban institution or utilitarian edifice (from bus stops to fire stations) as a potential attraction, you broaden the scope of what is worthy of capturing your imagination in a new place.

DON'T JUST EAT OUT; SHOP LOCALLY TO CREATE YOUR OWN MEALS

I've never had a bad time in an open-air market overseas. I often go to markets several times a day just to clock the different smells and colors and activities, letting my natural curiosity lead me.

—Henry Rollins, *Travel Slideshow* (2018)

One of the ironies of the world's most iconic public food markets is that tourists often go there without buying any food. Travelers will visit Marrakech's Jemaa el-Fna square and photograph the snake charmers, meander through Seattle's Pike Place Market shooting videos of fishmongers hurling halibut and salmon, or go to the Kashgar Sunday Market and buy Uyghur pottery souvenirs—then, having just spent hours walking past stalls of food, wander off and eat a prepared meal at a restaurant. As it happens, buying ingredients from those markets and creating one's own picnic (or, if staying in a place with a kitchen, cooking one's own meal) offers a cross-cultural eating experience that can prove far more interactive and immersive than formally eating out.

Moreover, such tourist-itinerary markets are just a sampling of what's on offer. While, say, La Boquería in Barcelona might be associated with colorful expanses of food stalls (as is Khan El-Khalili in Cairo, or Chatuchak in Bangkok), it reflects the rich bounty that can be found in scores of smaller neighborhood market squares in the same city. Traditional market stalls aren't the only places travelers can go to assemble a meal; even workaday supermarkets and convenience stores (Carrefour in France, OXXO in Mexico, FamilyMart in Japan) offer a window into how people find food locally. In addition to revealing the cultural nuances of a place, assembling meals with market ingredients is inevitably cheaper than seeking all your travel sustenance at restaurants.

May 24

DON'T LET TECHNOLOGY DISTRACT YOU FROM WHERE YOU ARE

We devise astounding means of communication, but do we communicate with one another? We move our bodies to and fro at incredible speeds, but do we really leave the spot we started from?

—Henry Miller, *The World of Sex* (1940)

In the postscript to her 1985 book *Tourism in History,* author Maxine Feifer commented on the ways new electronics technologies were altering the experience of travel. "Now there is the portable tape-deck," she noted, "with headphones to enable the [tourist] to remain in a place of his choice mentally while he is physically traveling around."

Though by the mid-1980s the debut of the Sony Walkman was indeed altering the travel experience in distinct ways, technology had been blurring travel life with the habits of home since at least 1912, when the American banker J. P. Morgan journeyed to Egypt hoping to improve his health with leisure and relaxation. "I am going up the Nile from Cairo in a steel dahabeah that I have had constructed after my own ideas of comfort," he boasted to the *New York Times.*

As one of his companions later noted, however, the custom-designed railcar offered Morgan all-too-easy access to cablegrams from New York, which invariably sent him into "long glowering calculations, hours upon end, while the incredible, half-ruined pyramids of other emperors and other ages which he had come to gaze at drifted by his window unnoticed."

Decades after the advent of convenience technologies like the cablegram (or the Walkman), it's tempting to try to "optimize" our travels using smartphone apps that have literally been designed to monopolize our attention. To reflexively reach for such technologies in moments of discomfort or uncertainty is the surest way to tether the potential novelties of a journey to the dull habits of home.

SEEK TRAVEL PHOTOS THAT GO BEYOND THE OBVIOUS

> Many snapshots made by tourists complete a hermeneutic cir-
> cle, which begins with the [photos] that advertise and antici-
> pate a trip, moves on to a search for these pictures in the
> experience of travel itself, and ends up with travelers certifying
> and sealing the very same images in their own photographs.
>
> —Patricia C. Albers, "Travel Photography" (1988)

In the late 2010s, articles in places like BuzzFeed and Uproxx began to lampoon travel "influencers" who braved the crowds at famous viewpoints or overlooks in Yosemite and Cappadocia and Angkor Wat, patiently waiting in line so they could take photos that made it look as if they were the only ones there.

Easy as it is to make fun of people who take great pains to pretend they had the world's most famous tourist sites to themselves, we all indulge in this kind of photographic fiction from time to time—in part because we tend to travel in the footsteps of the very images that first inspired us to travel.

In a sense, many of the pictures we seek to take as we travel—especially the ones that edit out tourist crowds—are photos of our own expectations. Indeed, even as the splendor of the world's iconic sights can sometimes be compromised by litter, road signs, scaffolding, parking lots, toilet facilities, and tour buses, we often prefer to photograph the place as it exists in our idealized imaginations.

Sometimes the best way to create memorable travel photographs is to leave in the little imperfections that might one day remind you of actually being there. Anyone can, after all, take travel-attraction snapshots that mimic a previous century of idealized touristic images; finding creative ways to include real-life imperfections in these photos is a way of making them your own.

THE GUEST-HOST DYNAMIC CHANGES
WHEN A PLACE GETS POPULAR

A tourist clientele tends to replicate itself. As a host community adapts to tourism, in its facilitation to tourists' needs, attitudes, and values, the host community must become more like the tourists' culture.

—Theron Nunez, in *Hosts and Guests* (1989)

In Rattawut Lapcharoensap's 2003 short story "Farangs," the young Thai narrator and his family mark the summer months by which nations' travelers arrive to cavort on their small island. Germans tend to show up in June, Italians in July, Japanese in August. The free-spending foreign visitors are good for the island's commerce, but at times it can be hard to keep track of who wants what from their travel experience. Brits expect to find hashish on offer; Americans seek out hamburgers and pizza. Europeans know how to bargain for their purchases, while Japanese are too polite (and Americans too oblivious) to haggle. Local vendors do their best to accommodate, struggling to meet the needs of "guests complaining in five languages."

While Lapcharoensap's story satirizes tourist desire from a host-community perspective, it also reveals how sincere gestures of hospitality can become wearying once one's hometown becomes a holiday attraction. Whereas the presence of a few travelers can be a source of curiosity and goodwill, the relentless incursion of hundreds makes human connection difficult. "Catering to guests is a repetitive, monotonous business," anthropologist Valene L. Smith noted in her 1989 anthology *Hosts and Guests*. "[If] the occasional visitor is replaced by a steady influx, individual guests' identities become obscured."

Thus, while hospitality is seen as a virtue most everywhere in the world, it's good to keep in mind that the guest-host dynamic of a given place will depend on how many outsiders show up from week to week.

May 27

DON'T LET GROUP EXCURSIONS BE JUST ABOUT THE GROUP

For the group traveler, Yucatán is the plane, the Holiday Inn, the cafeteria offering a juicy bacon burger, the air-conditioned bus trip to the ruins. In other words, everything necessary to feel like Florida, only with pyramids.

—Juan Villoro, *Swift Breeze Palms* (1989)

Decades after its 1969 debut, the movie *If It's Tuesday, This Must Be Belgium* is remembered as much for its title as its plot, both of which lampoon prepackaged European group tours. "It's not traveling; it's a mad dash through nine bloody countries in eighteen bloodier days," muses Ian McShane, who portrays an English guide saddled with the task of shepherding a cohort of neurotic tourists on an all-inclusive bus journey from London to Rome. "I have to be mother and father, psychiatrist, a host, teacher, interpreter, peacemaker and joke-maker to a silly crowd of Americans."

Group tours are easy to ridicule as a modern indulgence, but their origins trace back to the enterprising guides who organized pilgrimage parties to Jerusalem and Mecca in the Middle Ages. Since a central goal of such group excursions was religious fellowship, socializing with other pilgrims often took precedence over the lands and cultures encountered en route to the holy places. To this day, the biggest drawback of group travel is how—in replacing the routines and social obligations of home with travel-oriented equivalents—it can insulate you from the very places you're traveling through.

Since even staunch independent travelers can find themselves taking group excursions from time to time (often wilderness treks or safaris), it's important to resist the passivity and insularity that can come with traveling by cohort, and actively attune yourself to the subtleties and surprises of the landscapes and cultures you've all come there to experience.

A TRAVELER'S UNDERSTANDING OF A PLACE IS PARTIAL AT BEST

A person can't travel somewhere and then suddenly proclaim themselves an expert on that culture.

—Kenyan writer Carey Baraka, in a 2021 interview

One of the oldest clichés of travel writing is the tendency for some writers to assume that travel has afforded them special insight into new places and cultures. When novelist D. H. Lawrence visited Florence in 1921, for instance, Norman Douglas poked fun at him for the fact that he was "vehemently and exhaustively describing the temperament of the people" within a few days of arriving there. Two decades later, when George Orwell reviewed Henry Miller's *Colossus of Maroussi,* he quipped that it bore "all the normal stigmata of the travel book, the fake intensities, the tendency to discover the 'soul' of a town after spending two hours in it."

The best anecdote in this regard comes from nineteenth-century philosopher Herbert Spencer, who wrote about a French traveler who was ready to write a book about England three weeks into his visit. Three months later, the Frenchman decided he wasn't ready yet—and after three years he determined that he had no authority whatsoever to write a book about England.

Fortunately, travel writing was never really about pure reportage; it has always existed in the vicarious tension of what a traveler from one culture experiences (and attempts to comprehend) when visiting another. Indeed, for all of the discovery that can come with a journey to a new place, it's useful to remember that a great majority of that discovery is subjective, personal, and pegged to a more nuanced understanding of the small space we occupy in a much wider world.

RESPECTING OTHER WAYS OF LIVING HELPS YOU APPRECIATE YOUR OWN

> I must admit that Eskimo customs are gentler than those of my own people.
>
> —Tété-Michel Kpomassie, *An African in Greenland* (1981)

When Tété-Michel Kpomassie was a teenager in the West African country Togo he was collecting coconuts up in a tree one day when he was attacked by a python and fell more than twenty-five feet to the ground. While he was recovering from his injuries, he found a children's book at the local Jesuit library. Entitled *Eskimos from Greenland to Alaska,* the volume depicted a place where no trees grew, the sun disappears for weeks each winter, and hunters clothe themselves in animal skins.

Determined to see the place for himself, Kpomassie embarked on a working journey that took him through the countries of West Africa as well as France and Denmark. He learned languages as he went, working at a variety of odd jobs for eight years before finally booking passage on a boat from Copenhagen to the southern Greenlandic town of Julianehåb.

The adventures Kpomassie found in this new landscape were eventually compiled in his book *An African in Greenland,* an entertaining and sympathetic memoir that recounts the wonder of a young man from one non-Western culture getting to know the intricacies of a different non-Western culture. Everywhere he traveled, he used memories of (and pride in) his own culture not to judge what he encountered, but to serve as a benchmark by which he could make sense of what he encountered. "We shared the meal, all digging fingers into the same dish," he recalled of a salmon feast in the settlement of Fiskenæsset. "The way we were stuffing ourselves with food and swapping stories reminded me so much of Africa."

TRAVEL IS A WAY TO SEEK OUR COMMON HUMANITY

Perhaps travel cannot prevent bigotry, but by demonstrating that all peoples cry, laugh, eat, worry and die, it can introduce the idea that if we try to understand each other, we may even become friends.

—Maya Angelou, "Passports to Understanding" (1993)

The word *barbarian* originated in ancient Greece as a term for people who did not speak Greek. Its very intonation was understood as an onomatopoeia (something along the lines of "blah-blah") that mimicked the sound of unfamiliar languages. Though not initially a derisive term, *barbarian* in time became a catchall to describe people who were considered primitive or uncivilized. Having a pejorative term for outsiders was not unique to that part of the world: The Chinese had a number of slurs to describe non-Chinese peoples; the Inca used the term *purum awqa* (wild enemy) to describe the people living outside their rule; Aztecs called nomadic outsiders *chichimeca* (dog people).

Germanic tribes, themselves technically "barbarians," called outsiders *Walhaz*—a word that influenced the Old English *welsh* (meaning "foreigner"), which the Anglo-Saxons applied to the people now living in Wales (who in their own language call themselves Cymry, or "friends"). And while such indigenous peoples as the Ainu and Bantu are known by their own term for "human," the name Comanche comes from the Ute word for "stranger," and Apache is thought to derive from the Zuni word for "enemy."

In short, cultures have always defined themselves in contrast to people whose customs seem strange and whose words sound like babble. Travel, in its ongoing process of deepened familiarity and hopeful appreciation, allows us to get past the labels we've assigned to each other and seek out a common humanity.

LET THE INEVITABLE FAILURES OF A JOURNEY TEACH YOU

- -

A man who fails well is greater than one who succeeds badly.
—Thomas Merton, *No Man Is an Island* (1955)

My attitude toward the frustrations and failures that can arise on a journey was shaped not by a travel mentor, but by my writing mentor, a chain-smoking Korean War veteran named John Fredin. He'd been my English teacher in high school, and I approached him in my early twenties for feedback on what I'd hoped would be my first book. When subsequent months of revision left Mr. Fredin equivocal about my work, I admitted to him that the whole undertaking felt like a failure. My old teacher didn't argue with my conclusion; he just posed a simple question: "What will you let failure teach you?" As it happened, my unsuccessful attempt to finish that would-be first book gave me the hard-won skills and instincts to write a real one years later. When *Vagabonding* came out in 2003, one of the people I dedicated it to was John Fredin.

Just as that frustrated attempt to write a book made me a better writer, the knowledge that all failures carry inherent lessons has made me a better traveler. This is in part because a journey that doesn't risk failure isn't a true journey, and in part because stumbling into mistakes on the road (and learning from them) is inseparable from evolving into a more seasoned and humble traveler. "There are two kinds of failure," wrote American author Robert Greene in his 2012 book *Mastery*. "The first comes from never trying. . . . The second kind comes from a bold and venturesome spirit. If you fail in this way, the hit you take . . . is greatly outweighed by the things you learn. Repeated failure will toughen your spirit and show you with absolute clarity how things must be done."

AWAY FROM HOME HABITS, YOUR RECEPTIVITY DEEPENS

In every long journey there is a moment when you perceive that travel has truly begun. It does not usually happen at the beginning, but when you feel that your soul has fled from the habits of daily life.

—Javier Reverte, *Corazón de Ulises* (1999)

In his 2002 book *The Art of Travel,* Swiss-British philosopher Alain de Botton described how travel, in taking us away from the ingrained habits of home, puts us into a state of heightened awareness. "Receptive, . . . we carry with us no rigid ideas about what is or is not interesting," he wrote. "We irritate locals because we stand in traffic islands and narrow streets and admire what they take to be unremarkable small details. . . . We find a supermarket or a hairdresser's shop unusually fascinating. We dwell at length on the layout of a menu or the clothes of the presenters on the evening news."

Indeed, in making you newly curious about what you don't quite understand—in forcing you to use newly learned phrases or sets of directions just to get around—a journey has a way of blowing your days wide open. In embracing intriguing new options rather than routines or prescriptions, travel compels you to play games not just with the way you experience each day, but with the more whimsical idea of how you might want to experience the rest of your life: You imagine yourself living in some unfamiliar place, solving small problems and soaking in subtle thrills in this exotic new context.

"Foreignness can be an intoxicant," Pico Iyer mused in the 2004 anthology *A Sense of Place.* "As when we're drunk, we don't know how much it's our true selves coming out and how much it's the drink speaking through us."

TRAVEL ALLOWS YOU TO SEE YOUR OWN CULTURE FROM THE OUTSIDE

It might be a good idea if the various countries of the world occasionally swap history books, just to see what other people are doing with the same set of facts.

—Bill Vaughan, in "Sunbeams" (1962)

When American missionary Bryan Webb first traveled to the Pacific island nation of Vanuatu, he was puzzled by the local trade system, which bore little resemblance to what he'd known back home. "In Western trade . . . we buy only what we need or want," he noted in his 2014 memoir *Sons of Cannibals*. "Ni-Vanuatu will purchase items . . . because . . . they seek to initiate a relationship. Their idea of a good sell or buy is one that builds a bond between the two parties. . . . Can such a system work? Sure, especially in a context that grants status to people who disperse wealth rather than accumulate it."

In noting the personal texture of Vanuatuan trade, Webb thus gained perspective on the more abstract, materialistic nature of commerce in the United States. In a similar way, living in Korea for two years allowed me to understand how American notions of individualism don't always translate in a culture that prioritizes obligations over rights, and traveling to Beijing with my parents (whose gray hair earned them the reflexive respect of Chinese people) offered me a useful perspective on America's fixation on youth.

Travel has also deepened my appreciation for healthier aspects of my own culture, including America's comparative social mobility and lack of corruption, in a way I might not have appreciated had I not traveled. As Anthony Aveni wrote in his 1989 book *Empires of Time*, "Other societies become mirrors to gaze into, so that we can see ourselves more clearly—as but one culture in the context of manifold possibilities."

SOMETIMES DEVIATIONS CAN BE AS APPEALING AS PLANS

When you get lost—when you essentially go the opposite direction from the way you should—all kinds of marvelous and illuminating adventures can ensue.

—Don George, "On Getting Lost" (2010)

When I arrived in Morocco from Spain some years ago, my initial plan upon disembarking the ferry was to head for Chefchaouen, a picturesque backpacker haunt in the Rif Mountains. As it happened, I pronounced the town's name in the two-syllable Anglophone manner ("CHEF-chwan") instead of the more accurate French transliteration ("Shef-SHA-wan"). Thus, out of simple linguistic misunderstanding, my taxi driver took me to a completely different two-syllable town, Tetouan ("TET-wan").

Exploring the streets of one Moroccan city using a map for a different one is an interesting exercise in both optimism and credulity. I must have wandered, lost, among the low, cube-like white houses of Tetouan for more than an hour before I realized my mistake. As accidental discoveries go, my timing couldn't have been better, since farmers from the surrounding mountains were taking advantage of a monthly tax break for ethnic Berber vendors: Tetouan's narrow market alleyways were jammed with women in colorful costumes selling little piles of spices and onions and goat meat. I meandered through Tetouan's market for the better part of a day, strangely thrilled to be there.

I later made it to Chefchaouen, but its lovely blue alleyways and peaceful travelers' teahouses didn't compare with the heady, chaotic buzz I'd felt while accidentally wandering the market alleyways of Tetouan. As the comedian Ari Shaffir pointed out in a 2017 interview, travelers need not worry about ending up in the "wrong" place by mistake. "You're already where you're supposed to be, which is somewhere in this new place," he said. "There's no getting lost because you're already there."

THE PAST WAS GRAND, BUT TRAVEL PLAYS OUT IN THE HERE AND NOW

A persistent nostalgia infected most surfers, even young ones—
the notion that it was always better yesterday, and better still
the day before.

—William Finnegan, *Barbarian Days* (2015)

In Woody Allen's 2011 movie *Midnight in Paris,* an American writer named Gil Pender is obsessed with the city's "golden age," which he reckons took place in the 1920s. Through a twist of magic, Gil is transported back in time, where he socializes with people like Ernest Hemingway and Pablo Picasso. Thrilled to be in the company of his artistic heroes, Gil is perplexed that these folks don't regard the 1920s as a golden age—not compared with the Belle Époque of the 1890s, when a prior generation of artists (people like Gauguin and Toulouse-Lautrec) wandered the streets of Paris. Realizing that people of all eras idealize the past, Gil has no choice but to return to present-day Paris and embrace what it has to offer.

Though there is a satiric tinge to Gil's *Midnight in Paris* nostalgia, romanticizing the bygone realities of a place is a time-honored travel ritual—one that is tied into our very motivations for seeking out such destinations in the first place. Just as Paris's imagined 1920s aura is part of why Gil traveled there, it's common to blend a longing for Las Vegas with its 1950s "Rat Pack" mystique, or a yen to see Thingvellir with visions of how it was depicted in thousand-year-old Icelandic sagas.

Envisioning the past glories of places can in fact enhance present-day journeys, so long as such fantasies don't overwhelm the experience of the present moment, which—even with its inevitable imperfections and disappointments—may someday be looked back upon with a similar sense of longing.

WHAT YOU FIND IN A PLACE MATTERS MORE THAN WHAT YOU BRING

> There are people everywhere who form a diaspora of their own.
> When you are among them you will not be mocked or resented,
> because they will not care about your race, your faith, your sex,
> or your nationality.
>
> —Jan Morris, *Trieste and the Meaning of Nowhere* (2001)

In the course of writing more than fifty books about such places as South Africa, Italy, and India, Welsh author Jan Morris established herself as one of the most insightful travel writers of the twentieth century. At the outset of her career, when she covered the first ascent of Mount Everest in 1953, Morris sent dispatches home under the by-line James Morris. But, after a "lifelong conviction that I had been born into the wrong sex," Morris underwent gender reassignment surgery in 1972 and changed her name to "Jan."

At this point Morris could easily have focused her writing on the idiosyncrasies of traveling as a trans woman, but instead—after having documented her journey across the boundaries of gender in a 1974 book entitled *Conundrum*—Morris returned to reporting about the world with a sympathetic focus on the people and places she encountered. Instead of seeing her own identity as a litmus test for what a place might offer, she used place itself as a metaphor for the way we all relate to the world.

In doing so, Morris didn't just create classic travel books; she showed how what you find in a place is more essential than what you bring there. As the poet Kapka Kassabova noted upon the author's death in 2020, Morris's outward-focused curiosity showed "how to really see the world: to hold it in your gaze, then in your prose, then in your heart."

HOST CULTURES DON'T EXIST SIMPLY FOR YOUR PLEASURE

> Low Man believed the Coeur d'Alene Reservation to be a mo-
> notonous place—a wet kind of monotony that white tourists saw
> as spiritual and magic. Tourists snapped off dozens of photo-
> graphs and tried to capture it—the wet, spiritual monotony—
> before they climbed back into their rental cars and drove away
> to the next reservation on their itineraries.
>
> —Sherman Alexie, *The Toughest Indian in the World* (2000)

In *A Small Place,* Jamaica Kincaid's 1988 critique of the legacies of colonialism and misgovernment in the Caribbean, the Antiguan American novelist saved some of her harshest language for tourists. "An ugly thing, that is what you are when you become a tourist," she wrote. "Every native would like to find a way out," she added later in the essay, "every native would like a rest, every native would like a tour. But some natives—most natives in the world—cannot go any-where. They are too poor. . . . They envy you, they envy your ability to leave your own banality and boredom, they envy your ability to turn their own banality and boredom into a source of pleasure for your-self."

Harsh as Kincaid's assessment of tourism was, it wasn't a call to abolish the act of travel so much as a reminder to be aware of one's role as a guest, and to avoid seeing distant places as a static backdrop for your own pleasure. If, as travelers, we cannot change the complex histories that inform a place, we can at least make ourselves aware of them—and seek experiences that go beyond our own amusement.

THE TRUEST "INFLUENCERS" DON'T LIVE IN THE VIRTUAL WORLD

> Before the development of tourism, travel was conceived to be
> like study, and its fruits were considered to be the adornment of
> the mind and the formation of judgment.
>
> —Paul Fussell, *Abroad* (1980)

A few years ago, I was invited to talk about long-term travel at a SXSW-style "influencer" festival in Kazakhstan. Since my travel media expertise didn't extend to digital metrics and algorithms, I kept my message focused on things like staying vulnerable to surprise and meeting new people on the road. Though my talk got a nice response from the Kazakhs who attended, I was vexed by a question that went something along the lines of "I loved your talk, and you clearly understand travel, so why is it that you only have four thousand Instagram followers?"

The idea that "influence"—that is, dynamic, life-enhancing ideas—should somehow be measured by a digital metric is not an idea unique to young Kazakhs. But for me, the truest travel influencers haven't been people I've encountered on social media; they've been people like Valentina from Trentino, who taught me to savor each aspect of a meal, or Marcel from Havana, who showed me you don't need much money to have a great night out on the town. People like Johannes, a Namibian Damara souvenir vendor who gently disabused me of my individualist ideas of what constitutes satisfying work. "What I do here is not work; it's love," he said. "Love for my daughter, for my wife. Love is how I know what success is."

Receiving wisdom from people like Johannes or Valentina or Marcel is not the same as reading it in an Instagram caption (or the pages of this book); it's something you show up for—and endeavor to apprehend—in person.

DISTANT PLACES REVEAL THE MIRACLE OF THE FAMILIAR

> There are only two ways to live your life. One is as though nothing is a miracle. The other is as though everything is a miracle.
> —Albert Einstein, quoted in Reichenstein's *Die Religion der Gebildeten* (1941)

In her 2013 book *The Faraway Nearby,* Rebecca Solnit recounted a parable about a novice monk who complains that paying attention to his own breathing—a fundamental Zen meditation ritual—is boring. His teacher responds by plunging the young man's head into a stream and holding it down for a long moment. When the student is allowed to resurface, gasping as he catches his breath, the teacher asks him: "Do you still find breathing boring?"

Just as Solnit's monk gained a deepened appreciation for breathing when his head was submerged in water, travel allows us to see the beauty of our own familiarities—in part because it takes us away from the comforts we've come to ignore in our own lives, and in part because it affords us a fresh perspective on the way people in other parts of the world engage in their ordinary routines. For all of the experiences Paul Theroux has evoked in his many travel books, for instance, his most plaintive sense of longing came not from beholding some exotic spectacle, but when, as he noted in *The Old Patagonian Express*, he witnessed Costa Ricans engrossed in their daily routines. "I saw a young couple picking out a vacuum cleaner," he wrote, "and I felt homesick."

Oftentimes, the most poignant experiences on the road don't occur in the presence of some sprawling vista or grand monument, but in those quiet moments when we recognize beauty in the ordinary, and miracles in what we might otherwise have written off as mundane.

June 9

HOSTELS AREN'T JUST FOR
YOUTHFUL TRAVELERS

We cherish even lowly lodgings, because in a place where all
our senses are stretched—a new city, a foreign land—they make
it OK to fall asleep.
   —Thomas Swick, "The Place You Could Be Looking For" (2004)

Though the word *hostel* now calls to mind an international cohort
of young travelers slumbering and socializing in shared facilities
near global tourist attractions, the word originally denoted cheap
housing reserved for itinerant craftsmen, salesmen, and sailors. In his
1910 book *A Vagabond Journey Around the World,* American traveler
Harry A. Franck described sleeping in grungy working-class hostels
on the outskirts of cities like Edinburgh and Marseille, where he
shared bunkrooms and kitchen facilities with European laborers.

Around the same time, a German teacher named Richard Schirr-
mann got the idea to create "youth hostels" to house students taking
educational field trips. In 1932, Hosteling International was founded
to administer the hundreds of youth hostels that had sprung up
around Europe, and by the end of the twentieth century backpackers
could sleep at hostels in more than eighty countries worldwide.

Hostels remain a popular fixture on the global vagabonding circuit, and they cater to more than just youthful travelers. Some of my
fondest hostel memories involve staying at Prague's Czech Inn and
Beijing's Zhaolong Youth Hostel with my parents just after they re-
tired, and (despite the fact that they were in their sixties at the time)
my folks thrilled at being included in the hostels' game nights, walking tours, and communal dinners. Indeed, hostels are no longer just
for youth: They're an enjoyable, inexpensive lodging option for anyone willing to forgo a few comforts and embrace their communal energy.

AS A GUEST, STRIVE TO BE HUMBLE AND RECEPTIVE

> There is nothing so strange in a strange land as the stranger who comes to visit it.
>
> —Dennis O'Rourke, *Cannibal Tours* (1988)

The most iconic moment in the documentary film *Cannibal Tours* comes when a group of Westerners visits a remote village in Papua New Guinea. As the sweaty white folks wander around haggling for souvenirs, a handsome young Papuan speaks earnestly to an offscreen interviewer. "When the tourists come to our village, we are friendly towards them," he says, his words translated in subtitles. "We accept them here." While he's saying this, an elderly tourist creeps into the background, and—oblivious to what the tribesman is saying—snaps a picture of him before scuttling back out of the frame. This scene thus encapsulates the strained dynamic that can come with travel: Even as the Papuan takes pains to affirm the humanity of tourists, the tourist's first instinct is to treat him like scenery.

Cannibal Tours scenes convey a cringe-inducing reality as the tourists bargain hard for already cheap souvenirs, make dumb speculations about Papuan customs, and snap photos of everything. Yet while it's easy to ridicule these tourists' suitcase-sized camcorders and entitled assumptions, the present-day elegance of smartphone cameras and guidebook advice does not absolve us as travelers. Indeed, the oblivious behavior of the onscreen tourists has less to do with their dated 1980s aura than with the timeless ethos of touristic self-absorption.

Hence, the best way to avoid the gaffes of the tourists in *Cannibal Tours*—the best way to interact with host cultures in general—is simply to slow down, ask questions, and listen in earnest before taking photos of what you're only just beginning to understand.

WHAT SEEMS FOREIGN CAN HELP US EMPATHIZE WITH OUR OWN PAST

Even a brief glimpse of what we were is valuable to help understand what we are.

—Dervla Murphy, *Full Tilt* (1965)

When I visited Mumbai in the early 2000s, its shanty towns—communities like Dharavi, where six hundred thousand residents were crammed into an area of less than one square mile—felt alien, and somehow unique to a moment when India's urban population was exploding. It wasn't until I visited the Tenement Museum on New York's Lower East Side a decade later that I learned that Manhattan's slums had had a similar population density in 1894—the very year my great-grandmother immigrated there from Germany at age fifteen.

In this way, travel can offer insights into one's own cultural history that might otherwise have seemed incomprehensible. In 1953, a Swiss student named Nicolas Bouvier was traveling across Pakistan when he thumbed through a 1920 issue of *La Vie Parisienne* that someone had squirreled away in his Quetta hotel. Whereas back in Geneva Bouvier might have regarded the old French magazine as a relic of a quainter era, his immersion in Muslim South Asia made its bare-shouldered, kohl-eyed movie starlets appear nearly as titillating as they must have seemed to European audiences at the outset of the Jazz Age. "I had misjudged the period," he recalled in his travel memoir *The Way of the World*. "Having been surrounded by women enveloped in white veils, clouds rising from studded slippers, the graces of the flappers knocked me sideways."

Such moments of historical perspective don't just happen in societies more traditional than our own. Indeed, something as simple as a depleted smartphone battery (which can send one back to around 1999, when travelers still relied on paper maps) can also result in a kind of accidental time travel.

RESPECTING HOSPITALITY IS A TIME-HONORED TRAVEL RITE

No amount of money can pay for hospitality. The true traveler is a guest and thus serves a very real function, even today, in societies where the ideals of hospitality have not yet faded from the "collective mentality." To be a host, in such societies, is a meritorious act. Therefore, to be a guest is also to give merit.

—Hakim Bey, "Overcoming Tourism" (1994)

One common fixture of modern travel literature is authors' self-consciousness at the generosity of comparatively poor hosts. William Finnegan's *Barbarian Days* depicted this feeling in Samoa, Sarah Macdonald's *Holy Cow* in India. In Nanjala Nyabola's 2020 book *Traveling While Black*, the African author marveled at the generosity of people on her own continent. "In Burkina Faso, I experienced so much hospitality I was embarrassed," she wrote. "Strangers welcomed me into their homes and overfed me because they'd never seen a Kenyan before. They were bowled over by my broken French. They couldn't wait to show me off to their friends."

Hospitality is, in fact, so ingrained in various world cultures that many religions consider it a spiritual duty. The Hindu-Buddhist philosophy of *atithi devo bhava,* for example, suggests that one should revere guests with the same respect as one would a god; the Jewish book of Leviticus declares, "You shall treat the stranger who sojourns with you as the native among you"; the Christian Epistle to the Hebrews asserts that one should "show hospitality to strangers, as some have entertained angels unawares."

If we modern travelers sometimes feel embarrassed in the face of hospitality, it could be because we've lost our own connection to this time-honored human virtue. If in doubt, the best response is to accept such generosity with openhearted gratitude and the sincere conviction to one day pay it forward, when you receive guests in your own home.

TRAVEL REVEALS WHAT YOU DON'T KNOW ABOUT OTHER PLACES

To travel is to discover that everyone is wrong about other countries.

—Aldous Huxley, *Jesting Pilate: An Intellectual Holiday* (1926)

Studying the history of European writing about the rest of the world can be an exercise in how people got things wrong when trying to comprehend other places. Ancient Greeks were taught that India's gold was mined by gigantic ants; early Christian geographers claimed that Abyssinia was full of dog-headed men. One millennium later, Christopher Columbus insisted American rivers were filled with mermaids (which were in fact manatees), and Italian historian Peter Martyr d'Anghiera asserted African rivers were full of ox-headed fish (which were actually hippopotamuses).

In the nineteenth century, Zanzibar-born memoirist Emily Said Ruete became so exasperated with Romantic-era exaggerations about Arab cultures that she dedicated a portion of her 1886 book *Memoirs of an Arabian Princess* to refuting them. "The East is too much considered the land of fairy-tales, about which all sorts of stories may be told with impunity," she wrote, adding that the average European geographer "throws the reins over the neck of his imagination, and gallops away into fable-land."

Though such cultural exaggerations were also known to play out in the opposite direction (as late medieval Arab accounts of Spain and France will attest), this only underscores Ruete's frustration with travelers who cling to preconceptions and first impressions rather than seeking out the ongoing nuance of firsthand encounter.

Such preconceptions still taint our understanding of the world as travelers—and we can over-idealize the presumed kindnesses of places like Costa Rica or Zambia or Kiribati as readily as we can overemphasize their presumed dangers. If in doubt, be skeptical of received impressions about the places you visit, and embrace the challenges and surprises of experiencing those places in real time.

DON'T MAKE THE DESIRE TO DO GOOD BE ABOUT YOURSELF

> As admirably altruistic as it sounds, the problem with voluntourism is its singular focus on the volunteer's quest for experience, as opposed to the recipient community's actual needs.
> —Rafia Zakaria, "The White Tourist's Burden" (2014)

When I first began to teach travel writing workshops, I found that my students went through three inevitable steps when composing essays about volunteering abroad. The first step involved the author recounting a visit to some distant place—Nepal or Uganda or Guatemala—and teaching skills that forever changed the lives of the people living there. When this version of the story didn't elicit much enthusiasm in workshop, the author would compose a second draft asserting that *he*—that is, the person volunteering—was the person whose life was forever changed. When this draft received middling feedback, the author's third version of the story finally began to examine the topic in a more nuanced and satisfying way.

The problem with the early drafts didn't lie in the quality of the prose, but in the author's focus on himself. This tendency for travelers to portray themselves as ideal-driven protagonists has only become more pronounced in an age when we narrate so many aspects of our lives on social media. Whenever we post photos depicting ourselves as virtuous do-gooders in distant places, we run the risk of diminishing the real-life needs, abilities, and complexities of the people we seek to help.

BE CONSCIENTIOUS WHEN YOU
TAKE PHOTOS OF PEOPLE

The camera is a kind of passport that annihilates moral boundaries and social inhibitions, freeing the photographer from any
responsibility toward the people photographed.
—Susan Sontag, *On Photography* (1977)

In 2013, a Namibian Himba woman named Uatanaua Nduri made national headlines when she nearly assaulted a tourist for photographing her without consent. "The woman drove off while I was still holding onto the door of her car," she told a local newspaper. "She was lucky to get away, because I would have punched her." Nduri's ire was more than an issue of privacy: In Namibia's Kunene Region, where pastoral Himba women are known for plaiting their hair with a striking orange-red cosmetic ochre known as *otjize,* posing for paid tourist photos is a coveted source of hard currency. When the tourist offered a handful of sweets in lieu of cash, Nduri was furious. "The woman had taken me for a fool," she said.

Taking photographs of people as we travel can be a complicated ethical task. In addition to invading people's privacy (or refusing to tip when asked), taking photos of people like Nduri can result in "zooification"—a term scholars use to describe situations where tourists show more interest in ethnic costumes than the people who wear them. Moreover, many travelers who would be mortified if strangers walked up and started snapping pictures of their own children think nothing of photographing kids in developing countries.

Curiously, the global ubiquity of smartphone cameras has added a new wrinkle. As a recent visit to Sumatra revealed, local people were as interested in taking smartphone photos of me as I was of them. In any case, a simple request for permission is common courtesy.

June 16

ENCOUNTERING BEGGARS IS A PART
OF THE TRAVEL EXPERIENCE

> The routine of the beggars is heart-rending. The little girl who
> suddenly appeared at the window of my taxi, the utterly lovely
> smile with which she stretched out her hand, and then the extin-
> guishing of the light when she drew it back empty.
>
> —Thomas Merton, *Asian Journal* (1975)

O f all the things in India that vex the hapless protagonist of William Sutcliffe's 1997 novel *Are You Experienced?*, perhaps the
most unnerving is a beggar he encounters in Delhi. "It felt as if she
were an inhabitant of hell who had been sent to haunt me," he says, "to
remind me how rich and lucky I was, and how I didn't deserve anything that I had."

Indeed, the presence of beggars can be emotionally complicated
for travelers—in part because handing out money doesn't necessarily
solve the problem of begging. Childhood begging can be a particular
dilemma in tourist areas—in part because kids cadging money from
disproportionately wealthy outsiders can disrupt community hierarchies, and in part because the ritual is often exploited by criminal elements (an unfortunate reality depicted in the plot of the 2008 movie
Slumdog Millionaire). "Too many foreigners bring candy or drop
coins behind them, rewarding children for their begging," noted
Eddy L. Harris in *Native Stranger*. "We cannot ignore these poor, nor
can we save them with a few coins dropped here and there. Perhaps
the best we can do is know they are there and feel for them, feel with
them, and not distance ourselves from their poverty."

Inconclusive as this advice might sound, attuning ourselves to
poverty as travelers can be a way of understanding how local communities deal with their less fortunate members. Since most societies
have culturally specific (often religiously motivated) ways of respond-
ing to beggars, it's useful for travelers to follow the lead of locals.

TRAVEL OFFERS A WINDOW INTO HUMAN GENIUS

If you took all the genius that allowed us to put a man on the moon and applied it to understanding the ocean, what you get is Polynesia.

—Wade Davis, "On Native Ground" (2008)

When scientists Ozlem Tureci and Ugur Sahin helped Pfizer develop a Covid-19 vaccine in 2020, publicity around the development celebrated the couple's Turkish heritage. "Science only becomes powerful when it can benefit from greater diversity," read a UNESCO statement. The implication was that Turkish innovation was new to European medicine—though anyone familiar with the travels of Lady Mary Montagu would know otherwise. During a 1717 sojourn in Constantinople, at a time when smallpox was the leading cause of death in Europe, Montagu had noted that "smallpox is here entirely harmless by the invention of engrafting." In taking the Turkish technique home, Montagu effectively introduced the science of vaccination to England.

Though most travelers aren't in a position to bring home historic science innovations, the act of visiting foreign cultures can become an ongoing ritual of appreciating otherwise unfamiliar expressions of human genius. Before I traveled in Sri Lanka, for example, I'd never heard of Sigiriya—and it wasn't until I climbed up the fifteen-hundred-year-old complex of plateau-top palaces and hydraulic channels that I came to appreciate what a testament to urban planning the ancient rock fortress city was. I walked past the site's caves, pools, and shrines not certain what I was seeing, yet convinced nonetheless that it belonged in the global pantheon of civic engineering.

One of the keenest pleasures of travel comes in the way it compels us to appreciate the innovations—be it Icelandic sagas, or Persian architecture, or Peruvian Moche metallurgy—that we might never know about had we not left our own home cultures.

NUANCES REVEAL A PLACE MORE THAN STEREOTYPES

Our dualistic minds do not process paradoxes very well. . . . We are better at rushing to judgment and demanding a complete resolution to things before we have learned what they have to teach us.

—Richard Rohr, *Falling Upward* (2011)

There is a noticeable shift in Benjamin of Tudela's twelfth-century *Itinerary*, when the Jewish traveler's account departs the Arabian Peninsula and begins to describe India and China. Whereas his earlier descriptions of Europe and the Levant were straightforward descriptions of cities and their Jewish populations, his China account tells of sailors who outwit man-eating griffins by disguising themselves as seals, and his India account claims that the people of Kerala display the bodies of their dead after preserving them with spices. "The embalmed bodies look like living beings," he wrote. "Every man can recognize his parents and other members of his family for many years."

Scholars have concluded that Benjamin's *Itinerary* becomes more colorful after Arabia not because India and China were more exotic, but because the great Jewish wanderer hadn't gone to those places in person. Hearing secondhand stories about these lands, he recounted fantastical reveries rather than the workaday subtleties he might have witnessed had he actually spent time there.

As travelers, we're always presented with the temptation to see unfamiliar places through exotic stereotypes rather than more intricate distinctions. To visit faraway lands is to discover that all places contain parts of each other (as Benjamin saw firsthand in the Jewish communities of Marseille and Constantinople and Baghdad), and no place exists outside of time and reason. Though our first instinct might be to fall back on dualistic thinking—Here and There, Us and Them—travel allows us to plumb a place's nuances as we explore the fullness of our humanity.

SEEING OTHER CULTURES HELPS YOU
SEE YOUR OWN

It is hardly possible to overrate the value, for the improvement of human beings, of things which bring them into contact with persons dissimilar to themselves. . . . [T]here is no nation which does not need to borrow from others.

—John Stuart Mill, *Principles of Political Economy* (1848)

When Anne P. Beatty traveled to Nepal as an American Peace Corps volunteer in the early 2000s, she was startled by how seemingly dangerous life was for the children who lived there. Preteens carried infant siblings through rickshaw-crowded bazaars with no parental supervision; preschool boys shepherded thousand-pound water buffalo around rice fields; prepubescent girls cooked meals over flame-spewing kerosene stoves.

It wasn't until years later, when Beatty was living back in the United States, that she realized her safety anxieties were more about her own cultural conditioning than the realities of life in Nepal. "More than any souvenir, Nepal gave me an idea of how big the world is and how small my own place in it," she wrote in a 2018 essay. "My years there gave me some distance from my own culture, which seems obsessively, often to its detriment, focused on protection, whether for our children or for our borders. . . . It may be better for kids to be brave and happy than safe and bored."

Indeed, travel has a way of showing us how our own culture has formed even our most basic assumptions. When Koreans (or Ghanaians) eat rice for breakfast, it makes us wonder why our own compatriots prefer cold cereal; when the Japanese bow (or Ukrainians kiss, or Thais *wai*) their hellos, it makes us consider why people back home prefer to shake hands. In this way, pondering what seems peculiar about other cultures gives us the opportunity to ponder the peculiarities of our own.

THE LESSONS OF TRAVEL CAN INSPIRE CULTURAL CHANGE

The graduate of the Grand Tour did return home contaminated in some sense by the foreign. He had seen that there are many models for being civilized—which is one beginning of true civilization, and civility.

—Susan Sontag, "Questions of Travel" (1984)

The founding of the European Union in 1992 is commonly seen as a top-down event (with leaders from a dozen countries gathering in Maastricht to sign the unification treaty), but this gesture of international cooperation was in some ways the bottom-up result of the youth travel boom after World War II. Thanks to the rise of hostels and inexpensive train passes, two generations of Europeans had come of age with a less rigidly nationalistic sense for who they were. "The young of Western Europe were encouraged to interact and think of themselves as a transnational community based on age," noted historian Richard Ivan Jobs in his 2017 book *Backpack Ambassadors*. "They developed a transnational travel culture vital to the broad ideological trajectory of postwar Europe."

The deepened sense of cross-cultural understanding that evolved in late-twentieth-century youth hostel lounges was in some ways a legacy of the Grand Tour of prior centuries, when Continental travel was treated as an educational endeavor for young aristocrats. While the Grand Tour was designed as a prestige-oriented form of applied learning, however, its young travelers embraced intuitive lessons as well as formal ones—often bringing home nuanced attitudes and cultural sensibilities that went against the fixed prejudices of their elders.

Indeed, even as travel offers us practical lessons, it also sharpens our instincts for how we might understand the world's rich complexity. In making us more comfortable with other cultures and customs, a journey allows us to deepen and diversify our own.

MASS TOURISM CAN MAKE A PLACE
LESS LIKE ITSELF

The buildings which destroyed the [Torremolinos] landscape
were being erected not for Spaniards but for . . . wealthy north-
erners who would use the area only as their playground.
—James Michener, *The Drifters* (1971)

The first place in recorded history to be ruined by tourism was the
beach town of Hippo Diarrhytus, in modern-day Tunisia, which
attracted a tame dolphin nearly two thousand years ago. Since a
friendly dolphin was seen as a blessing from Neptune, word spread,
and the sleepy town was inundated with visitors hoping to touch the
creature. As local residents struggled to feed and house the dolphin-
obsessed guests, they began to feel that the town was no longer theirs.
"Finally," wrote Pliny the Younger in his first-century *Epistulae*, "the
place was losing its character of peace and quiet. It was then decided
that the object of the public's interest should be quietly destroyed."

What was a curious footnote in Pliny's day became so common as
mass tourism boomed in the twentieth century that scholars gave it a
name—the "Torremolinos Effect," named after the quiet Spanish fishing village that was transformed into a tourist slum as vacationers
began to flock to its balmy climate each winter in the 1960s.

Indeed, as places become more and more popular with tourists,
they have a way of feeling less and less like the place that originally
attracted those tourists. Some of the world's most iconic travel attractions (including, but not limited to, Puerto Vallarta, Santorini, and
Koh Samui) have, over the years, come to feel like they have more in
common with each other than with their host cultures. Finding a
purer vision of these cultures is often as simple as veering away from
a country's famous vacation destinations and seeking out lesser-
known landscapes.

ROMANTICIZED VISIONS OF PLACES TEND TO BE INACCURATE ONES

- -

The romantic gaze involves . . . the deserted beach, the empty hilltop, the uninhabited forest, the uncontaminated mountain stream and so on. Notions of the romantic gaze are endlessly used in marketing and advertising tourist sites.

—John Urry, *The Tourist Gaze* (1990)

During a 1953 location-scouting trip for the movie *Brigadoon*, producer Arthur Freed visited such bucolic Scottish locations as Braemar, the Firth of Forth, and Loch Fyne, but he ultimately elected to shoot the movie on an MGM soundstage in metropolitan Los Angeles. Asked why he didn't film the musical in the country where it was set, Freed quipped, "I went to Scotland, but I could find nothing that looked like Scotland."

Absurd as this sounds, being disappointed by the reality of exotic shooting locations is an ongoing Hollywood tradition—as evidenced in 1999, when producers planted dozens of coconut palms on a Thai beach to make it look more stereotypically beach-like for Leonardo DiCaprio's *The Beach*; or in 1961, when producers shipped hundreds of tons of white New Jersey sand to Tahiti to make it seem more stereotypically Tahiti-like for Marlon Brando's *Mutiny on the Bounty*.

In doing this, Hollywood was simply mirroring our own romanticized visions of what we think places should look like—visions that have been reinforced in recent years by the idealized, selectively filtered travel images we see on social media. The thing is, few places are going to live up to the Platonic ideals we project onto them in advance. Fantasies aside, the reality of the destinations we dream of visiting can involve bad weather, uninterested locals, and, inevitably, clusters of other tourists. Encountering these things need not compromise our experience of places so much as bring them to life in imperfect and intriguing ways.

EXPLORE NEW CITIES ON FOOT, AS A FLÂNEUR MIGHT

> The flâneur is attracted to the city's dark corners, to chance en-
> counters to confront the unexpected, to engage in a kind of
> counter-tourism that involves a poetic confrontation . . . unclut-
> tered by the dominant visual/tourist images of that place.
> —Carol Crawshaw, in *Touring Cultures* (1997)

The French art of *flânerie* involves aimlessly strolling through a city with no goal beyond blending into crowds and paying attention to the subtlest details around you. Though it has, over the years, been embraced by travelers as a dynamic way to experience new places, it began as a ritual Parisians used to explore their own city as it modernized in the mid-nineteenth century. Poet Charles Baudelaire noted in an 1860 essay that the task of the *flâneur* is "to be away from home, and yet to feel at home anywhere . . . [to move] into the crowd as though into an enormous reservoir of electricity."

Directly translated, a *flâneur* (derived from the Old Norse verb *flana*, "to wander with no purpose") is a saunterer who witnesses the utilitarian life of a city without feeling compelled to participate in it. Though *flâneur* is masculine in its original noun form (*flâneuse* is its feminine equivalent), *flânerie* need not be a gendered pursuit— although, depending on your environment, your gender can affect how it plays out. The task of the *flâneur* is to achieve a kind of introspective solitude among strangers—to focus your energies not on external goals, but on simple observation (novelist Honoré de Balzac equated *flânerie* to "gastronomy of the eye").

When, as a traveler, you choose to become a *flâneur,* you don't seek out tourist zones that have been curated for your enjoyment; rather, you move through in-between spaces, invigorated by the notion that, in not knowing what to expect, you enable yourself to commune with the unexpected.

MUSEUMS REVEAL A PLACE'S CONVERSATION WITH ITSELF

> We do not just keep and collect things, amass and restore them.
> We trouble ourselves to repurpose, create, and invent things just
> to carry, a little easier, those stories we cannot live without.
> —Kendra Greene, *The Museum of Whales You Will Never See*
> (2020)

As Egyptians took to the streets of Cairo in 2011 to demand the overthrow of then-president Hosni Mubarak, protestors set up what they called the "Museum of the Revolution" in a tent near the Presidential Palace. Exhibits featured things like empty tear gas canisters and photographs commemorating a movement that was literally still happening. The makeshift museum's purpose wasn't just to honor the revolution, but to make it feel more official.

In her book *The Museum of Whales You Will Never See*, American artist Kendra Greene described how Iceland's national museum—established almost a century before the country secured independence from Denmark—played a role in creating the country's sense of self. "It became a fashion for the nation-states of Europe to . . . consolidate their national identities, through the founding and development of national museums," she wrote. "If you are going to make a bid for independence, one thing to do is make a claim for who you are." By showcasing its identity through its cultural relics (many of which had to be reclaimed from Denmark's own national museum), the museum was asserting Iceland's sovereignty before it became properly sovereign.

In this way, part of the reason travelers seek out museums—be they national galleries or local relics put on display in a small-town gas station—is that visiting them can be like sitting in on the conversation a place is having about itself.

TRAVEL ENABLES A BROAD AWARENESS
OF SMALL DETAILS

> Journeys are the midwives of thought.... There is an almost
> quaint correlation between what is before our eyes and the
> thoughts we are able to have in our heads: large thoughts at
> times requiring large views, and new thoughts, new places.
> —Alain de Botton, *The Art of Travel* (2002)

Years ago, as I was waiting for the Egypt-bound ferry to arrive in
Aqaba, Jordan, I found myself observing a group of men making
bricks. Before long, the workers waved me over and gave me a tutorial
in their craft. The first step, they showed me, was mixing straw and
water into a pile of clay-rich soil to achieve the right viscosity of mud.
From there, sticky wads of mud were peeled off, pressed into sand-
primed wooden molds, and shaken out as damp rectangles that were
left to dry in neat rows under the sun. The dozen or so bricks I pressed
with the men's help that day weren't particularly well made, but the
experience changed the way I looked at buildings for the rest of the
trip.

Sometimes the lessons you learn on a journey are less about specific skills and understandings than a broader awareness of small details. "Those who travel heedlessly from place to place, observing only
their distance from each other, and attending only to their accommodation at the inn at night, set out fools, and will certainly return so,"
British statesman Philip Stanhope wrote in a 1747 letter to his son.
"But those who observe, and inquire into . . . the trade, the manufac-
tures, the government, and constitution of every place they go to; who
frequent the best companies, and attend to their several manners and
characters; those alone travel with advantage, and as they set out wise,
return wiser."

Indeed, travel doesn't just teach us how to move through the world
beyond our home; it can reveal to us the everyday processes and in-
terrelationships that make those places what they are.

CULTURE ANYWHERE IS A FLEXIBLE CONCEPT

> Seeking to impose a cultural identity on a people is equivalent
> to denying them the most precious of liberties—that of choosing
> what, how, and who they want to be.
>   —Mario Vargas Llosa, in a 2003 interview

In the mid-twentieth century, Mexican restaurants in Kansas City began to put parmesan on tacos for the simple reason that the cheese was inexpensive and easy to find locally. This innovation proved so popular that a "Kansas City taco" became synonymous with its parmesan flavor. With the twenty-first-century rise of social media, however, many Mexican Americans in Kansas City had to defend their "inauthentic" way of making tacos. "All these Yelpers [are criticizing] things they have zero experience in culturally or emotionally," one exasperated local restaurateur told *Eater*. "Access to Twitter or Yelp does not make you an expert on how my grandparents made our food."

Just as the parmesan tacos of Kansas City are a unique expression of Mexican immigrants who found themselves adapting to a new place, culture anywhere is a fluid process that continually bends to new circumstances. Travelers who become fixated on unchanged traditions in new places risk overlooking the ways healthy societies have always adapted to outside influences.

In this way, baseball can be enjoyed as a touchstone of national pride in the Dominican Republic, just as Bangladeshi death-metal music can be understood as a sincere expression of Dhaka youth culture. As a friend in Havana once told me, playing the Asturian bagpipes was for him a celebration of his Cuban identity, in part because Cubans have always put their own stamp on outside traditions. "One of the reasons Cuban culture is so strong," he said, "is because we're not afraid to listen to the rest of the world, and keep the best parts as our own."

BUSES BRING YOU INTO THE RHYTHMS OF LOCAL LIFE

> There are train buffs; there are no bus buffs. A bus is simply a way to get from one place to another cheaply.
> —Thomas Swick, *The Joys of Travel* (2016)

One of the more memorable literary evocations of commonplace long-distance transport comes in Norman Lewis's 1951 Southeast Asia travel memoir *A Dragon Apparent*, when the British author described how his Laotian bus driver sent an assistant out to repair an electrical issue while the bus was speeding through the countryside. "With the bus leaping and lurching beneath him he crawled barefoot all over the front end," Lewis wrote, "opening first one and then the other side of the bonnet, wielding his pliers to strip and join wires and insulating the joints with oblongs of tape he carried stuck to the skin of his legs." In witnessing this, Lewis got a window into the intrepid improvisational spirit with which the people of central Laos lived their lives.

Though buses are popularly regarded as the least glamorous way to travel ("we wave instinctively at trains . . . [but] nobody ever waves at buses," Canadian novelist Douglas Coupland quipped), they move more people from place to place than any other form of transport in the world. Particularly in the developing world, inexpensive buses and shared taxis are the way most people get from home to work and from town to town—which means that riding them brings you into the rhythms of local life.

In committing yourself to travel by bus (and in many parts of the world it can be hard to get around if you don't), you aren't just making your way to another destination—you are invariably joining a self-enclosed local community, a practical-minded microcosm of the culture you're visiting.

IMPROVISED COMMUNICATION IS PART OF THE JOURNEY

Language lessons remind me again and forever that there are things in this life which cannot belong to us, but which we might pick up and carry along anyway.
—Kristin Van Tassel, "Swamp Creatures" (2018)

When journalist William Finnegan traveled around the South Pacific as a young surfer, drinking kava with groups of Fijians helped him understand how communication isn't always tied to language itself. "I loved watching people chat, even when I understood nothing," he recalled in his memoir *Barbarian Days*. "They used their mouths, hands, eyes—all the usual communication apparatus—but also chins, brows, shoulders, everything. Watching people listen was even better. There was a lovely . . . shifting of the head from side to side; a constant cocking of the neck, notch by notch . . . [as if] the listener was continually resetting his mind at different angles in order to take in different speakers, different impressions, with maximum equanimity."

Finnegan's Fijian realization is a reminder that, as travelers, we can communicate in ways that go well beyond spoken language. Employing what linguists call "intersemiotic" communication, physical gestures and non-linguistic sounds, we can share our basic feelings and needs with the people we meet on a journey, even if we can't have a fully articulated conversation. Moreover, augmenting intersemiotic efforts by learning at least a few words of local languages—even phrases as simple as "hello" and "thank you"—doesn't just help us communicate; it's a good-faith way to show people we're making an active effort to be understood.

In this way, engaging with unfamiliar languages need not be a structured classroom task; it often flows out of the informal effort of trying to get our point across on the road, of being patient when misunderstandings arise, and of knowing that imperfect attempts to communicate are always better than no attempt at all.

EXERCISE A SENSE OF EXTROVERSION ON THE ROAD

Thou hast made me known to friends whom I knew not. Thou hast given me seats in homes not my own. Thou hast brought the distant near and made a brother of the stranger.
—Rabindranath Tagore, *Gitanjali* (1910)

One of my more charming days as a traveler in Myanmar began when I asked an old man in the town of Pakkoku about the music I'd heard booming out of a Buddhist temple the night before. The old man didn't speak much English, so he fetched his grandson, who invited me to come to his school. There, the English teacher asked me to stay and speak to his classes, which compelled a gaggle of teenagers to take me to the local *pwe* festival, which—as it happened— was the source of the music I'd heard the previous night. That evening, I was delighted to witness my first-ever Myanmar *pwe*, which featured dancers, puppet shows, stand-up comedians, and a lip-synching drag cabaret troupe from Yangon known as the Thunderbirds.

Though getting to know people in distant lands is one of the most rewarding aspects of travel, it can at times feel like a daunting task. The solution, as I was reminded in Myanmar, is to exercise your extroversion and ask a friendly question about some aspect of the place you're visiting. This question can be as simple as asking what people do for fun on weekends, or where one can get a decent meal, or if it's possible to join a soccer game in the town square. Given the right blend of courtesy and patience on your part, I've found that people are happy to help, proud to show off their community, and willing to take a happenstance interaction into fascinating new directions.

THE CHANCE TO MAKE LOCAL FRIENDS
IS A BLESSING OF TRAVEL

Here's what I love about travel: Strangers get a chance to amaze you. Sometimes a single day can bring . . . a simple kindness that opens a chink in the brittle shell of your heart and makes you a different person when you go to sleep—more tender, less jaded—than you were when you woke up.

—Tanya Shaffer, *Somebody's Heart Is Burning* (2003)

When European Christian pilgrims made the arduous journey to Jerusalem in the Middle Ages, many of them expressed affinity for the Muslims they met there. Fifteenth-century English pilgrim Margery Kempe, whose mystic eccentricities were known to irritate her fellow travelers, wrote that her Muslim guides showed her more kindness than her own companions. When Swiss pilgrim Felix Fabri made his second Jerusalem pilgrimage in 1483, he brought a gift of European stirrups for a local Muslim named Cassa, who had befriended him and offered him the use of a donkey on his previous pilgrimage to the city.

To be sure, most pilgrimage memoirs from that era focused on religious sites and Christian companions, but that only makes such heartfelt moments of cross-cultural connection resonate. In a similar way, modern-day travelers are statistically more likely to befriend fellow travelers than local people, even in study-abroad programs designed to foster international friendship ("Semester Abroad Spent Drinking with Other American Students," quipped one early 2000s headline in the satirical newspaper *The Onion*).

Yet if making genuine local friends is less common on the road, that's all the more reason to honor the human connections that do arise. Do favors for these friends; keep in touch with them, return bearing gifts, find ways to host them in your own part of the world, and savor the blessing that true friendship represents.

FINDING RICHER TRAVEL EXPERIENCES

EMBRACING UNCERTAINTY MEANS
THE REAL JOURNEY HAS BEGUN

It is good to come to a country you know practically nothing about. Your thoughts grow still, useless . . . there is no reference point. You struggle to associate colors, smells, dim memories. You live a little like a child, or an animal.

—Andrzej Stasiuk, *On the Road to Babadag* (2004)

To read travel reports from many centuries ago—particularly travel reports prepared for kings and emperors back home—is to marvel at the amount of mythical apparitions adventurers encountered in distant lands. Chinese pilgrims headed to India, it seemed, encountered a curious number of ghosts and dragons in the deserts of Central Asia; Spanish sailors continually spotted griffins and mermaids along coastal stretches of the Americas.

In truth, these travelers weren't encountering legendary creatures in distant lands: They were encountering uncertainty. Since statements like "I'm not sure what I saw; we need to spend more time there" didn't go over well in official expedition reports, mythological reveries tended to stand in for what could not yet be explained. In an age when affecting an air of certainty is still a rewarded gesture (particularly on social media, which features "like" buttons, but none indicating "let's wait for more information and then make up our minds"), travel offers a rare opportunity to let uncertainty structure your days.

In fact, it often isn't until your travels become less pegged to certainties—less beholden to expectations and plans—that the most satisfying part of the journey begins. "I love that thrill of being somewhere else, and not knowing how things work, and being a little bit untethered from the confines of what you think of as your daily existence," American author Pam Mandel wrote in her 2020 book *The Same River Twice*. "I love that. It's like a drug."

DON'T SET LIMITS ON HOW YOU NAVIGATE THE JOURNEY

"Maps are liars," [my father] told me. . . . "The truth of a place lies in the joy and the hurt that comes from it."

—Prince Modupe, *A Royal African* (1958)

When Prince Modupe brought a map home from his urban Conakry colonial school in the 1930s, his father, a Susu tribal leader in what is now Guinea, told him it was an absurd object. By depicting the river as a squiggly line (with no indication of water depth) and rendering the landscape in uniform kilometers (with no sense for the physical challenges within that landscape), the map struck the elder Modupe as dishonest. "I understand now that my airy and easy sweep of map-traced staggering distances belittled the journeys he had measured on tired feet," Prince Modupe recalled in his memoir, *A Royal African*. "With my big map-talk, I had effaced the magnitude of his cargo-laden, heat-weighted treks."

In a 1989 essay entitled "Deconstructing the Map," geographer Brian Harley pointed out that all maps spin a story about what is important within a landscape—and even something so simple as a road atlas can constrain and misrepresent a journey. "Once off the interstate highways, the landscape dissolves into a generic world of bare essentials that invites no exploration," he wrote. "Context is stripped away and place is no longer important."

Even the interactive nature of GPS navigation can mislead travelers—less by prioritizing landscape features than by centering the desires of the person who uses it. In showing you the most direct route to places you already wanted to go, digital maps have a way of stripping away the contexts that can make travel meaningful. If in doubt, following maps is less essential to a journey than creating a more organic and intuitive relationship with the landscapes they represent.

TRAVEL WITHIN LOCAL ECONOMIES WHENEVER YOU CAN

> When we travel, we observe distant standards of living, experience local economies, and develop empathy and interest in people's lives.
>
> —Sharon Bohn Gmelch, *Tourists and Tourism* (2009)

When I took my first long-term journey across Asia in the late 1990s, I discovered I had two basic travel economies to choose from. The first, which was custom-designed for people like me, consisted of convenient tour buses, luxurious chain hotels, and air-conditioned rental cars that ensured a comfortable journey. The other economy consisted of figure-it-out-as-you-go commuter bus routes, mom-and-pop guesthouses, and getting from place to place with the assistance of tuk-tuk, jeepney, or rickshaw drivers.

Because I had more time than money at that point in my life, I tended to seek out the latter. Traveling within local economies—sharing buses and ferries with area commuters, and eating and sleeping in places that catered to a regional clientele—was not always easy when compared to Asia's luxury-travel circuit, but I invariably had more dynamic travel experiences as I embraced the socially engaged problem-solving routines that went hand in hand with saving money.

Though my initial decision to travel this way was a self-interested budget strategy, I soon learned that spending my money in this way was healthier for the communities I visited. In sleeping and eating at, say, a locally owned $12-a-night beach hut in a place like East Java, you don't just put money directly into the community you're visiting (rather than "leaking" those funds to corporate shareholders in Jakarta or Houston)—you're also providing the community with a profitable alternative to less-than-sustainable enterprises such as dynamite fishing and palm oil plantations. Thus, when you're on the road, make a point of spending your money in local economies. The habit will strengthen your host communities, even as it saves you money.

BE DARING IN TRYING UNFAMILIAR FOODS

Eat what is put in front of you. They are not making fun of you.
The rooster's head floating in the soup really is given to the hon-
ored guest. If you insist on being a picky eater, stay home.
—Tim Cahill, *Hold the Enlightenment* (2002)

When the ancient Greek botanist Theophrastus interviewed soldiers returning home from Alexander the Great's campaigns
in Asia, he was intrigued by their reports of plucking food from a tree
that "had pods like a bean, ten inches long and as sweet as honey."
Though Theophrastus expressed scientific skepticism at this, the
Greek men who'd tasted the oversized beans in India swore they were
delectable. So it was that Europe came to know of the banana.

One of the great joys of travel has always been the opportunity it
provides to sample foods that are unfamiliar to our palates—and to let
those curious new flavors deepen our relationship to what we consider delicious. When I first traveled to Busan as a young man, the
spicy, pickled-cabbage texture of *kimchi*, Korea's staple side dish, felt
strange and slimy on my tongue; now, decades later, *kimchi* (along
with *kalbi, gochujang,* and other Korean flavors) is my comfort food.

The more I've traveled, in fact, the more I've come to savor the
possibilities of trying unfamiliar foods in new places. This has not
only left me with a sharpened knack for finding cheap and delicious
street food (like *kushari* in Egypt, *pylsur* in Iceland, or *ulundu vadai* in
Sri Lanka)—it has made me realize how dishes that might at first
seem strange (guinea pig *cuy* in Andean Ecuador, or grasshopper *tak
ka tan* in Thailand's Isaan region) can be a curiously tasty window
into how geography and culture shape what and how we eat.

EVERY SO OFTEN, SKETCH (RATHER THAN TAKE) A PICTURE

Cameras replaced sketching by the last century; convenience trumped engagement, the viewfinder afforded emotional distance, and many people no longer felt the same urgency to look.
—Michael Kimmelman, "At Louvre, Few Stay to Focus" (2009)

One of my students' favorite journal prompts when I teach travel writing classes involves taking a pen or pencil and drawing a vista they might otherwise have photographed. Some students are at first frustrated by this exercise—in part because they're self-conscious about their art skills, and in part because the task forces them to spend a decent portion of the day sketching a sight their smartphone lens would have captured in an instant. The longer they sit with their notebook, however, the more they come to savor the way the assignment forces them to investigate the smallest details of their environment. Often, my students become tourist attractions in their own right, as the very ritual of making the drawing compels people to stop and see what has inspired such careful attention.

A couple of centuries ago, travelers packed sketchbooks as reflexively as modern travelers carry cameras, and popular travel guidebooks included listings of the best vantage points from which to draw or paint iconic landscapes and street scenes. Part of the point of packing the sketchbook was to slow the traveler down and force her to spend time considering the panoramas and landmarks that made being in a new place so extraordinary.

Despite the efficiency and convenience of documenting your journey with digital photographs, endeavor to set your camera aside from time to time and sketch the scenes that capture your attention. In breaking out of old visual habits, you transform the passive act of noticing the world's splendor into a more active rite of appreciating it.

July 6

YOUR MODE OF TRANSPORT CHANGES HOW YOU SEE (AND ARE SEEN)

> We've forgotten the benefit of surface travel: It forces you to understand, deep in your bones, the distance you've covered; and it gradually eases you into a new context that exists not only outside your body, but inside your head.
>
> —Seth Stevenson, *Grounded* (2010)

How one chooses to travel from place to place invariably affects how one experiences a given part of the world. Just as a bike ride offers an essential window into the textures of life in Amsterdam, riding a ferry from Java to Sulawesi can compel one to embrace the cheerful patience that defines life in Indonesia, and a *sherut* taxi from Jerusalem to Jericho offers a peek into Israel/Palestine not visible from tour buses.

If there's a classic example of how one's mode of transport changes how one sees (and is seen in) the travel landscape, it came in the person of Bessie Stringfield, who spent most of the 1930s exploring the United States by motorcycle. At a time when Black Americans were often denied basic services on railroads and in hotels, riding a Harley-Davidson allowed Stringfield to blaze her own trail—often because it had never occurred to folks that what she was doing was possible. "People were overwhelmed to see a Negro woman riding a motorcycle," her biographer later noted.

When Stringfield needed money, she performed motorcycle stunts at carnivals; when she was denied accommodation, she would sleep on her bike at filling stations; when she wasn't sure where to go next, she would flip a coin onto her map and ride where it landed. In this way, Stringfield's motorcycle didn't just enable her to travel across America; it preempted the need to ask permission before she did so.

FIND THE TASTE (OR TOUCH) EQUIVALENT OF SIGHTSEEING

> Most tourists feel compelled to put the camera between them-
> selves and whatever is remarkable that they encounter. Unsure
> of other responses, they take a picture.
> —Susan Sontag, *On Photography* (1977)

The aesthetic notion of the "picturesque" dates back to the late eighteenth century, when a travel-obsessed Anglican minister named William Gilpin became fixated on "that kind of beauty which is agreeable in a picture." In a 1782 book that encouraged travelers to examine "the face of a country by the rules of picturesque beauty," Gilpin expressed sorrow at not being able to immediately "fix the scenes" he saw in his travels.

Less than a century after Gilpin spelled out his theories of the picturesque, the simultaneous emergence of photography and leisure tourism didn't just enable travelers to "fix the scenes" they saw—it transformed eyesight into the most important sensual aspect of the travel experience. Terms like *sightseeing* and *scenic viewpoint* and *eye-catching* date back to this era, and visually magnificent regions formerly considered wild and barren—places like mountains and wilderness beaches—suddenly became popular tourist destinations.

While the rise of digital media has only underscored the predominance of eyesight in seeking out (and recalling) travel experiences, it's important to remember that the novel environments of a journey provide delights for all five senses. What is the auditory version of sightseeing? What is the smell equivalent of a postcard vista? What taste is as awe-inspiring as a scenic viewpoint? What touch or temperature demands the kind of creative attention that goes into an Instagram post?

As you travel, don't overlook the pleasure and discovery that come with engaging your non-visual senses.

TRAVEL ALLOWS YOU TO REINVENT THE NOTION OF LOITERING

Not that long ago, the nomad was basically the vagrant, the hobo, the gypsy, and all of the things that white people in Western Europe and North America were not too keen on.

—Felix Marquardt, in a 2021 interview

One faintly absurd aspect of modern vacation travel is the fact that so many people from wealthy countries pay thousands of dollars (and travel thousands of miles) to pass their days soaking up the sun on resort beaches and luxury-hotel verandas. In this way, vacation travel becomes a weirdly complicated way of finding societal permission to do nothing for a few days.

In his 2019 essay collection *The Book of Delights,* poet Ross Gay unpacked the notion of "loitering"—and how, in America, it is often defined as a criminal act (particularly for people who don't happen to be wealthy or white). "The Webster's definition of loiter reads thus: 'to wait around idly without apparent purpose,' and 'to travel indolently with frequent pauses,'" Gay wrote. "Among the synonyms for this behavior are linger, loaf, laze, lounge, lollygag, dawdle, amble, saunter, meander, putter, dillydally, and mosey. . . . All of these words to me imply having a nice day. They imply having the best day. They also imply being unproductive. . . . [T]he crime of loitering, the idea of it, is about ownership of one's own time, which must be, sometimes, wrested from the assumed owners of it, who are not you, back to the rightful, who is."

The sooner we come to see loitering as an expression of freedom, rather than a misdemeanor or a costly self-indulgence, the sooner we can make the most of it on the road. Beaches and cafés are officially sanctioned venues for doing nothing, but as travelers we can also grant ourselves permission to loiter at street corners and on shipping wharfs and in village squares—to stop moving through a place for a few hours, and allow that place to move through us.

ONE GIFT OF TRAVEL IS THE DIFFICULTIES IT PRESENTS

It is precisely by falling off the bike many times that you eventually learn what the balance feels like. . . . People who have never allowed themselves to fall are actually off balance, while not realizing it at all.

—Richard Rohr, *Falling Upward* (2011)

Perusing travel articles and social media photos occasionally reminds me of the time I spent helping film a fast-food commercial during my summer intern stint at a Wichita television station many years ago. While it's no secret that line-cooked hamburgers come out of the wrapper a bit smushed and smeared, the producers spent the better part of a day wafting smoke and spraying chemicals on dozens of on-camera burgers in an attempt to make them appear succulent and smoking hot, topped with gently melting cheese and water-dewed lettuce. Just as these TV-commercial burgers scarcely resembled the ones you might find in real life, travel media can leave you with the impression that journeys revolve around blissful reveries, and that difficulties are something to be prepared against and avoided.

In truth, difficulties aren't something to be evaded so much as embraced as an intrinsic part of any journey. The comforts we find on the road have less to teach us than the challenges, and the most life-affecting journeys begin with the conviction to risk failure and travel in a more vulnerable way. "We have no reason to harbor any mistrust against our world, for it is not against us," Rainer Maria Rilke wrote in *Letters to a Young Poet*. "And if only we arrange our life in accordance with the principle which tells us that we must always trust in the difficult, then what now appears to us as the most alien will become our most intimate and trusted experience."

DON'T LIMIT YOUR TRAVELS TO MAJOR CITIES AND RESORTS

The worst big-city vice is forgetting that the hinterland exists—
the unglamorous reality of the country.
> —Paul Theroux, *On the Plain of Snakes* (2019)

When Mexico City–based novelist Juan Villoro traveled through the Yucatán by car in the late 1980s, he felt like he was visiting a foreign country, even though his mother's family hailed from the region. Villoro visited the peninsula's well-touristed Mayan pyramids, but he was particularly intrigued by the culturally distinctive "country within the country" that he encountered in this largely rural part of Mexico. As influenced by Cuba and Miami as it was by Mexico City or Guadalajara, Yucatán was home to Mexicans who played baseball, listened to merengue-infused rock music, and did sweatshop labor for distant export markets. "Yucatán has developed a border economy," he wrote in his 1989 book *Swift Breeze Palms*, "even though it is the most remote region in the country."

As travelers, we find it easy to forget that a given country consists of far more than its major cities, historical monuments, and recreation areas. This is in part because the travel industry showcases these attractions, but also because the first things we learn about the rest of the world as schoolchildren are capital cities and iconic tourist sites. Add to this the rise of cheap air travel and two centuries of urbanization, and the very notion of world travel can begin to resemble a giant game of hopscotch that connects cosmopolitan capitals with assorted tourist resorts and World Heritage sites.

In truth, some of the richest travel experiences can be found in the simple willingness to seek out places that haven't adapted themselves to global visitors—to wander through a country's comparatively anonymous hinterlands and discover experiences that haven't been created for our amusement.

BE WARY OF PLACES THAT HAVE BEEN CREATED FOR TRAVELERS

> The main mistake made by pro-tourist planners is that they . . . try to build tourist factories, called "resorts" and "amusement parks," through which people are run assembly-line fashion and stripped of their money.
>
> —Dean MacCannell, *The Tourist: A New Theory of the Leisure Class* (1976)

In his book *Abroad*, cultural historian Paul Fussell uses cruise ships (which he calls "small moveable pseudo-places making an endless transit between larger fixed pseudo-places") as a metaphor for how modern consumerism has made the experience of travel feel less like travel. "I don't want to sound too gloomy," he wrote, "but there's a relation here with other 'replacements' characterizing contemporary life: the replacement of coffee-cream by ivory-colored powder, for example, or of silk and wool by nylon; or glass by Lucite . . . eloquence by jargon, fish by fishsticks . . . and travel by tourism."

Indeed, in attempting to sanitize the complexities that come with encountering a new place, the travel industry has a way of insulating us against the very foreignness we travel to experience. Though amusement parks and all-inclusive resorts clearly qualify as "pseudo-places," many ecotourism and adventure-travel experiences are designed to take place in settings that—while not involving fast food or passive entertainments—tend to involve "the systematic removal of uncertainty and randomness from things" (which is how statistician Nassim Nicholas Taleb, in his 2012 book *Antifragile*, defined the "touristification" of life experiences).

While most journeys will at times take us to places that have been created for our pleasure, it's useful to keep in mind that the very embrace of randomness and uncertainty—not homogenized comforts and predictabilities—is what makes travel so rewarding.

TRAVEL CONVENIENCES CAN GET IN THE WAY OF SERENDIPITY

> The nomad who walks or rides, with his baggage stowed on a camel or an ox-cart, may suffer every kind of discomfort, but at least he is living while he is traveling; whereas for the passenger in an express train or a luxury liner his journey is an interregnum, a kind of temporary death.
>
> —George Orwell, "The Road to Wigan Pier" (1937)

George Orwell's essay "The Road to Wigan Pier" was a prescient meditation on the contradictions of travel and technology. On one hand, he wrote, traveling to London from Scotland by train erases the organic experience of walking the countryside between the two places. On the other hand, restoring the travel experience is not as simple as refusing the technology. "In order that one may enjoy primitive methods of travel," he noted, "it is necessary that no other method should be available."

What in Orwell's day was a matter of rail transit is now an issue of constant connectedness. At one level the ubiquity of smartphones and Wi-Fi connections makes travel easier; on another level, part of travel's charm has always been its disorienting uncertainty. Thus, it's important to seek balance—and seasoned travelers over time learn to sense when their gadgets are enhancing new experiences, versus when such gadgets are getting in the way of new experiences.

Most of us aren't going to discard our smartphones any sooner than Orwell was going to walk to London when he didn't have to. That said, just as walking to London on occasion is going to yield serendipitous travel experiences that aren't possible on a train, setting aside your electronic devices and putting yourself at the mercy of your exotic new surroundings can yield the types of experiences that make travel surprising and worthwhile.

GETTING OFF THE BEATEN PATH IS A SIMPLE TASK

There is not very much comfort when one leaves the beaten tracks of travel, but any loss is far more than made up for by the intense enjoyment.
—Isabella Bird, *The Golden Chersonese and the Way Thither* (1883)

The notion of "getting off the beaten path" has become such an ingrained part of the travel vernacular over the years that it can at times seem like a complicated task. As critic Lucy R. Lippard noted in her 2000 book *On the Beaten Track,* the commercial travel industry has capitalized on this compulsion to travel where most people don't. "The tourist industry has gotten into the off-the-beaten-track business," she wrote, "which is usually more expensive and fundamentally more snobbish in its appeal for places where other tourists won't be."

The reason that tour companies have monetized the very notion of avoiding other tourists has less to do with the difficulty of avoiding beaten paths than it does with our own pre-formed ideas about what makes a place appealing. Falling into the habit of seeking out the popularly identified "attractions" in new places, it's easy to lose track of what you're supposed to do when you aren't being passively entertained in these places.

In truth, walking a few miles in any direction from obvious tourist sites is the surest way to begin a diversion from the beaten path—and taking an active interest in the most intricate details of a new place is the surest way to enjoy it, regardless of whether or not other tourists are around. This way of travel can be less comfortable than on-the-beaten-path travel, but this discomfort is invariably more psychic than physical—and the more you do it, the easier it becomes.

GOING BY BICYCLE IS A GREAT WAY TO EXPERIENCE A PLACE

One of the advantages of cycling is that it automatically prevents a journey from becoming an Expedition.
—Dervla Murphy, *Full Tilt* (1965)

When Dervla Murphy received a bicycle for her tenth birthday in Ireland, she felt the curious urge to pedal it all the way to India. Two decades later—in low spirits after the death of her mother—she packed a few changes of clothes and headed east on a fixed-gear bicycle she'd dubbed "Roz." In her travelogue of the ensuing six-month journey, *Full Tilt: Ireland to India with a Bicycle,* Murphy reveals herself as an unpretentious, good-humored sojourner who navigates icy roads in France, suffers severe sunburn in Iran, cracks three ribs in Afghanistan, and savors sleeping on teahouse floors in Pakistan. Murphy delights in the way bicycling allows her to establish rapport with locals as she pedals from country to country.

Bicycle memoirs like Murphy's have become their own vibrant travel writing subgenre (more recent classics include Andrew X. Pham's *Catfish and Mandala* and Kate Harris's *Lands of Lost Borders*), in part because pedaling across entire countries has a way of immersing a person in the day-to-day rhythms of the cultures one encounters en route.

Yet bicycle travel need not always be an epic undertaking. I pedaled a fixed-gear bicycle across central Myanmar for three weeks in 2001 (subsisting on fresh mangoes and sleeping in Theravada Buddhist monasteries), but I've typically used shorter-term bike rentals as a dynamic way to cover ground on islands (Sifnos in Greece; Koh Samui in Thailand), in beach communities (Florida's Pensacola; Mozambique's Tofo), and in cities (thanks to Bogotá's *ciclovia* routes and Paris's Vélib' bike shares).

Given the ubiquity of inexpensive bike rentals worldwide, pedaling your way around a place is invariably a great way to experience it.

TO BETTER GET TO KNOW A PLACE, GO SHOPPING THERE

> The basic difference between going shopping and going to a museum is that, in a shop, one doesn't have to just look.
> —Paula Marantz Cohen, "The Last Taboo" (2007)

Though the history of travel is usually traced to endeavors like pilgrimage and exploration, some of the most remarkable journeys of yore were motivated by trade. In the sixth century B.C.E., for example, Phoenician merchants from Tyre (in modern-day Lebanon) traveled to the western coast of Africa looking for new sources of the mollusk *Stramonita haemastoma,* which was prized as a source of purple clothing dye. In the thirteenth century, Chinese traders ventured as far as Persia in search of cobalt, which was used as a coloring agent in kilns that produced ceramic dishes.

Indeed, for as long as people have endeavored to travel, trade has been a pretext for cooperation, friendly exchange, and seeking out common aims among people who might otherwise view each other as a threat. To this day, marketplaces are not just a setting for peaceful cross-cultural interaction—the very act of shopping as a traveler is a great way to experience another culture in a cordial and colorful setting. Shopping in Florence's Mercato Centrale offers a unique window into Italy, just as Seoul's Namdaemun Market offers a glimpse into Korea, Minnesota's Mall of America reveals cultural aspects of the United States, and the Chichicastenango Market is an expression of Guatemala.

Famous marketplaces aside, most any act of shopping—be it for souvenirs, a snack, or a new pair of socks—puts travelers into dynamic interactions with the vendors and shoppers who live in that place. More than any museum or monument, markets offer an intimate, hands-on encounter with the place you've come to experience.

FELLOW TRAVELERS DIVERSIFY THE JOURNEY EXPERIENCE

> By becoming a traveler, the individual becomes part of a mobile, decentralized subculture whose daily existence revolves around the pursuit of leisure. The journey travelers undertake, therefore, involves not only immersion in a series of foreign cultures, but also participation, en route, in a multitude of temporary [traveler] settings.
>
> —Klaus Westerhausen, *Beyond the Beach* (2002)

One of my most memorable experiences during a six-week European sojourn in July 2013 was the day I participated in the Islamic Ramadan fast with a woman from Brunei named Huwaida.

Huwaida was enrolled in my Paris travel writing classes, and when her classmates and I learned that observing Ramadan meant fasting for sixteen-hour stretches of northern-summer daylight (as opposed to the twelve-hour days of her equatorial homeland), we offered to join her on a rotating basis as a show of support the first week of the ritual. Each day, a different person joined Huwaida in fasting during daylight hours, and each evening we all gathered at the outdoor tables of Place de la Contrescarpe for an informal *iftar* meal. In this way, our experience of Paris became, in its own small way, an experience of Brunei as well.

As much as travel is an endeavor to experience the places we visit, a journey can sometimes intertwine with the cultures of our fellow travelers. Travel is, in fact, one of the rare times in life when we can experience what social scientists have termed *communitas*—the egalitarian bond that arises when people let go of their homebound notions of difference and status, and celebrate their common humanity through shared rites of passage. On the road, it's instinctive to seek out the company of our fellow travelers, and—in sharing life experiences with them, far from the constraints of our homes—to learn from each other, even as we learn about the places we visit.

A TRAIN ISN'T JUST A VEHICLE; IT'S A PLACE

> A wonderful aspect of traveling by train is the transactional re-
> lationship between passengers who feed off one another, pick-
> ing up tips, offering advice, guarding each other's belongings,
> and generating a trust that is unique to railway travel.
> —Monisha Rajesh, *Around the World in 80 Trains* (2019)

Almost two hundred years after the advent of railroad travel, it's easy to forget just how revolutionary trains felt when people first began to use them. Though railroads made travel faster and more convenient, many people were bewildered to see the scenery outside spooling by at breakneck speeds of twenty-five miles per hour, compelling some to assert that trains made transit feel like being blasted across the landscape like a projectile. "All traveling becomes dull in exact proportion to its rapidity," English philosopher John Ruskin complained. "A fool wants to shorten space and time; a wise man attempts to lengthen both."

Despite such criticisms, trains expanded the scope of overland travel for the average citizen, and democratized the notion of who had ready access to distant lands and unfamiliar landscapes. These days, when the ubiquity of airplanes has made travel even faster and more removed from the natural landscape, taking a train feels like a throwback to a simpler, more languorous era. Moreover, while planes and cars keep passengers buckled into a single seat, railroad travel allows passengers to wander, socialize, and treat the train as a culturally vibrant destination in and of itself.

Thus, it's good to remember that a journey isn't just about where you end up, but how you get there—and a classic train trip (be it the Trans-Siberian across Russia, the Ghan across central Australia, or the Coast Starlight up the West Coast of the United States) is a great way to combine both.

UNCERTAINTY MAKES FOR THE TRUEST ADVENTURES

An adventure is never an adventure when it's happening. Challenging experiences need time to ferment, and adventure is simply physical and emotional discomfort recollected in tranquility.
—Tim Cahill, *Hold the Enlightenment* (2002)

The most popular American travel writer of the 1920s and 1930s was Richard Halliburton, a flamboyant Memphis native who went around the world performing such travel stunts as swimming the length of the Panama Canal, attempting to cross the French Alps on an elephant, living with the French Foreign Legion in North Africa, climbing Japan's Mount Fuji in winter, reenacting Robinson Crusoe's solitude on an island near Venezuela, and retracing the routes of Ulysses, Lord Byron, and Alexander the Great. He disappeared at sea in 1938, while attempting to sail a Chinese-style junk from Hong Kong to San Francisco.

Halliburton's books were a wild success in their own day, but later critics asserted that his theatrically staged "adventures" were symbolic of a moment when true adventure was no longer possible. "Halliburton became popular at the very time when travel was becoming a bland and riskless commodity," wrote historian Daniel Boorstin in his 1962 book *The Image*. "Nowadays it costs more and takes greater ingenuity, imagination, and enterprise to fabricate travel risks than it once required to avoid them. Almost as much effort goes into designing the adventure as into surviving it."

In the years since Boorstin made this observation, "adventure travel" has grown into a full-fledged (and reliably enjoyable) market within the tourist industry itself. Yet the truest legacy of adventure travel might well come in the willingness to embrace uncertainty on the road—that is, not in creating arbitrary travel stunts, but in being willing to not know what will happen next in unfamiliar places, and steering the journey accordingly.

July 19

LOCAL AUTHENTICITY ISN'T DETERMINED
BY TRAVELERS' WHIMS

> Authenticity exists when people have a degree of control over
> how change occurs in their societies. "Authentic" cultures . . .
> have the wherewithal to participate in processes shaping their
> lives.
>
> —Erve Chambers, *Native Tours* (1999)

When Danish anthropologist Christina Anderskov interviewed
independent travelers in Central America in the early 2000s,
she found that Western backpackers had a curious sense for what was
and wasn't authentic about the cultures they encountered. "The more
colorfully the locals dress, the more 'real' they seem [to backpackers],"
she reported in a 2002 research paper. "'Real' culture and 'real' locals
are perceived to exist to a higher extent in remote and less developed
areas." The travelers she met thus considered the most authentic part
of Central America to be rural Guatemala, where local people donned
traditional costumes, whereas the modern cities of Costa Rica—home
to locals who wore T-shirts and jeans—were written off as inauthentic.

Arjun Appadurai wrestled with a similar conundrum when pondering tourists' perceptions of cuisine in a 1986 *Anthropology Today*
article. "Authenticity is typically not the concern of native participants
in a culinary tradition, except when they (and the food) are far from
home," he wrote. "New foods come in and go out of vogue in all complex culinary traditions. The idea of authenticity seems to imply a
timeless perspective on profoundly historical processes."

Ultimately, of course, the question of what is authentic about a
place—be it food in Italy or clothing in Central America—isn't ours to
determine as travelers. What is "real" has never been a static signifier
of a community's past; it always has been an ever-changing set of
choices that people who live within that community make to serve
their ongoing needs.

July 20

WHEN YOU FIND A TRAVEL "PARADISE," SEEK OUT ITS CONTEXT TOO

A *paradise* is a traditional type of tourist community . . . [situated] not merely outside the borders of urban industrial society, but just beyond the border of the peasant and plantation society as well.

—Dean MacCannell, *The Tourist: A New Theory of the Leisure Class* (1976)

When Leonardo DiCaprio's *The Beach* hit movie screens in the winter of 2000, its dark plot revolved around a group of backpackers degenerating into violence on an isolated island in Thailand. The DiCaprio movie was based on Alex Garland's 1996 novel, which skewered the assumptions travelers bring to distant places. Garland's book didn't just explore how the backpackers' escapist utopia devolved into murderous savagery—it challenged the reader to consider why the backpackers desired such a utopia in the first place. The beach in *The Beach* wasn't just idealized because it was unknown to tourists; it was idealized because it was also devoid of locals.

In his groundbreaking 1976 study *The Tourist*, sociologist Dean MacCannell noted that what travelers call a "paradise" is invariably a fantasy environment—a market-driven fiction that mimics isolation from human society without requiring any of the discomforts and inconveniences that result from that isolation. "All-inclusive" resorts—where vacationers are invited to enjoy the beaches of, say, Egypt without having to interact with any Egyptians—are the ultimate distillation of this fiction.

Any passive enjoyment of a beach "paradise" has a way of stripping travel of the very cultural contexts that make it so rewarding. Restoring that sense of context is often as simple as traveling a few miles in any direction from a given beach resort and regarding that new place—imperfect, human, and vibrant in subtler ways—as its own kind of paradise.

DON'T CONFINE THE NOTION OF
WHAT A SOUVENIR CAN BE

To me the most striking characteristic of a souvenir is its openness, its readiness to carry the mind in all directions. There might
be millions of tiny brass Eiffel Towers distributed over the globe,
but no two of them carry the same meanings.

—Orvar Lofgren, *On Holiday* (1999)

When astronaut Neil Armstrong died in 2012, his estate ex-
ecutors discovered that he'd saved a few mundane technical
items—a mirror, an emergency wrench, a waist tether—as keepsakes
from his 1969 moon landing. Somehow, for all of the millions of
words that had been written about the Apollo 11 mission to the moon
and back, Armstrong chose to keep a handful of souvenirs from the
journey that told a story only he could intuit.

While the notion of travel souvenirs is sometimes equated with
tacky kiosks selling keychains and shot glasses near tourist attractions, it's useful to remember that souvenirs aren't just objects—they
are narrative devices that we use to create stories about our own lives.
Sometimes these stories are for other people (particularly when we
bring souvenirs home as gifts), but usually they represent a subtler
conversation we're having with ourselves.

On the road, travel keepsakes are often purchased in gift shops
and craft markets, but the notion of a souvenir goes beyond objects
that are sold as such. A souvenir can be anything from a travel
experience—something as simple as a volcanic pebble or a train
ticket, or as formal as a piece of art or a journal entry—that honors a
certain moment in your life, certifies the journey that took you there,
and celebrates the confluence of people and places and actions that
made it possible.

DARE TO BE LONELY, LOST, AND BORED ON THE ROAD

> The luxury that I advocate cannot be bought. It has nothing to do with money. It is the reward of those who have no fear of discomfort.
>
> —Jean Cocteau, *Letter to the Americans* (1949)

In my various podcast appearances in recent years, I've often wound up underpinning my travel advice with the phrase "lonely, lost, and bored"—a verbal tic I wasn't fully aware of until a young podcaster named Jalen Vasquez pointed it out to me in 2020. As Jalen noted in our interview, I tended to reiterate those words not as states to avoid on the road, but as states travelers should embrace.

Indeed, over the course of the 2010s, as smartphones had made loneliness, lostness, and boredom easier to avoid on a journey, these three words became my unwitting catchphrase as I encouraged travelers to break out of their phone-tethered routines and leave themselves vulnerable to new places. Jalen told me that my repetition of this phrase had compelled him to set the words LONELY, LOST, BORED as the background of his phone's lock screen. His rationale was to simply create a concrete reminder to not use his phone as a buffer every time he felt uncomfortable in a new place.

Loneliness on the road need not be assuaged by reflexively texting friends back home, since feeling lonely has a way of attuning you to people you might meet in a new place. Being lost doesn't necessitate GPS navigation; it simply requires closer attention to your environment, and openness to people who might help you navigate it. Boredom isn't an irritant to be assuaged with digital distractions: It's an invitation to pay closer attention to possibilities you have yet to notice in the place you've traveled so far to see.

DISCOMFORTS AND INCONVENIENCES
IMMERSE YOU IN A CULTURE

I had this unsatisfied feeling . . . when confronting the rich, full-of-variety, colorful, often hard-to-define reality of [African] cultures, customs or beliefs. The everyday language of information that we use in the media is very poor, stereotypical and formulaic. For this reason huge areas of reality we deal with are beyond the sphere of description.
—Ryszard Kapuscinski, "Herodotus and the Art of Noticing" (2003)

When the Polish journalist Ryszard Kapuscinski joined a global cadre of reporters covering Africa in the early 1960s, he had a hard time keeping up with the cosmopolitan protocols of his colleagues from richer European countries. Whereas British and French journalists stayed in fancy hotels and had exclusive access to officials at the highest levels of government, Kapuscinski's modest Polish resources forced him to travel by bus, sleep in cheap guesthouses, and interview everyday Africans.

In time, Kapuscinski came to realize that his relative poverty was a gift—a useful limitation that allowed him to get past a formulaic understanding of the cultures he was covering. "It is not the story that is not getting properly expressed: it's what surrounds the story," he noted in a 1987 *Granta* interview. "The climate, the atmosphere of the street, the feeling of the people, the gossip of the town, the smell; the thousand, thousand elements of reality that are part of the event you read about in 600 words in your morning paper."

As was the case for the resourceful Polish journalist, it is useful to remember that the discomforts and inconveniences of a journey are a reliable way to immerse us in the realities of another culture. Freed from the burdens of arbitrary luxuries and official public relations narratives, we put ourselves in a better position to experience other cultures as they experience themselves.

DISCONNECTING CAN CREATE A HEIGHTENED SENSE OF CONNECTION

I wanted to experience the walk as the walk, in all of its inevitably boring walkiness. To bask in serendipitous surrealism, not just as steps between reloading my streams. I wanted to experience time.

—Craig Mod, "The Glorious Boredom of My Walk in Japan" (2019)

In 2019, American writer Craig Mod embarked on a six-week walk centered on the Nakasendo—the Central Mountain Way—across Japan. Though his 620-mile route had no shortage of physical trials, Mod's key challenge on the walk was to become less dependent on his smartphone. "I can't help but feel that I am the worst version of myself, being performative on a very short, very depressing timeline," he wrote of his social media habits.

Instead of ditching his phone entirely, Mod chose to block his favorite social media apps and use the device only to access information that wouldn't distract him from the hike itself—information like maps, Japanese history blogs, and Wikipedia. "My phone ceased to be a teleportation machine and became, instead, a context machine," he wrote.

In the early days of his hike, deprived of reflexive distractions, Mod experienced something resembling boredom—but in time he realized this unsettled feeling was an important gift of the hike. "In the context of a walk like this, 'boredom' is a goal," he wrote, "the antipode of mindless connectivity and constant stimulation. Boredom fosters a heightened sense of presence."

In Mod's case, this reinvented sense of presence inspired him to embrace an expansive attitude of extroversion, offering gregarious greetings to every person he met on his walk. "The walk was powerful because I could choose to be a new person," he recalled later. "Kind hellos begetting kind hellos: It was something I rarely felt when plugged in online."

July 25

AVOID POINTLESS COMPETITION WITH OTHER TRAVELERS

> I had ambiguous feelings about the differences between tourists and travelers—the problem being that the more I traveled, the smaller the differences became.
> —Alex Garland, *The Beach* (1996)

After Alex Garland's backpacker-noir *The Beach* was made into a Leonardo DiCaprio movie in 2000, a number of British-authored pop novels—books like Emily Barr's 2001 *Backpack* and Katy Gardner's 2002 *Losing Gemma*—began to feature plots involving travelers on the vagabonding trails of Asia. Some plots leaned toward potboiler intrigue and others toward romance, but they all featured self-absorbed young backpackers trying (and mostly failing) to use travel in Asia as an escape from the superficial, directionless, consumerist lives they led back home. Cut loose from the social pecking orders of home, the travelers in these stories tended to obsess over their status within the backpacker milieu itself.

Though the characters in these novels were fictional, they echoed real behaviors among independent travelers. In 1992 the Danish anthropologist Anders Sorensen, utilizing the same techniques ethnographers used to study indigenous cultures, conducted fieldwork on backpackers in Southeast Africa. Sorensen analyzed the Western backpackers' values and practices, and discovered that the young Europeans and North Americans maintained hierarchies, ideologies, and symbols of exchange distinct to their own insular cohort. Instead of looking for nuances and complexities within host cultures, the independent travelers tended to fixate on signifiers of subcultural authenticity in each other.

While comparing oneself to other travelers is perhaps inevitable, it's important not to get caught up in the false elitism that can pervade some indie-traveler circles. To do so—particularly at the expense of staying attuned to the culture you're actually visiting—is a way of traveling halfway around the world without fully leaving your home.

LIKE IT OR NOT, YOU TRAVEL AS AN AMBASSADOR OF YOUR HOME

> At home, we can roam the streets for days and few could give a toss who we are. But when you travel, you represent your country to people who may have never met someone like you before.
> —Dave Seminara, *Mad Travelers* (2021)

After the 2003 U.S.-led invasion of Iraq, an act that was deeply unpopular in many parts of the world, rumors began to circulate on Usenet newsgroups and then-nascent weblogs that American travelers were sewing maple-leaf flags onto their backpacks in an attempt to pass themselves off as Canadian. I was traveling in Thailand at the time, and while I never met any Americans who'd pasted their gear with Canadian flags, older travelers told me that this was a ruse that dated back to the Hippie Trail era, when young American travelers posed as Canadian to avoid criticism for the equally unpopular Vietnam War. By the mid-2010s, this dubious stratagem garnered a satirical nickname—"flag-jacking"—complete with its own Wikipedia page.

To this day, I have yet to meet any "flag-jackers" in my travels, and—even if such travelers do exist—it feels like a craven way to account for your country's least-popular political policies and cultural stereotypes. Concealing your national identity on the road makes far less sense than traveling in a way that reflects well on your home country.

Sometimes this will involve explaining your country's idiosyncrasies (particularly its political ones), but as much as anything it's a matter of practicing kindness and respect—of asking questions and listening in earnest; of recognizing your role as a visitor, and not condescending with your good intentions; of leaving behind more than you bring away as a traveler, and giving more than you take.

OVERTOURISM IS A REAL
(AND AVOIDABLE) THING

> What we sell to tourists is perishable. The silence on the mountaintop or the expansiveness of a pristine beach are gone when hordes invade.
> —Shamubeel Eaqub, "The Downside of Too Many Tourists" (2018)

When I traveled to Indonesia a few years ago, rice farmers on the island of Bali were struggling to maintain their traditional *subak* irrigation system due to the fact that tourist demand for golf courses, laundered linens, and infinity pools was depleting local water supplies. Around the same time, travelers to Bali's southern resorts were griping about traffic-snarled roads, long lines at temples, and garbage-littered beaches.

The irony here is that as I read about these developments I was traveling in Sumatra, just two islands away from Bali in the same archipelago, and I rarely encountered other tourists. Other culturally rich and scenic Indonesian regions—places like Flores, Sumba, or even Bali's less-touristed north—offered the country's visitors a similar aura of touristic isolation.

"Overtourism" of the sort one can encounter in Bali is a perplexing spectacle, in part because destinations that are deemed trendy or "must-see" become deluged with visitors, while nearby places remain curiously pristine by comparison. This in mind, if Venice feels overrun with cruise-ship traffic, you have the right to explore Padua (or Verona, or Ljubljana) instead. Similarly, Kings Canyon attracts far fewer Sierra Nevada sightseers than Yosemite, Choquequirao is a quieter Inca setting than Machu Picchu, and Utrecht is a pleasant urban alternative to Amsterdam.

As you travel, keep in mind that almost any tourist-clogged attraction will likely have a quieter alternative nearby. Seeking out those alternatives (even if you don't initially know what or where they are) is an experience that will make your journey more dynamic, even as it benefits those less-trendy host communities.

IN AN AGE OF DISTRACTION, PAYING ATTENTION IS A LUXURY

In an age of distraction, nothing can feel more luxurious than paying attention.

—Pico Iyer, *The Art of Stillness* (2014)

The most interesting advice from Francis Galton's 1871 book *Hints to Travelers* (which was, over the years, used by such British explorers as Ernest Shackleton, Robert Falcon Scott, and Percy Fawcett) didn't involve the task of planning and logistics, but the simple art of paying attention. "It is a loss, both to himself and others, when a traveler does not observe," Galton wrote. "Remember that the first and best instruments are the traveler's own eyes. . . . In short, describe to yourself at the time all you see."

While Galton's advice had a scientific bent (encouraging travelers to record things like mountain glaciation and prevalent winds), the art of paying attention is still one of the most useful skills a traveler can hone. This can apply to such practicalities as avoiding scams and finding your way around, but it also applies to the subtler details of unfamiliar places, and the spiritual texture of paying attention to life itself.

A travel friend I met in Beirut once pointed out to me that while the English language compels one to "pay" attention, French speakers "lend" attention, and Arabic speakers "give" attention. When we regard our attention as a gift rather than an expense, she said, we're less likely to hoard it, and more compelled to give it out freely.

This in mind, travel can allow you the heightened opportunity to immerse yourself in the subtleties of a place and a moment—to ignore the twenty-four-hour news cycle and relentless stream of algorithm-driven smartphone distractions, and sharpen your ability to give attention in the here and now.

TRAVELING WITH FAMILY MAKES YOU MORE RELATABLE

- -

Because children pay little attention to racial or cultural differences, junior companions demolish barriers of shyness or apprehension often raised when foreigners unexpectedly approach a remote village.

—Dervla Murphy, "Murphy's Laws of Travel" (2011)

Bruce Kirkby's 2020 book *Blue Sky Kingdom,* which recounted the Canadian adventurer's journey across Asia with his wife and young sons, depicted a harrowing instant when one of his boys was snatched up by a stranger. After a moment of bewilderment, Kirkby realized his son's abductors were simply Chinese tourists who—delighted by the presence of a cute kid—wanted to take his photo. "It was hard to imagine a Canadian stranger plucking up a child and carrying them away without asking a parent first," he quipped, "or going to jail after."

Though this incident was a source of irritation for Kirkby, many cultures' natural affinity for children can be an unanticipated delight for people who travel with their own kids. I've known road-hardened indie travelers who've worried that becoming parents might somehow compromise their journeys—only to discover that the presence of children made them more approachable in places as far-flung as Argentina and Botswana and Mongolia.

Similar serendipities happen in the other generational direction, as I discovered when I visited Beijing with my parents. Whereas I was received as an exotic outsider when I'd traveled alone on previous visits to China, the addition of two affable, gray-haired Americans made me instantly relatable to local residents.

Of the many lenses through which people relate to the rest of the world, one of the most intuitive is family. To travel with your own children, parents, siblings, or cousins is a way of sharing this core expression of common humanity.

IN AN AGE OF HASTE, TRAVEL LIBERATES OUR SENSE OF TIME

- -

> The poet does not lament that a beautiful afternoon has passed, because every time has a scent proper to it. . . . The scent of the afternoon will be followed by the pleasant smell of the evening. And night, too, exudes its own fragrance.
> —Byung-Chul Han, *The Scent of Time* (2017)

There is a moment in Eddy L. Harris's travel memoir *Native Stranger* when the author realizes that his journey through Africa has reinvented the way he experiences each day. "My sense of time had blurred and time itself had become nearly meaningless," he wrote. "I never checked my watch. It didn't matter what day it was. You woke up at the beginning of day, and went to sleep at the end of it. In between you ate when you could and did what you had to do to see you to the day's end. . . . Long days contracted into nothing, and the shortest moment seemed sometimes to take forever."

Part of the reason travel had transformed Harris's sense for time was that getting around in places like Mali and Mauritania and Senegal could be full of delays and inefficiencies. Yet in learning not to cling too tightly to rigid itineraries and expectations in Africa, he found that time could be experienced in a more open-ended manner. Unshackled from all notions of predictability and haste, Harris found that each day unspooled on its own terms.

At a certain point in the journey, time can come to feel deliciously irrelevant. Whereas back home we regard it as a consumable commodity—chopping each day into streamlined, bite-sized chunks—travel has a way of making time feel raw and spacious and open to possibility.

GO YOUR OWN WAY, AND ADAPT TO THE JOURNEY THAT RESULTS

I'm a big believer in winging it. I'm a big believer that you're never going to find the perfect travel experience or the perfect meal without a constant willingness to experience a bad one.

—Anthony Bourdain, in a 2012 interview

When I first visited Southeast Asia, I soon began to suffer "temple fatigue" in the face of so many spectacular Buddhist shrines. Temple details that at first seemed exquisite—gold-leaf stupas, massive tiered roofs, intricate frescoes, jewel-encrusted statues—eventually became a tad wearying. Within a week in Bangkok, I'd been to a half dozen temples, yet I had trouble remembering which photos I'd taken where.

The problem was not that the Thai temples were too similar, but that I'd tried to see so many without knowing much about them (first-time visitors to Europe report suffering a similar "cathedral fatigue" in the face of so many historical churches). Eventually I left Bangkok to wander through the small villages that dotted the Thailand-Laos border. Intrigued by the rural landscapes I found there, I bought a small fishing boat with two other travelers and drove it nine hundred miles down the Mekong River—an engrossing (and at times harrowing) experience that remains one of my most memorable travel experiences anywhere in the world.

When you first arrive in new places, it's natural to visit well-known sites and prescribed attractions, but as the journey deepens, it's good to follow your instincts and curiosity, even if it takes you into directions that haven't been certified by travel guidebooks or formal tourist infrastructure. In seeking to go your own way—and adapting to the unexpected adventures that result—you put yourself into a position to find experiences no amount of advance planning could have prepared you for.

August 1

INDEPENDENT TRAVEL MAKES FOR A MORE DYNAMIC JOURNEY

I've yet to find that longitude and latitude
can educate those scores of monumental bores
Who travel in groups and herds and troupes.
—Noël Coward, "Why Do the Wrong People Travel?" (1961)

Early in my travel writing career, I drove across the Americas as an embedded journalist in a Land Rover expedition that was raising money for charity. Our convoy featured nine team members (including a three-member film crew) driving four vehicles through twelve Latin American countries. Though the expedition enabled me to see places like Machu Picchu and Torres del Paine for the first time, I was perplexed when the documentary about the trip later appeared on cable TV, and acquaintances who watched it said it looked like "the trip of a lifetime."

Enjoyable as the expedition had been in certain moments, I didn't regard it as a "trip of a lifetime"—in part because the independent journeys I'd taken worldwide over the course of the previous decade (the very trips that gave me the credentials to embed with the Land Rover expedition as a travel writer) were far more meaningful to me than what played out on the TV documentary. By its very design, the Land Rover expedition meant that I always traveled in the company of the other eight team members, and we couldn't change our route or stay in any one place for more than a day or two.

If in doubt, a "trip of a lifetime" need not involve film cameras or an "expedition team" wearing matching uniforms. As often as not, the best journeys are the quieter, self-funded ones done alone or with friends—journeys that allow you to savor the unexpected, linger in places that intrigue you, and follow instincts rather than itineraries.

August 2

DON'T ASSUME PLACES WERE BETTER
A FEW YEARS AGO

- -

Nobody goes there anymore. It's too crowded.
—Yogi Berra, describing a St. Louis restaurant to friends (1959)

When anthropologist Claude Lévi-Strauss traveled through the Amazon in the 1930s, he found himself stricken with the desire to have been there earlier. "The paradox is irresoluble," he recalled in his 1955 book *Tristes Tropiques*. "Either I can be like some traveller of the olden days . . . or I can be a modern traveller, chasing after the vestiges of a vanished reality. . . . [Yet] I may be insensitive to reality as it is taking shape at this very moment. . . . A few hundred years hence, in this same place, another traveler, as despairing as myself, will mourn the disappearance of what I might have seen, but failed to see."

What Lévi-Strauss saw as an anthropological conundrum was in fact a common anxiety among travelers. "There is no mystery left," D. H. Lawrence groused in his 1927 book *Mornings in Mexico*. "We've done the globe, and the globe is done." Half a century before that, Mark Twain contrasted the leisurely life he remembered on the Mississippi River in the 1850s with the frenetic pace of life in the 1870s—while, back in the 1850s, English clergyman Henry Christmas warned: "Those who wish to see Spain while it is still worth seeing must go soon."

This reflexive nostalgia for earlier times has only gotten sharper in a time when we can go online and glimpse most any corner of the world before we go there. But even as anxieties about tourist oversaturation make us long for earlier eras, it's useful to remember that—as Lévi-Strauss noted—obsessing on the perceived purity of yesterday only serves to make us risk missing out on nuances of the moment we're experiencing right now.

STAY OPEN TO UNPLANNED
TRAVEL EXPERIENCES

If you go into a place with your itinerary mapped out down to every meal and bus ride, you're not leaving room to learn anything new. More often than not, serendipity is going to be what leads to the most treasured memories and the best stories.

—Sebastian Modak, in a 2020 interview

In her 2005 book *A Field Guide to Getting Lost,* American essayist Rebecca Solnit noted that the English word *lost* derives from the Old Norse *los,* which refers to the disbanding of an army. This etymology implies that losing one's way is less about being in the wrong place than it is about letting go of planned endeavors, and embracing surprises rather than avoiding them. "The things we want are transformative, and we don't know what is on the other side of that transformation," Solnit wrote. "That thing the nature of which is totally unknown to you is usually what you need to find, and finding it is a matter of getting lost. . . . I worry now that many people never disband their armies, never go beyond what they know."

Indeed, as travelers we all too often enforce busyness among each other ("Why didn't you do ____ and ____ in Slovakia?") rather than fostering a willingness to seek the unplanned and embrace the unknown. In taking us away from the routines and certainties of home, travel offers the rare opportunity to leave ourselves open to whatever comes our way, without knowing the outcome in advance.

ALLOW YOURSELF THE LUXURY OF TAKING YOUR TIME

- -

We left Serbia like two day-laborers, memories full of new friendships. We had enough money for nine weeks. It was only a small amount, but plenty of time. We denied ourselves every luxury except one, that of being slow.
—Nicolas Bouvier, *The Way of the World* (1963)

One of the more ostentatious rituals reported among the fashion-obsessed dandies of nineteenth-century Paris was putting turtles on leashes and walking them, as slowly as possible, along avenues like the Champs-Élysées. This was in part a self-conscious gesture of dissent against the efficiency and anonymity of the emergent Industrial Age, but it was also an assertion that the purest expression of luxury in life was taking one's time.

In his 2017 book *The Scent of Time*, Korean Swiss philosopher Byung-Chul Han used the sense of smell as a metaphor for how we might resist the compulsion to hurry our way through life. "A scent is slow," Han wrote. "Thus, as a medium, it is not adapted to the age of haste. . . . The age of haste is an age without scents." That is, unlike with sights or sounds, technological efficiencies haven't offered us a way to fast-forward smell. The phrase "stop and smell the roses," which admonishes us to ease up and appreciate moments in life, resonates because scent is something that cannot be rushed.

In an age when the notion of "luxury travel" is marketed in terms of high-priced amenities like infinity pools and in-room pedicures, it's good to remember that the truest travel luxury—an amenity available to all travel budgets—is the ability to slow down, take your time, and savor the experience of being in new places.

August 5

THE BEST JOURNEYS ARE NOT
A CONSUMER EXERCISE

> Travel is one of the few activities we engage in not knowing the outcome and reveling in that uncertainty. Nothing is more forgettable than the trip that goes exactly as planned.
> —Eric Weiner, "Travel Should Be Considered Essential" (2020)

Once, during a visit to Mombacho Volcano National Preserve in Nicaragua, I met a Canadian woman named Suzanne who'd been returning to explore the cloud forest each year for the past decade. The first time she'd visited, she told me, she expected to see howler monkeys—but she had only allowed herself a one-hour hike in the preserve because she had a dozen other places she wanted to see during her week in Nicaragua. Like so many other travelers, she had approached her destination with a concrete to-do list—a clear rundown of items she felt needed to be checked off in Nicaragua—and that ended up leading to experiential disconnect. Frustrated because she saw no monkeys during her hour at Mombacho, she ultimately realized that the problem lay in what she called her "consumer approach" to seeing the country.

The following year Suzanne decided to go back to Mombacho and stay there until she saw a howler monkey in the wild. It took six days of hiking in the cloud forest before she saw one, she said, but it felt like this ritual allowed her to see Nicaragua for the first time. It wasn't until she stopped filling her time with activities that she was able to be fully present.

As Suzanne realized in Nicaragua, sometimes the surest path to disappointment as travelers is to see the journey as a checklist of consumer options rather than a continually unfolding mystery—an embrace of uncertainty that can deepen your experience of the world.

OFFSET VISIONS OF THE PAST WITH WHAT IS HAPPENING NOW

> We may fancy an exotic past that contrasts with a humdrum or unhappy present, but we forge it with modern tools. The past is a foreign country whose features are shaped by today's predilections, its strangeness domesticated by our own preservation of its vestiges.
>
> —David Lowenthal, *The Past Is a Foreign Country* (1985)

When the Austrian poet Rainer Maria Rilke visited Rome in the early years of the twentieth century, he felt as if he were traveling through two foreign places that crashed up against each other in the same moment—one that belonged to the present, and another that belonged to previous eras. "Rome makes one feel stifled with sadness through the abundance of its pasts," he wrote, "laboriously upheld pasts, sustained by philologists and copied by the average traveler, which are essentially nothing more than accidental remains from a life that is not and should not be ours."

Gloomy as Rilke's observation was, it hints at what can happen when, as travelers, we approach a place in terms of what it used to be, rather than what it offers right now. As common as it is for tourists to seek out museums, landmarks, cathedrals, monuments, and battlefields, it's important to balance such endeavors with equal attention to the newer textures of a place. Standard real-time travel attractions tend to include things like restaurants, nightclubs, and arts performances, but they can also include the subtler aspects of a place.

In his *Arcades Project,* an unfinished avant-garde text-map of 1930s Paris, philosopher Walter Benjamin suggested that the smallest experiences of a given location—aimlessly strolling its streets, talking to children in public squares, sipping cognac at a streetside café—interweave to create a subtler evocation of history that plays out in the present moment.

WORKADAY ROUTINES ARE A PART OF THE TRAVEL ADVENTURE

Leave home, leave the country, leave the familiar. Only then can routine experience—buying bread, eating vegetables, even saying hello—become new all over again.
—Anthony Doerr, *Four Seasons in Rome* (2008)

In all his years of traveling the world as a musician in the 1980s and 1990s, D.C. native Ian MacKaye seldom visited tourist attractions. This was in part because shoestring punk-rock tours entailed relentless performances (his band Fugazi once played sixty-five European shows in seventy days), but also because growing up in Washington left him hypersensitive to how oblivious people could become in the presence of monuments and museums. "I wanted to be a part of the places I traveled to," he said in a 2018 interview. "I didn't want to see the world as a snow globe I wasn't in; I wanted to be inside the globe."

For MacKaye, this meant immersing himself in the workaday rituals of the places he visited—seeking laundromats rather than landmarks, grocery stores instead of gift shops, auto mechanics rather than maîtres d'hôtel. "I love the world that way," he said. "I go out into it to be a part of it." MacKaye thus learned to savor the same seemingly banal routines some travelers might regard as tedious obstacles to more satisfying experiences. To see such quotidian rituals as part of the adventure is to embrace the journey in a deeper, more all-encompassing way.

"There are two phases of enjoyment in journeying through an unknown country," Dervla Murphy wrote in her 1968 travel memoir *In Ethiopia with a Mule*. "The eager phase of wondering interest, and the relaxed phase when one feels no longer an observer of the exotic, but a participator in the rhythm of daily life."

VISITING FEWER PLACES CAN YIELD RICHER EXPERIENCES

When you hurry, time is filled to bursting, like a badly-arranged drawer in which you've stuffed different things without any attempt at order.

—Frederic Gros, *A Philosophy of Walking* (2015)

One of the biggest challenges for travelers hoping to visit every country in the world entails just how one defines "country" and "visit." Strolling the Manhattan-sized nation of San Marino is a different task than journeying across all forty-six oblasts of Russia (a country encompassing seventeen million square kilometers), and spending one year in Madagascar is a different endeavor than spending a few days there between brief stop-offs in Mauritius and the Seychelles.

In 1954, an organization called the Traveler's Century Club was founded to help folks tally countries, eventually assembling a list of 329 eligible states and territories. A rival organization, MostTraveled People.com, founded in 2005, asserted that one could choose from 573 eligible territories (a list that later grew to 875); Nomad Mania, founded in 2011, tabulated 1,281 far-flung territories (a list that later grew to 1,301). Thus, the notion of visiting every place in the world has been transformed into a faintly absurd task involving millionaires spending weeks on military boats, hoping to disembark for a few minutes at obscure sub-Antarctic outposts like Bouvet Island.

The problem with checking countries off lists is that it reduces travel to a geographical parlor game. Even among travelers with more modest ambitions, we all too often seek quantity rather than quality—packing, say, ten nations into a one-month Europe sojourn, when the monthlong experience of a single European country would yield much richer rewards. If in doubt, the number of places you seek on a journey counts for less than the willingness to slow down and savor each new place on its own terms.

TRAVEL IS ONE OF LIFE'S MOST EFFECTIVE FORMS OF EDUCATION

Wisdom is not finally tested in schools,
. . . Now I re-examine philosophies and religions,
They may prove well in lecture-rooms, yet not prove at all under
the spacious clouds and along the landscape and flowing
currents.

—Walt Whitman, "Song of the Open Road" (1855)

At the time, the dinner I prepared with a pair of American travelers in the kitchen of a Cairo hostel two decades ago didn't feel all that portentous. The older of the two, Paul, worked as a city planner in California; the younger, Dan, worked as a whitewater raft guide in Colorado. What I didn't realize was just how attuned Dan was to Paul's insights into how urban environments were designed and managed. Months later—having wandered through the Middle East and Europe with a sharpened sense for how cities function—Dan joined the Peace Corps. Though he didn't have any formal training in city planning, he managed to finagle a municipal-development assignment in Honduras. He now works as an emergency-preparedness advisor for the city of Wellington in New Zealand.

All these years later, Dan still points to that moment in Cairo as a key step in his professional development. "Travel plants seeds and opens ideas and possibilities," he told me in a 2020 podcast interview. "Just being out on the road and paying attention to everything you encounter can expand your idea of what life can be."

The more you learn on the road, the more you open yourself up to further learning, and this can create a butterfly effect that generates results you won't appreciate until years later. Indeed, the most life-altering rewards of a journey aren't tied up in "finding yourself" so much as in *creating* yourself—of expanding your sense of possibility in a way that can come to benefit your whole being.

THERE IS MORE TO A PLACE THAN ITS SIMPLE AMUSEMENTS

> I don't believe you know a place until you've been really bored in it.
>
> —Ian Frazier, in *They Went* (1991)

A central appeal of travel is that, in taking us to new environments, it gives us a constant flow of stimulation. Some of this stimulation is so hard-wired to tourist attractions that it can be easy to conclude that a journey consists entirely of straightforward amusements. As we seek out tourist diversions in the same manner in which we fill our days with tasks and distractions at home, it can be easy to overlook the more nuanced realities that a place can offer. Finding these subtler textures in a place can be as easy as allowing ourselves to become bored in it.

Russian novelist Leo Tolstoy famously called boredom "a desire for desires," though when he wrote that (in 1878, in *Anna Karenina*) daily life was not so infused with artificial desires as it is now. In an age when instant, low-stakes diversion is a smartphone screen away, mindfully leaving ourselves open to boredom on the road can be a way of forcing our attention onto what we have yet to notice—a way of actively stimulating our senses to the subtleties we've overlooked, rather than passively expecting to be entertained.

"Your true traveler finds boredom rather agreeable than painful," wrote Aldous Huxley in his 1925 book *Along the Road*. "It is the symbol of his liberty—his excessive freedom. He accepts his boredom, when it comes, not merely philosophically, but almost with pleasure." In other words, travelers need not seek to fill idle moments with random amusements, since experiencing moments of boredom—and being receptive to the subtle gifts those moments offer—is part of the point of the journey.

August 11

A JOURNEY CAN STRENGTHEN
THE BOND OF FAMILY

> The idea seemed wild at first: what if I quit my job and spent a
> year traveling the world to complete the journey my mother
> never had a chance to make?
> —Maggie Downs, *Braver than You Think* (2020)

One of the great travel chroniclers from world history was a man
named Xu Xiake, who spent three decades exploring inner
China and Central Asia in the early 1600s. Xu's mother had encouraged him to study history and geography as a young man, ostensibly
in preparation for the imperial civil service examination, but when
these readings inspired him to drop out of school and travel to the
places he'd read about, his mother wholeheartedly supported him.

While most historical Chinese travel accounts from the era are
lean and laconic, Xu's diaries resonate with ebullience as he travels on
foot through places like Yunnan and Tibet, describing wildlife and
geographical features ("I've lost all desire to sleep," he enthuses upon
seeing a snow-flecked rainbow glowing over a waterfall in Sichuan).
As he traveled, Xu remained grateful for his mother's support, returning home to spend time with her between journeys, and—
remarkably—bringing her along on a shorter trip when she was eighty
years old.

As Xu's example shows, in-depth journeys need not be undertaken
at the expense of family connections—and even solitary journeys can
be an extension of familial love. Journalist Maggie Downs's travel
memoir *Braver than You Think*, for example, recounts a solo round-
the-world journey that her mother, receding into Alzheimer's disease,
was not able to take. "I am confident that those who are dying want
their loved ones to live, which is exactly what my mom would have
wanted for me," she wrote. "And so I have carried her with me from
Machu Picchu to the Great Pyramid to the convergence of seas. I
chose life over her death."

234 – THE VAGABOND'S WAY

PRESUMED ALTRUISM COUNTS FOR LESS THAN RESPECTFUL ENGAGEMENT

> Orphanages are incentivized to maintain low standards of living because voluntourists and visitors want to see poverty.
> —Pippa Biddle, *Ours to Explore* (2021)

Greg Mortenson's 2006 memoir *Three Cups of Tea* became a best-seller on the strength of its inspirational narrative, in which the American author became motivated to build schools in rural Pakistan when local villagers assisted him after a mountain-climbing mishap. By 2010 Mortenson's charity claimed to have built more than 170 schools for girls in Central Asia—though a *60 Minutes* investigation later concluded that most of these structures were either abandoned, never completed, or being used for things like grain storage.

Though Mortenson's charity didn't cater to travelers, its sentimental narrative and dubious practical outcomes have a lot in common with "voluntourism"—a multimillion-dollar global enterprise that uses images of inequity and "save the world" promises to connect paying travel-volunteer clients from wealthy countries with communities in poorer ones. As journalist Pippa Biddle wrote in *Ours to Explore*, however, voluntourism is a growth-driven, for-profit industry that tends to misrepresent the suffering of host communities, exaggerate what untrained outsiders can accomplish during short-term visits, and emphasize the virtue narratives of visitors rather than the real-life needs of the people they presume to help.

"Millions of voluntourists are booking trips based on what they want to do and where they want to go, not what skills they have or what communities really need," she wrote. "Blindly following altruistic intentions has led to half-built libraries [and] exploitative orphanages." Biddle's suggested alternative for well-meaning travelers? "Swap out service for engagement by embracing the role of a visitor. . . . Take the time to sit, observe, and think before consuming." In short: Remember your role as a guest, and don't let presumed altruism preclude respectful interactions.

THE BEST MUSEUMS ARE SOMETIMES NOT MUSEUMS

When you think about it, department stores are kind of like museums.

—Andy Warhol, *America* (1985)

One of the strangest attractions in Los Angeles is the Museum of Jurassic Technology, a surreal gallery that leaves the visitor wondering just what it is she's looking at. There, amid dim lighting, one can see displays of antique dice, oil portraits of cosmonaut dogs, and complex theoretical diagrams about how memory works. Each display is captioned with the meticulousness of conventional museums, yet the more one examines the objects, the more one wonders if these items belong to the world of fact or fiction. Such confusion is part of the point of the Museum of Jurassic Technology, which author Lawrence Weschler has called "a museum, a critique of museums, and a celebration of museums, all rolled into one."

In toying with the notion of what (and how) a museum is supposed to display, the MJT draws on long-held anxieties about what these displays are supposed to represent. Philosopher Theodor Adorno noted that the German word *museal*, which means "museum-like," describes objects "to which the observer no longer has a vital relationship"—and indeed it can at times be hard to know how to respond to artistic and historical ephemera that have been deemed worthy of museum display.

Though traditional museums will always figure on travel itineraries, the focused curiosity with which we are encouraged to explore these galleries need not be reserved for formal institutions. Indeed, we can bring the same open-ended sense of wonder to the artifacts on display in everyday places—secondhand stores, libraries, shopping malls, open-air markets—and engage these items with a less structured, more playful sense of reverence and imagination.

August 14

LOOK BEYOND THE RECEIVED STEREOTYPES OF A PLACE

Foreign reporting can be depressingly narrow. . . . Sometimes it seems as if there are only two possible subjects: people we should fear and people we should pity. But those aren't the individuals I met when I was abroad.

—Peter Hessler, *Strange Stones* (2013)

The most widely read article in the history of *Granta* began as an email that Kenyan author Binyavanga Wainaina wrote out of exasperation upon reading the British literary journal's "Africa" issue. Entitled "How to Write About Africa," Wainaina's satirical response is a wicked sendup of all the clichés—starving children, anthropomorphized animals, an entire continent treated as if it were one cultural entity—that have come to define generations of Western writing about Africa.

At the heart of Wainaina's frustration was the way stereotyped narratives fail to depict such everyday events as "having African characters laugh, or struggle to educate their kids, or just make do in mundane circumstances." One decade after the *Granta* satire, Kenyan filmmaker Wanuri Kahiu put together a three-point test to assess storytelling about Africa, including: Are the characters healthy? Are they in need of saving? Are they having fun? "We need to show images of Africans who are not dying, not in need of saving, and living a joyous, thriving African life," Kahiu said in her 2017 TED Talk.

Though as travelers we often follow the standard narratives of what there is to do in distant cultures, we need not limit ourselves to wildlife safaris and charity projects when we visit a place like Kenya (or Bangladesh, or Guatemala, or Papua New Guinea). The more we seek travel experiences that go beyond our received ideas of a culture's attractions or shortcomings, the more we can see that culture for what it really is.

TRAVEL CAN REINVENT WHAT
AND HOW YOU LEARN

- -

Travel has forced my mind open in a way that books alone could not.

—Nanjala Nyabola, *Traveling While Black* (2020)

Of the many kinds of fellow wanderers I encounter on journeys, I invariably enjoy the company of people who've dropped out of university to travel. Freed from the constraints of the classroom, these folks have a knack for rediscovering the joy of learning in a more nuanced and immersive way. Language is an obvious learning focus overseas, but I've also seen people throw themselves into studying Muay Thai and cooking in Thailand, flamenco and oenology in Spain, yoga and photography in India. Oftentimes, these endeavors aren't aimed at expertise so much as enrichment: I've met non-artists on the road making video documentaries or decorative jewelry; non-athletes learning surfing or parkour; non-authors contextualizing their life stories in the pages of a travel journal.

Unlike in a formal class setting, the self-directed learning that happens on the road is (at any age) less about evaluable results than creative process. "Usage is like oxygen for ideas," American entrepreneur Matt Mullenweg wrote in a 2010 essay. "Nothing can recreate the crucible of real usage." While Mullenweg was alluding to technology development, the same principle can apply to trying out new things on the road. In constantly presenting you with what you didn't know you didn't know, a journey provides a constant flow of oxygen for personal growth.

Oftentimes, the most essential thing you learn on the road isn't a skill so much as the adaptive savvy—instincts like time management, goal-setting, negotiation, networking, cultural awareness—that arises along the way. Moreover, since travel to distant places allows you to risk failure in a setting where nobody you know will see your mistakes, it emboldens you to learn in a more vulnerable way.

DEVOTE A PORTION OF THE JOURNEY TO BEING IN NATURE

> Now I see the secret of the making of the best persons,
> It is to grow in the open air and to eat and sleep with the earth.
> —Walt Whitman, "Song of the Open Road" (1855)

The people of Norway have, over the years, developed a system for dealing with frigid subarctic winters: Faced with shortened days and sinking temperatures, they actively embrace the cold and spend as much time outdoors as possible. Known in Norwegian as *friluftsliv* (open-air living), the concept was popularized in the 1850s by playwright Henrik Ibsen, who extolled the spiritual benefits of escaping indoor confinements and interacting with nature. As life in Norway has become increasingly modern and urban, *friluftsliv* is something Norwegians schedule year-round (for periods as short as a lunch break) as a bulwark against the workaholic, hyperconnected stresses of indoor life.

The cultural instinct to embrace one's aliveness by going outside is not unique to subarctic Europe (a similar outdoor ritual, *shinrin-yoku*—"forest bathing"—is practiced in Japan), in part because spending the bulk of one's day indoors is a recent human phenomenon that is at odds with a spiritually balanced life. At a time when the outdoors is often regarded as an in-between space that one encounters while going from one indoor place to another, *friluftsliv* allows one to mindfully experience a world that is not regulated by artificial lighting and temperature control.

While a journey naturally makes one less beholden to indoor routines, travelers can still be tempted to regard the outdoors as an in-between space, especially in cities. On the road, find ways to balance the experience of human-built environments with the willingness to head outside and spend open-ended days in the soul-enriching splendor of the natural world.

ONE CAN TRAVEL IN DIFFERENT MODES ON A SINGLE JOURNEY

A tourist may grow into a deeper traveler, just as a journeyman
sawyer becomes a master wheelwright; and further, all travelers, even the most awakened, at times move through the world
as mere tourists.

—William Least Heat-Moon, "Here, There, Elsewhere" (2013)

As commercial tourism took hold in Europe in the mid-nineteenth century, commentators among Britain's elite began to describe tourists with metaphors usually reserved for invasive insects. "The cities of Italy are now deluged with droves of these creatures," grumbled a British consul in 1865. "Of all noxious animals," an upper-class clergyman lamented around the same time, "the most noxious is the tourist."

Such observations betray the fact that disdain for tourists originated as an expression of an aristocratic class that resented having to share the marvels of travel with what they considered an inferior grade of compatriot. To this day, denigrating tourist amusements is a reflexive practice among those who feel they belong to a more sophisticated class of wanderer.

In truth, all modes of travel can have their merits—and a single journey can mix urbane discoveries with tourist indulgences in a way that makes for a more rewarding experience. Indeed, for all the times I've stumbled into quaint art galleries in the quiet corners of Paris, some of my fondest memories in that city have taken place on the Champ de Mars, where first-time tourists from Guangzhou and Indianapolis, Minsk and Brasilia, Nairobi and Brisbane all shared in the simple thrill of picnicking beneath the evening glitter of the Eiffel Tower.

On the road, snobbish hierarchies need not determine what is worth seeing or doing, and engaged journeys can embrace the generic diversions of mass tourism, even as they seek out subtler, more refined epiphanies.

HANDWRITING A LETTER HOME IS AN ICONIC TRAVEL RITE

One of the most prolific kinds of travel narratives, whether informal or formal, has always been the letter.
—Percy G. Adams, *Travel Literature and the Evolution of the Novel*
(1983)

When I was a teenager, still years away from possessing a passport, I associated international travel with the aerogrammes that would sometimes arrive at my house from overseas missionaries and family friends. Now something of a rarity, an aerogramme is a single sheet of postage-embossed paper onto which one can write a letter, fold along indicated lines, seal shut using pre-gummed tabs, and mail anywhere in the world. On my initial overseas journeys through Asia in my mid- and late twenties, carefully fitting a handwritten missive onto an aerogramme and mailing it home was a rite that made travel feel real.

Sending handwritten messages back home is in fact part of a folk travel-writing tradition, dating back to the days when Roman soldiers in Egypt (or Chinese merchants in Indonesia) went to great trouble to find homeward-bound travelers to carry messages to family and friends. Many classic seventeenth- and eighteenth-century books (particularly those written by women like Mary Wollstonecraft and Lady Mary Montagu) started out as letters—and it wasn't until the rise of international wireless and telephone connections in the nineteenth and twentieth centuries that travelers had other options for getting a message home.

While the current ubiquity of digital communication has made it possible to livestream our travels in a way that makes handwritten letters seem obsolete, there is nevertheless a concrete expression of commitment (and decreased odds of digital feedback distraction) baked into the task of sitting down, organizing your thoughts onto a sheet of paper in pen, and mailing your travel story home.

MAILING A POSTCARD CERTIFIES YOUR TRAVELS IN PLACE AND TIME

> The postcard is an extraordinary device for anchoring memory, for making the trivial momentous, for challenging a sense of what is distant and what is close.
>
> —Stephanie Coyne DeGhett, "Icons of the Everyday" (2013)

In the first decade of the twentieth century, mailing out picture postcards became so popular (750 million were sent in the United States alone in 1906) that some commentators saw the trend as a harbinger of cultural decline. A 1906 *American Magazine* article declared that postcards would lead to a "faddy degeneration of the brain"; in 1910, the magazine published an anti-postcard screed entitled "Upon the Threatened Extinction of the Art of Letter Writing."

While postcards might have been dismissed as lowbrow detritus one century ago, there is something elegant in the way they serve to evoke a relationship (evidenced by the sender's signature and the addressee's name), a moment in time (certified by the cancellation stamp), and a place (depicted with a scenic image on the front). Unlike, say, an Instagram post, mailing a postcard isn't a public declaration; it's a decision to handwrite a message on an object and send it to a single person. It contains no data that will be harvested for algorithms, and no obligation on the part of the recipient (beyond, perhaps, getting a magnet and hanging it on a refrigerator).

In contrasting postcards to Instagram, I realize I'm echoing the very misgivings critics expressed in the face of the postcard boom a century ago. That said, there is a sense of retro joy in the ritual of buying a postcard in a distant place—of embossing it with a message, affixing a stamp, and mailing it off as a physical token of your presence (and absence) to someone far away.

TRAVEL INTENTIONS YIELD TO REALITY IN SUBJECTIVE WAYS

When you're headed out with your happy travel dreams, a guidebook is your magic key; it's your oracle, where all the answers await. But the world has its own agenda of trains that break down when it's 120 degrees outside, and goats that vomit on your shoes.

—Ed Readicker-Henderson, "Why You're Here Now" (2002)

One of the more curious aspects of perusing old guidebook texts lies in their suppositions about just what it was travelers needed to know for the journey. The thirteenth-century *English Manual of French Conversation,* for example, offered advice on washing your legs to protect against fleas while sharing inn beds with other travelers; the eighteenth-century Japanese *Ryoko Yojinshu* told hikers to smear ox dung on their sandals to ward off vipers; the nineteenth-century *Pretty Women of Paris* presumed English visitors to France needed to know how to conduct themselves at brothels. 1970s Hippie Trail guesthouse ledgers compared tips on where to find hash in Tangier and Kathmandu, while the 1996 *Visitor's Key to Iceland* was less focused on monuments and museums than hills, rivers, and rocks that had featured in ancient sagas.

Peculiar as these recommendations might seem, they illustrate how assumptions about what might make for a successful journey have varied from country to country, era to era, traveler to traveler. Invariably, the advice of people who have traveled before you should be taken with a grain of salt, as you come into a more dynamic relationship with the realities and subtleties of your own journey.

TRAVELERS OFTEN SEEK DISHONEST VISIONS OF PLACES

> It is said that the camera cannot lie, but rarely do we allow it to do anything else, since the camera sees what you point it at: The camera sees what you want it to see.
>
> —James Baldwin, *The Devil Finds Work* (1976)

Back when the camera had just been invented, many photographers who traveled through the Holy Land were less interested in the reality of nineteenth-century Palestine than visions of the biblical past. Employing local guides to recruit peasants as models, photographers staged scenes such as "Lazarus in the Tomb" and "The Good Samaritan" in the Levantine landscape. "Indigenous Muslims were asked to play unfamiliar biblical roles," Israeli sociologist Erik Cohen noted in a 1992 article. "Local models were sometimes posed in studio portraits before painted European-style, bourgeois-salon backdrops."

As absurd as this pseudo-biblical nineteenth-century Holy Land ritual might sound, travelers are still obsessed with fantasy visions of the places they visit. Late in the twentieth century, for example, tourists were so persistent in seeking traditional-looking photos of otherwise modern African people that the Tanzanian government considered setting up a fake Maasai village for tourist buses. "Tourists want to see the most primitive people in their most primitive state," one exasperated Tanzanian official reported. "Setting up artificial villages may be fake, but it's less aggravation."

In traveling the world, it's useful to remember that the sights we expect to see in places—conditioned over the years by the simplified visions of TV travel documentaries, *National Geographic,* and social media—tend to be stereotyped simplifications of how people in those places actually live. If in doubt, let go of your bygone visions of how a place is supposed to look, and embrace reality as it presents itself in the present moment.

August 22

LOOK BEYOND THE OBVIOUS VESTIGES
OF HUMANITY'S PAST

There are certain objects that strike the imagination, and inspire
awe in the very idea of them, independently of any dramatic
interest, that is, of any connection with the vicissitudes of human
life.

—William Hazlitt, "Shakespeare's Genius" (1818)

Overland travelers headed to Machu Picchu are often surprised to
find that northern Peru was once home to a fascinating pre-
Columbian civilization of its own. Known as the Moche, this irrigation-
farming culture is remembered for its innovative textiles and
metallurgy, as well as monumental pyramids like the Huaca del Sol.
Unlike Inca structures, Moche pyramids were made of mud brick,
which means they have eroded substantially over the past fifteen hundred years. Hence, while granite-buttressed Machu Picchu sits atop
many Peru bucket lists, adobe Moche pyramids are relatively unknown.

As travelers, we often overlook vestiges of human ingenuity for the
simple reason that those creations weren't engineered out of hard
stone or metal. Whereas generations of travelers have celebrated remnants of Stone Age and Bronze Age civilizations in Europe, for instance, parallel Asian civilizations flourished through a variety of
what might be called Bamboo Ages, when the fast-growing plant was
utilized to create medicines, tools, bridges, irrigation pipes, and housing complexes that don't show up on the archaeological record.

Most any sojourn through rural China will reveal that the Bamboo Age hasn't fully ended (particularly in Shanxi, where bamboo is
still an ingredient in a popular medicinal *baijiu*)—and the most vivid
legacy of Moche culture is not its eroded pyramids, but the ubiquity
of Peru's Moche-derived national seafood dish, ceviche. In this way,
the aging remnants of history you encounter on the road don't just
offer axiomatic lessons in human impermanence; they offer subtler
hints at human continuity.

August 23

TOURISM CAN STRENGTHEN LOCAL CULTURES

> When tourists from the Western world go to Third World coun-
> tries, it increases the locals' pride in their own culture. Tourism is
> the avenue on which we can exchange our cultures and learn
> from each other.
> —Tourism scholar Ranjan Bandyopadhyay, in a 2006 interview

Though travelers arriving at Panama City's Tocumen International Airport now see colorful posters in the arrival hall celebrating Emberá lifeways, there was a time when Panama's indigenous cultures were considered a dying vestige of the country's precolonial past. This began to change in the 1990s, when local initiatives compelled the Emberá to augment their small-scale farming/fishing economy by hosting international tourists. In the course of a few years, Emberá communities in Panama's isolated rainforest regions strengthened their economy by showcasing traditional music, dances, and handi-crafts to outsiders. Once consigned to earning hard currency by ship-ping plantains downriver to distant urban markets, the Emberá now thrived by shipping Western travelers upriver into their own villages.

Panama isn't the only place where tourism has reinvigorated re-gional economies by reigniting pride in traditional customs. In Papua New Guinea's Sepik River region, travelers' interest in indigenous art-work has diversified the economy in remote villages; in Poland's Tatra Mountains, tourists' taste for *oscypek* cheese has inspired young locals to learn traditional highland methods of preparing it; in Kyoto, wooden *machiya* townhouses once written off as outdated shanties are now being renovated as Japanese restaurants and travelers' inns.

In an age when tourism is a key source of foreign exchange for the world's poorest nations, traveling to the more isolated regions of a host country and spending your money there isn't just a way to inter-act with local cultures in a more traditional setting—it is often part of an economic dynamic that keeps those traditions healthy.

August 24

THE BEST TRAVEL MOMENTS AREN'T CAPTURED IN IMAGES

We felt that here at Lake Paradise, in the heart of Africa, we had really found peace on earth, goodwill toward men. I nestled closer to Martin. Neither of us spoke. We sat there into the dawn.

—Osa Johnson, *Four Years in Paradise* (1941)

The first travel "influencers" in mass-media history were a young Kansas couple named Osa and Martin Johnson, who revolutionized the then-nascent world of wildlife documentaries by depicting themselves having off-the-beaten-path adventures in films like *Wings over Africa* and *Borneo*. Osa's signature safari hats and riding pants landed her on a 1939 *New York Times* list of best-dressed women in America, and her travel memoir *I Married Adventure* was a 1940 best-seller.

Despite their celebrity status, however, the Johnsons' happiest travel memories tended to happen off-camera. Though Martin's state-of-the-art cameras pioneered the slow-motion wildlife sequences that appeared in their 1928 movie *Simba,* Osa's journal from that time celebrates simpler tasks, like fishing for tilapia, picking wild Abyssinian coffee beans, and collecting rainwater to wash her hair. Moreover, while in their movies the Johnsons appear to be self-directed American protagonists in an African landscape, Osa's Lake Paradise journal mentions their African collaborators by name and documents her enthusiasm for learning Swahili. And, fashion icon status aside, Osa savored her anonymity at Lake Paradise. "In the forest I feel as if everything belongs to me," she wrote. "There's no competition, no worry about what other women are wearing."

Nearly a century later, when social media technologies allow most anyone to broadcast their travels in real time, it's good to remember Osa's conviction that the most rewarding travel experiences aren't the flashy ones we perform for the camera, but the quieter ones we keep for ourselves.

USE TRAVEL TO EMBRACE (NOT ESCAPE) YOUR REAL LIFE

But I'm not running away. I'm running toward . . . toward adventure, toward discovery, toward diversity. I am free to live by the standards and ideals and rules I create for myself.
—Rita Golden Gelman, *Tales of a Female Nomad* (2001)

In a 2019 *Saturday Night Live* sketch, Adam Sandler plays a travel agent who's become weary of his clients' outsized vacation expectations. "If you're sad now, you might still feel sad there," he says in a satirical TV commercial. "If you're sad where you are, and then you get on a plane to Italy, in Italy you'll be the same sad you from before, just in a new place. Does that make sense? We can take you on a hike. We cannot turn you into someone who likes hiking. We can provide you with a wine tasting tour of Tuscany. We cannot change why you drink."

At a certain level Sandler's comedy satirizes the perky promises of the travel industry, but it also skewers the escapist fantasies that can arise in anticipating our journeys. Scholars have found that the pleasure people attach to travel actually begins in the planning stages, but it can unravel on the road if one's attitude toward the journey is tied to passive expectations rather than active pursuits. As researcher M. Joseph Sirgy observed in a 2009 article for the *Journal of Happiness Studies,* travel is statistically more satisfying when people seek "desired states" rather than avoiding "undesired states."

In other words, traveling to escape your real life is less likely to yield happiness than traveling to embrace your real life. A journey cannot, in and of itself, open your mind and inspire change; these attitudes are an active choice on the part of the person taking the journey.

STAY OPEN TO DETOURS AND
UNPLANNED DIVERSIONS

> I think unknown territory is where the imagination gets stimu-
> lated. It's where you find the thing you didn't know you were
> looking for, where your world gets enlarged.
> —Rebecca Solnit, "Terra Incognita" (2006)

One of my wife's favorite family travel experiences as a young adult started when her road-weary father mistakenly assumed the "15:00" on their flight itinerary meant 5 P.M. (rather than 3 P.M.), causing them to miss their Torino-to-Barcelona flight. Had my future father-in-law been a less imaginative man, he might have checked the family into an airport hotel and waited for the first flight out the next day. Instead, he took his mistake as a pretext to have an adventure in the Alps. Improvising a rental-car route toward Italy's border with Switzerland, the family stumbled into a village in the Aosta Valley, where they spent an enchanted evening in a mist-shrouded landscape that offered a quiet contrast to the tourist-crowded Cinque Terre coast they'd visited two days before. The joy of experiencing the Aosta Valley became inseparable from the accident of having found it, and to this day my wife's family regards their missed flight as a serendipitous event.

As you travel, it's empowering to regard your inevitable mistakes not as a compromise of your vision for the journey so much as an opportunity to create a new one. In feeling emboldened rather than disappointed, you'll allow yourself to see detours and diversions as unexpected travel blessings. As Pico Iyer noted in a 2006 speech: "Travel at its best is not really about going from A to C via B, but in accidentally getting there via P, or realizing that you wish you'd been in T all along. The goal in travel is, really, getting lost."

THE DEFINITION OF "TRAVELER" IS BROAD (AND VIBRANT)

> My Africanness gave me an opening into the lives of my hosts that other travelers—white, Western, or wealthy—may never be able to experience. I learned that the guidebook-writers conditioning people to be afraid of Africa might not be experiencing the same Africa as I am.
>
> —Nanjala Nyabola, *Traveling While Black* (2020)

When the American anthropologist Erve Chambers visited the traditional Hmong villages of northern Thailand in the 1980s, he was at first struck by how remote the mountain settlements felt. The longer he spent there, however, the more he realized that the seemingly isolated Hmong had close connections to relatives living in North America. "Consider the possibility," Chambers wrote, "that the 'exotically' dressed tribeswoman tourists sought to photograph there had only recently returned from visiting her sister in Los Angeles, where she was a tourist in her own right."

In my own travels, I am continually reminded that middle-class folks from industrialized countries aren't the only people out taking journeys. In a Medan shared taxi, I once met an Indonesian who worked as a busboy on a cruise ship and had seen far more European capitals than I had; in the Old City of Damascus, I stumbled into a church service filled with Sudanese refugees, all of them fluent in multiple languages, who'd been traveling out of necessity for years. Visitors to India are, statistically, three times as likely to share the road with domestic Indian tourists than with all non-Indian travelers combined; in Mexico the ratio of Mexican to international tourists is five to one.

On the road, it's useful to keep in mind that laborers, migrants, and domestic tourists aren't just legitimate fellow travelers—they are often a window into a richer understanding of the place you're visiting, and of the travel rite itself.

WAITING FOR TRAVEL EXPERIENCES INTENSIFIES THEM

Waiting greases the cogs in the machinery of marvels.
—Tim Cahill, *Hold the Enlightenment* (2002)

When we're at home dreaming of our travels, what we invariably imagine is a highlight reel of colorful bazaars, sumptuous outdoor meals, awe-inspiring cathedrals, forested mountain trails, and empty white-sand beaches. What we tend to forget in such fantasies is that getting to the world's wonders involves a lot of waiting: waiting in airport security lines; waiting for flights to take off and land; waiting in taxis stopped by urban traffic jams; waiting in buses stopped by rural mudslides; waiting in restaurant foyers and museum queues; waiting in ticket lines and visa offices.

Before a journey begins, waiting for the marvels we dream of takes the form of excited anticipation, yet once we're on the road, it's easy to assume that waiting is a diminished form of in-between time—a tedious irritant that gets in the way of the real experiences we seek. Yet while modern consumerist culture has convinced us that the greatest pleasure in having desires is gratifying them, the act of waiting for an experience has always been intertwined with the pleasure that comes with having it. The Spanish word for "to wait for," *esperar,* can also mean "to hope" or "to expect"; the German word for boredom, *die Langeweile,* which literally translates as "the long while," implies an intensified awareness of time.

On the road, waiting for experiences isn't just the price we pay for having them: It's a chance to meditate on the quotidian novelties of life away from home; an opportunity to savor what we're about to do, and earn—through patience—the wonders that await us.

August 29

TO REALLY GET TO KNOW A PLACE,
WORK IN IT

Teach English in Japan, aquaculture in the South Pacific, accounting in Brazil. Sink into an otherness that reflects a reverse image of yourself.

—Bob Shacochis, "Be an Expat" (2002)

When I moved to Busan to work as an English teacher a few years after graduating from college, I was less motivated by the prospect of getting to know South Korea than the promise of adding money to my nearly empty bank account. Had I been vagabonding there, I might have had some fun travel experiences and moved on, but working in Korea—spending hours each week overseeing classrooms of students—proved to be an unexpectedly vivid crash course in the Korean way of seeing the world.

Koreans, I discovered, valued formal pedagogy, yet my employers insisted that my core mission as a teacher was to be a clueless American who initiated conversations. The less I knew about Korea, the more my students had the chance to educate me—in English—about the country's cuisine and drinking rituals, its rivalries with Japan, and its up-and-coming pop stars. My favorite students were middle-aged housewives, who—freed from the stratified syntax of the Korean they spoke at home—savored the opportunity to opine and pontificate in the less patriarchal textures of English.

Formal employment hasn't been the only way working in a foreign place has offered me a window into local culture. Passing through Jerusalem as a backpacker, I found work handing out promotional flyers for a pub near Zion Square—an experience that allowed me to apprehend the idiosyncrasies and frustrations of catering to tourists from a local perspective. In this way, working in a place—be it a few years or a few days—has invariably given me the opportunity to appreciate that place in a more intuitive way.

PAUSE TO SAVOR THE BEST MOMENTS
OF THE JOURNEY

All night . . . we would look out over the immense sea, full of white-flecked and green reflections, the two of us leaning side by side on the railing, each of us far away, flying in his own aircraft to the stratospheric regions of our own dreams.

—Ernesto Guevara, *The Motorcycle Diaries* (1995)

In attempting to illustrate the spiritual task of embracing the moment, Buddhist monk Thich Nhat Hanh recalled the childhood memory of taking an entire hour to eat a single cookie. "I would take a small bite and look up at the sky," he wrote in his 1992 book *Peace Is Every Step*. "Then I would touch the dog with my feet and take another small bite. I just enjoyed being there, with the sky, the earth, the bamboo thickets, the cat, the dog, the flowers. . . . I was entirely in the present moment, with my cookie."

In her book *Alone Time,* journalist Stephanie Rosenbloom uses Nhat Hanh's cookie story as an analogy for the way we might seek to savor our travel experiences "in an age when it's not unusual for a meal to be eaten with one hand while the other is posting a photo of it to Instagram." Savoring, which Rosenbloom defined as "actively aiming for the most joy to be found in a moment," is not just an attempt to prolong the joy of good experiences; it's a way to feel more fully alive by doing so.

Part of the task of savoring the best moments of travel comes in shifting one's experiential focus. At home, we find satisfaction in achieving work and personal goals, but travel offers a unique opportunity to trade achievement for appreciation—to slow down and relish rapturous moments by embracing them with our whole being.

TRAVEL ENABLES YOU TO EXPRESS
LATENT PARTS OF YOURSELF

What a person does while abroad is not visible from home, and many of those acting in a nonconformist manner overseas will not have tested society's boundaries prior to their leaving.
—Klaus Westerhausen, *Beyond the Beach* (2002)

When Swiss explorer Isabelle Eberhardt was growing up in Geneva in the late nineteenth century, her greatest urge was to travel to North Africa. "I will never be content with a sedentary life," she wrote in her diary. "I will always be haunted by thoughts of a sun-drenched elsewhere." Since it was considered improper for European women to travel alone, Eberhardt sailed to Algeria disguised as a man. There, freed of gender expectations, she fraternized with soldiers, smoked hashish, converted to Sufism, and rode through the Sahara on horseback.

In his 2001 book *Sultry Climates,* scholar Ian Littlewood examined how setting out on journeys has offered generations of travelers the chance to try out unexpressed sides of themselves. "Easier foreign travel encouraged a tourism of escape . . . [making it] possible to reject at will the social and moral restriction of life at home," he wrote. Sometimes such journeys of discovery offered unexpected cross-cultural epiphanies. In the 1970s, Hippie Trail travelers who'd been forced to keep trans identities private back in Europe, for example, reported surprise at finding *hijra* intersex communities in India, or a culturally sanctioned third gender, *kathoey,* in Thailand.

The broadened personal expression that comes with travel goes well beyond gender identity, of course. Be it the freedom to leave behind workaholic routines, overcome introversion by chatting up strangers, or dance until dawn for the simple thrill of doing it, being far from home offers you the chance to try out whole new parts of yourself.

EXPANDING YOUR COMFORT ZONE

NOT KNOWING EXACTLY WHERE YOU ARE CAN BE A GOOD THING

Travel has become a way to remind myself how it feels to get lost, and then get unlost. It is a way to remember the discomfort of uncertainty and the unfamiliar. It's an exercise in receiving the unexpected.

—Kristin Van Tassel, "Swamp Creatures" (2018)

One time, during an overland journey across South America, I got hopelessly disoriented while looking for the Buquebus ferry terminal on the Buenos Aires waterfront. Though I wandered the shipping district for upward of two hours that day before I managed to circle back and find the ferry terminal, it proved to be one of my more gratifying afternoons in the city.

I came to savor this experience not because it led to some momentous travel epiphany, but because it kept me in the moment as I wandered through an otherwise unremarkable industrial neighborhood. Not knowing exactly where I was headed, I lingered longer at curbside flea markets and paid closer attention to the ad hoc soccer games dockworkers played amid the canyons of triple-stacked shipping containers.

The increased awareness that comes with not knowing where you are can, in fact, be good for your brain. In a study published in *Nature Communications* in 2017, research subjects who were forced to find their own way around cities in a travel simulation were found to have more dynamic hippocampal brain activity (thought to combat neurodegenerative conditions like Alzheimer's disease) than travelers who navigated those cities using GPS.

As the Norwegian explorer Erling Kagge enthused in his eponymous book about walking, "I've lost my way so many times that I wonder whether I'm secretly drawn to the little mystery of not knowing where I am. Suddenly, I get to know a neighborhood, a city, a forest in a new way."

TRAVELING ALONE MAKES YOU MORE VULNERABLE TO THE WORLD

> Don't travel with anybody of your own culture if you really want to understand another one. . . . People tend to gravitate to you if you're alone. You arouse their curiosity more. They may think you're lonely.
>
> —Colin Thubron, in a 2021 interview

Of the many insights Swiss adventurer Ella Maillart took home from her arduous thirty-five-hundred-mile journey from Beijing to Kashmir in 1935, one of the most affecting was a preference for traveling alone. "A companion is in himself a detached 'piece' of Europe," she later told an interviewer. "I dislike it because I want to forget my western outlook; I try to become blank inside so as to let the journey sink deep in me. In that way I can grasp better what I see; I can feel the whole impact made on me by the newness I meet at every step."

Maillart's implication here is that traveling solo need not consign the traveler to solitude—and in fact my own experience over the past two decades has shown that I am more open to local people when I'm on my own. Whereas at home I tend to be an introvert who doesn't compulsively seek the company of other people, I'm a lot more gregarious when I'm traveling by myself. Moreover, without a companion along for the journey—without giving off the sense that I am socially self-contained—I am more likely to get invited into other people's lives, and more open to such invitations when they happen.

As much as anything, traveling solo has a way of making you more vulnerable to your environment—more meditative, more aware, more open to new experiences, and more attuned to your own sensibilities as you take in the world around you.

HOW YOU GET PLACES AFFECTS HOW YOU EXPERIENCE THEM

The journey is part of the experience—an expression of the seriousness of one's intent. One doesn't take the A train to Mecca.
—Anthony Bourdain, *A Cook's Tour* (2001)

When American traveler Harry A. Franck made his way across Europe in the first decade of the twentieth century, he noticed that German trains offered the cheapest class of fare. Colloquially known as *Hundekarten* (dog tickets), fourth-class fare offered access to what Franck, in his book *A Vagabond Journey Around the World,* called "a boxcar with wooden benches around the sides, and a few apologies for windows." While he didn't find fourth class all that comfortable, Franck did find that it offered him a visceral perspective into working-class life in Central Europe.

In a similar way, taking a *matatu* minibus across Nairobi offers a purer experience of Kenya than getting shuttled around in some safari outfitter's Land Cruiser—and a Guatemalan *ruletero* (or Ghanaian *tro tro,* or Laotian *songthaew*) offers a colorful share-taxi perspective on local culture that air-conditioned tour buses could never provide. Sometimes, taking local transport can lead to unexpected adventures, like the time my Sri Lankan *tuk-tuk* driver offered (for an extra $8 or so) to bypass the Nuwara Eliya train station and drive me across the Central Highlands in his auto rickshaw. My trip to Adam's Peak ended up taking the better part of a day, but we stopped at several waterfalls (and had a happy-go-lucky lunch at his cousin's house) en route—an experience the more efficient train could never have offered.

One need not always opt for the cheapest, most local transport, of course—yet it's worth keeping in mind that embracing diverse and creative ways of getting from place to place can make for richer journeys.

USE "PSYCHOGEOGRAPHY" TO
EXPLORE A NEW PLACE

To wander is to leave behind the complications of living. You can forget the person you are supposed to be for a time, and become who you truly are—unhindered by duties, obligations, and nagging thoughts. To wander is to access your true self.
—Keri Smith, *The Wander Society* (2016)

In 1958, a French avant-garde philosopher named Guy Debord published a treatise entitled "Theory of the *Dérive*," which encouraged city dwellers to "drop their usual motives for movement, and let themselves be drawn by the attractions of the terrain." *Dérive*, which is French for "drifting," was a strategy for breaking out of habitual or utilitarian reasons for moving from point A to point B (work, shopping, social obligation) and wandering the streets out of whimsy and desire rather than obligation and necessity. In not knowing exactly where (or why) she is going, a person thus allows herself to be surprised by the spontaneous sights and encounters of the city.

According to Debord, drifting through a landscape allows one to experience a place not through its physical geography, but through its "psychogeography"—an imaginative and intuitive sense for what a place has to offer. For some people, this might involve following the color pink or the smell of pastry through a city; for others it might involve flipping coins at intersections (heads, turn right; tails, turn left), and changing one's route accordingly.

Though Debord's strategies were meant to jar city dwellers out of dull routines in their own hometowns, psychogeography is a great alternative to the prescribed tourist approaches of a journey. As travelers, we can give ourselves permission to find more playful and intuitive ways to discover the texture and spectacle of a new place.

BOREDOM ALLOWS YOU TO PAY
A NEW KIND OF ATTENTION

[Boredom] is your window on time's infinity, which is to say, on your insignificance in it. . . . Once this window opens, don't try to shut it; on the contrary, throw it wide open.

—Joseph Brodsky, "In Praise of Boredom" (1989)

In January 2019 I took an off-grid trek into the jungles of the Mentawai Archipelago, two hours by speedboat off the western coast of Sumatra. Of the many novelties I experienced during my week of hiking through calf-deep mud and sleeping in Mentawai longhouses, one was the unique opportunity the island afforded me to become completely, refreshingly bored.

The rise of the commercial travel industry has, I think, led too many travelers to believe that being bored on the road is akin to failure. Part of truly experiencing Mentawai culture, however, was coming to terms with the fact that nobody there organized their hours in the same micromanaged sense we have come to see as essential in the industrialized world. It was not, in fact, until I stopped feeling antsy—until I stopped saying to myself, "Okay, so *now* what do I do?"—that I began to truly appreciate where I was.

Of the many ways I learned to sit still and embrace boredom in the jungle, my favorite was swimming in a little stream not far from my host's house. Floating there, with beams of sunlight angling in through the jungle canopy, I realized that the trees all around me were alive with primates—shy, tan-brown macaques that I had, in five days of being there, never noticed before.

In coming to terms with the boredom of a given day—in being willing to do nothing, for its own sake—I thus learned to pay attention to what I hadn't expected to see.

WHAT WE HOPE TO SEE IN PLACES CAN BE AT ODDS WITH REALITY

The traveler is a sort of Heisenberg optic, eager to see what a country looks like when he's not there.
—Ted Scheinman, "The Grand Tour, 2.0" (2014)

My week of trekking through the Mentawai jungles was organized by Agus, a young man who'd grown up in the islands. Tough, thoughtful, and consistently cheerful, Agus was one of the best trekking guides I've had anywhere in the world—and it was telling when I returned to the Sumatran mainland and realized he'd appeared in almost none of the hundreds of photos I'd taken in the jungle.

I got a clue as to why this was when I watched my video of a Mentawai sago-processing ritual: As a tattooed tribesman clad in a loincloth danced atop the pulp, my guide's arm darted into the background and snatched a plastic bottle out of the shot. Apparently, years of working with trekking groups had conditioned Agus to remove anything that didn't look traditionally Mentawai—himself included—from the sightlines of his clients' cameras. Agus was as ethnically Mentawai as anyone there (and even the more traditional islanders used things like processed sugar and wristwatches), but with his fluent English and penchant for T-shirts, he'd learned he had too much in common with his clients to be the kind of Mentawai they were looking for.

When we visit new places, we are often subject to a travel variation of the "Heisenberg effect," wherein scientific systems are altered by the act of being observed. When we desire to see places as if we weren't there, it's easy to forget that those places have already changed in ways that have little to do with our fanciful reveries of what we'd hoped to find there.

DON'T LET PRECONCEPTIONS BLUR WHAT YOU SEE FIRSTHAND

> More and more I am trying to get used to African ways, trying to live them, trying to shed the snakeskin of assumptions and expectations and sensibilities of the world I come from.
> —Eddy L. Harris, *Native Stranger* (1992)

If there's a reason Eddy L. Harris isn't mentioned alongside Paul Theroux and Jan Morris as one of the great English-language travel writers of the late twentieth century, it might have something to do with the ironies of literary criticism. In 1992, when Harris followed up his bestselling 1988 debut *Mississippi Solo* with a travel book entitled *Native Stranger: A Black American's Journey into the Heart of Africa*, Afrocentrist critics took issue with the book's less-than-romantic depiction of the continent.

The irony here is that, despite the early 1990s academic vogue for Afrocentrism, Harris's naysayers tended to be ideologically minded Americans without much on-the-ground experience in the parts of Africa he'd written about. "My book was a clear-eyed, accurate picture of a place that I loved, but that I described in gritty fashion," Harris said in a 2006 interview. "I decried poverty and corruption. I hung out the dirty laundry, I guess, and nobody wants you to do that."

Three decades on, *Native Stranger* still speaks to the inherent contradictions of travel: to the complexities of making sense of one's own identity in a distant place, and how what we hope to discover in those places can be chastened (and deepened, and made more fully human) by what we find when we slow down and leave ourselves open to a full breadth of experience. "I had some eerie feeling Africa could teach me about life and what it means to be human, deepen my appreciation for all that I am and all that I have," Harris wrote, "help me . . . to step out of my cozy little world, out of myself so that I could see myself better."

TECHNOLOGY IS EASY TO CRITIQUE
(AND HARD TO AVOID)

Technology makes it easier to see the world almost as it is, but sometimes the harder parts are what make travel memorable.
—Susan Orlean, "Zooming In on Petra" (2018)

One of the more prescient prognosticators of the way technology has come to dilute real-world experiences was French theorist Jean Baudrillard. "Travel was once a means of being elsewhere, or of being nowhere," he wrote in his 1990 book *The Transparency of Evil*. "Today it is the only way we have of feeling that we are somewhere. At home, surrounded by screens, I am no longer anywhere, but everywhere in the world at once, in the midst of . . . a banality that is the same in every country. To arrive in a new city, or in a new language, is suddenly to find oneself here and nowhere else."

As it happened, the notion that physical journeys offer contrast to mediated reality was contradicted by Baudrillard's own 1986 travel book *America*. "To grasp [America's] secret, you should not begin with the city and move inwards to the screen," he wrote. "You should begin with the screen and move outwards to the city." Content to regard America through received images, Baudrillard thus cruised around the United States hypothesizing about Disneyland, Michael Jackson's androgyny, and Ronald Reagan's smile. Convinced that the America he'd seen on television was the real America, television visions were all Baudrillard saw in America.

As I explore the ways that information technology can compromise the experience of travel, I, like Baudrillard, often speak not as someone who has transcended technological distractions, but as someone who is still trying to strike a balance between the banal familiarities of the virtual world and the life-expanding possibilities of the real one. Seeking this balance is a key challenge for any twenty-first-century traveler endeavoring to take mindful journeys.

September 9

TECHNOLOGY CAN HELP (AS WELL AS HINDER) THE JOURNEY

> We might someday evolve the correct biological hardware to live in harmony with portable supercomputers that satisfy our every need and connect us to infinite amounts of stimulation. But for most of us, it hasn't happened yet.
>
> —Kevin Roose, "Do Not Disturb" (2019)

Optimism about new technologies has been offset by apprehensions since at least the fourth century B.C.E., when the Athenian philosopher Plato wrote a dialogue asserting that the written word was eroding the memory powers and intuitive associations of oral storytelling. In modern times, concern about how new technology affects organic activities has become somewhat reflexive: Novelist George Orwell, for example, lamented in the 1930s that the sound of the radio had become more familiar in daily life than the sound of birds; in the 1970s, social critic Susan Sontag wondered if point-and-shoot cameras would make "having an experience identical to taking a photograph of it."

In recent decades, continual digital innovations have made the technology conundrum an inevitable part of the travel conversation. On one hand, calling home on a Wi-Fi-connected laptop certainly beats shoving coins into public pay phones (as I did during my 1990s vagabonding journeys); on the other hand, my travels were inevitably more immersive—more committed to the place I was visiting—when I couldn't so easily be in touch with friends and family on the other side of the world.

Smartphones alone—which put digital maps, guidebooks, phrasebooks, exchange-rate calculators, music libraries, and weather radars (as well as a camera and a flashlight) onto one pocket-sized device—have become so useful and convenient it's hard not to bring them on a journey. The challenge, of course, is to discipline oneself in such a way that they enhance the experience of a place without continually interrupting it.

DIGITAL COMPULSIONS STEAL TIME FROM YOUR JOURNEY

- -

If you've only lived with social media, your first duty is to yourself. Quit social media for six months, experience travel; see how it affects your way of being in the world. You can't know yourself without perspective.

—Jaron Lanier, in a 2018 interview

In Sylvia Ardyn Boone's groundbreaking 1974 guidebook *West African Travels,* the American art historian enthused about how travel offered her respite from the constant distractions of life at home. "Your personality is not being shredded by a cascade of words and images . . . that corrodes your integrity and self-esteem," she wrote. "No beautiful people, no jet setters, no odious comparisons between yourself and your possessions and the vastly superior minds, bodies and possessions of . . . public figures constantly splashed on the TV screen. . . . With the pressure cooker off, your better self emerges."

The deluge of TV images that unnerved Boone was part of a then-nascent "attention economy" that has now come to dominate the way we make sense of the world. As legal scholar Tim Wu wrote in his 2016 book *The Attention Merchants,* living in a twenty-first-century digital media ecosystem—one that has been designed to exploit our anxieties and monopolize our thought processes—puts us at risk of missing out on the richer textures of being alive. "How we spend the brutally limited resource of our attention will determine [our] lives to a degree most of us may prefer not to think about," he wrote. "We are at risk, without quite fully realizing it, of living lives that are less our own than we imagine."

Travel is still a singular way of seeking out our better selves, but only if we allow it to be. In finding ways to focus our journeys on the here and now rather than digital distractions, we can give our lives the gift of true attention.

THE REAL WORLD COUNTS FOR MORE THAN THE VIRTUAL ONE

Technology . . . the knack of so arranging the world that we don't have to experience it.

—Max Frisch, *Homo Faber* (1957)

In a feature entitled "What's New in 1999," the *San Francisco Chronicle* enthused about a 300,000-square-foot Sony entertainment megaplex that was "designed specifically to counter the idea that in the future no one will leave the house," and featured things like virtual-reality games and 3D movies. "In the next century, some thinking goes, everyone will shop at home, watch movies at home, and communicate with all their friends through videophones," the article read. "We've all heard of that future, and it sounds pretty lonely."

Decades after the *Chronicle* made this observation, we don't just have a wealth of streaming entertainments and virtual communities available in our homes; we have the increasing ability to carry those diversions—and the screen-focused loneliness they portend—on the road with us as we travel. Whereas these diversions once offered the promise of experiencing the world without going to the trouble of leaving home, their portability now presents the temptation to leave home without going to the trouble of experiencing the world.

As we become used to the mediated experience of being alive (setting down our smartphone just before we fall asleep, then picking it up the moment we awake) it can become harder to avoid mediating our life experiences. We thus get so used to being "elsewhere" that we have trouble being where we are, even when we go to the literal trouble of journeying elsewhere.

DON'T PERFORM YOUR TRAVELS BEFORE YOU EXPERIENCE THEM

Technology has provided us with endless distractions and numerous ways to brag about our trips. We can post pictures, text updates . . . that, while impressing friends (and making others jealous), successfully take our minds off the fact that we're not really experiencing the moment we're recording.

—Thomas Swick, *The Joys of Travel* (2016)

Belgian surrealist René Magritte's 1929 painting *The Treachery of Images,* which depicts a photorealistic pipe over a caption reading "This is not a pipe," evokes a playful meta-message about the difference between images of objects and the actual items they depict. Magritte's painting is not, after all, a device that enables one to smoke tobacco; it's just a realistic-looking two-dimensional portrayal of one.

In a similar way, the digital travel photos we see on social media don't typically depict journeys so much as the hypothetical notion of what journeys might look like were the sunsets more vibrant, the beaches less crowded, and our smiles more dazzling. When we share these images and videos, we aren't documenting our experience of places so much as advertising a carefully filtered depiction of what we'd hoped we might experience there.

Staging such moments in the hopes of attracting social media feedback is a sure way of missing out on the subtler, more affecting textures of a journey. Capturing a moment on camera is not, after all, the same as experiencing it, and ragged moments of inquiry and unexpected discovery can't be framed in a viewfinder.

MEETING STRANGERS BEATS TEXTING FRIENDS ON THE ROAD

In hostels and guesthouses, one sees "independent" travelers eagerly settling down in front of computers instead of conversing with fellow travelers. They seem only partially "abroad," unable to cut their links with home.

—Dervla Murphy, in *The Tao of Travel* (2011)

The first time I visited Kenya, in the summer of 2008, I didn't converse with a single Kenyan. Granted, I was only in the frontier town of Lokichogio for a few hours in transit from South Sudan to Ethiopia, but nothing was stopping me from chatting up the ethnic Turkana diners I saw in the café during lunch. Nothing, that is, apart from the Samsung BlackJack (an early-model smartphone) a friend had loaned me for the trip. Seeing that I had a signal, I called my sister back home and spent the better part of my meal chatting with her.

At the time I was tickled that I could sit in a café in Kenya and chat with someone in Kansas; looking back, I realize I'd squandered my brief layover in Lokichogio. That same summer, I'd noticed that my fellow travelers and I were as likely to be communicating on phones or laptops in hostel lounges as we were with each other. The same technology that had enabled us to be socially present with people back home, it seemed, was making us socially absent where we were. I have since come to refer to these gadgets as "electronic umbilical cords."

Reaching out to people back home is a comforting ritual on the road, but reflexively doing so whenever you get lonely or bored can cut you off from the firsthand possibilities that make travel so rewarding. If in doubt, talking to strangers on the road beats messaging friends back home.

TAKE YOUR TRAVELS OFF-GRID

The internet has brought a change in the very concept of travel as a process taking one away from the familiar into the unknown. . . . Relatives and friends evidently expect regular reassurance about the traveler's precise location and welfare—and vice versa.

—Dervla Murphy, from *To Oldly Go* (2015)

In March 2020, police in England and Fiji coordinated an international task force to search for Lydia O'Sullivan, a twenty-three-year-old British woman who'd gone missing while taking a holiday on the Fijian island of Viti Levu. "She was last sighted in a hotel in the Western Division," the *Fiji Sun* reported. "Authorities ask anyone with knowledge of her whereabouts to contact police immediately." Within hours of this report, O'Sullivan was found alive and well at an eco-retreat two hours from the capital city, Suva. As it turned out, the young British woman hadn't disappeared in Fiji; she'd just spent a week in a place that didn't have a reliable internet connection. "Lydia was safe and well," her family told Sky News, "and oblivious to the worldwide search for her."

In an age when one week of silence can cause your family to assume you're in some kind of danger, the biggest travel challenge often isn't finding ways to immerse yourself in a new place so much as establishing an effective sense of separation from the place you left behind. For travelers, this can be as simple as clearly and courteously setting the terms of that separation—of letting friends and family know that being less reachable for a time is not a sign of peril in some distant place, but an expression of commitment in getting to know that place in a deeper, more life-enriching way.

SOME TRAVEL DISAPPOINTMENTS ARE TIED TO EXPECTATION ITSELF

How does one see a place better when others are absent? Is looking like sucking: the more lookers, the less there is to see?
—Walker Percy, "The Loss of the Creature" (1975)

In his essay-length meditation on the idiosyncrasies of sightseeing, novelist Walker Percy hypothesized about an American couple who, feeling faintly disappointed by the official attractions on offer in Mexico, gets lost in the mountains and stumbles across an indigenous corn festival. Ecstatic to see something that feels authentic—something they hadn't expected to encounter—the couple's first worry is that other tourists might be there. "The problem is to find an 'unspoiled' place," Percy wrote. "'Unspoiled' does not mean only that a place is left physically intact; it means also . . . that it has not been discovered by others."

Percy's essay occasionally plumbs academic abstractions ("their consciousness of the corn dance cannot escape their consciousness of their consciousness"), but even its more cerebral language hints at something true about tourist angst: "The highest point, the term of the sightseer's satisfaction, is not the sovereign discovery of the thing before him," he wrote. "It is rather the measuring up of the thing to the criterion of the pre-formed symbolic complex."

In other words, any experience of a designated "sight" automatically competes with our expectations—formed by guidebooks, photos, advertisements, word of mouth, et cetera—of what a person might see and do there. When we find ourselves anxious around other tourists, it's because they remind us that, as sightseers, we are essentially consumers of an experience that is constructed for us in advance.

Avoiding this consumer role, Percy noted, is "something one struggles for"—a process that begins when we wander away from what we're expected to see, and make ourselves vulnerable to uncertainty and surprise.

September 16

LONELINESS CAN BE A WAY OF SEEING THE WORLD MORE CLEARLY

> One of the great surprises at this point is that you find that the
> cure for your loneliness is actually solitude.
> —Richard Rohr, *Falling Upward* (2011)

In her 1969 essay "Trash, Art, and the Movies," movie critic Pauline Kael described how watching crappy movies can be a way of assuaging urban loneliness. "When we feel defeated, when we imagine . . . that home no longer exists . . . in whatever city we find ourselves we can duck into a theater and see on the screen our familiars," she wrote. "Movies are our cheap and easy expression, the sullen art of displaced persons."

While visiting the cinema can indeed be a way to commune with a version of one's home-self and feel a tad less alienated on the road (and I'll confess feeling joyously, ridiculously American while watching *Dude, Where's My Car?* on one lonesome Mumbai afternoon in 2000), the best journeys allow us to reinvent our own relationship with what it means to be alone. At home, our experience of solitude takes place in the context of the familiar, whereas encountering aloneness in a new place offers an intensified perspective on who we are and how we respond to the world.

Being on the road thus allows us to reinvent solitude in a way that makes it feel less lonely—to walk out of the cinema, as it were (or put down the smartphone), with an intensified resolve to interact with a new place. "Spells of acute loneliness are an essential part of travel," Jonathan Raban wrote in his 2010 book *Driving Home*. "Loneliness makes things happen."

TO TRULY EXPERIENCE A PLACE, SEEK TO LIVE LIKE LOCALS DO

> The secret of memorable travel is to approximate, as best you can in the short time allotted you, the life of a local.
> —Thomas Swick, *The Joys of Travel* (2016)

Moldova isn't a place that ranks high on people's travel bucket lists. This Eastern European post-Soviet Romanian-Russian mash-up of a republic doesn't boast many tourist attractions, nor does it figure favorably in travel literature (in *The Geography of Bliss*, Eric Weiner declared it the world's least-happy country, describing it as "a dirt-poor nation with no culture"). Still, my sister Kristin visits the place every few years—and raves about the unparalleled variety and delectability of its regional soups.

Granted, Kristin spends her time there with the friends and family of a former student from Moldova, which means she lives like a local person when she's there. In the regions of the country she visits, this means putting a lot of thought, time, and effort into making soups. "Each family has its favorite recipes and ingredients, which they take great pride in preparing," she told me. "People argue about their favorite ingredients and methods of preparation, moving back and forth between Romanian and Russian, depending on which language suits their point best."

Not everyone can arrive at their destination with contact information for local hosts, of course, but Kristin's experience in Moldova is a reminder of what can happen when you move beyond a place's tourist attractions—or lack thereof—and get a sense for what life is like for the people who live there. Oftentimes this can be as simple as looking past a place's prescribed "sights" and seeking the same activities—farmer's markets, sporting events, concerts—that local people seek for themselves.

RANDOM FACTORS GUIDE THE JOURNEY AS MUCH AS PLANNED ONES

The random, the unscreened, allows you to find what you don't know you are looking for, and you don't know a place until it surprises you.

—Rebecca Solnit, *Wanderlust* (2000)

One perk of being an author in the digital age is that it offers interesting windows into how people respond to your work. The "most highlighted" ebook passage from my 2008 essay collection *Marco Polo Didn't Go There* involves a topic people don't bring up much with me in person: "The simultaneous charm and risk of travel is it shakes up the paradigms and habits that help you simplify and interpret day-to-day life. Life on the road, for better or for worse, vivifies a muted aspect of reality: it makes you realize that random factors influence your life just as much as planned ones."

That people highlight this passage on e-readers more than they verbalize it in person might point to the fact that life's randomness catches people off guard, even as it feels obvious. In a heady 1996 essay entitled "How to Get from Space to Place in a Fairly Short Stretch of Time," American philosopher Edward S. Casey suggested that places everywhere contain an "ontological wildness" that does not hew to conventional understandings of what is considered wild. "In the very heart of the most sophisticated circumstance is a wildness that no culture can contain or explain, much less reduce," he wrote. "The wildness exceeds the scope of the most subtle set of signifiers, despite the efforts of painters to capture it in images and of storytellers to depict it in words."

On the road, such moments of wildness—that is, moments so random as to feel ineffable—are easier to stumble into than they are to describe. To paraphrase John Steinbeck, sometimes we don't take journeys so much as journeys take us.

EASY AS IT IS TO SAVE MONEY ON THE ROAD, DON'T BE CHEAP

Tourists who spend $4,000 on a two-week tour package will bargain the price of a carving down from $5 to $3, since part of tourist discourse is that naive tourists pay higher prices than local residents, and the tourists do not want to be duped.
—Edward M. Bruner, "Of Cannibals and Tourists" (1989)

According to the travel veterans interviewed in *A Season in Heaven*, David Tomory's 1996 oral history of the Hippie Trail, in-group prestige among Westerners wandering Asia in the 1970s was achieved by endeavoring to spend as little money as possible. Travelers who had plenty of money pretended not to, and rumors abounded that resourceful vagabonds could hitch from Damascus to Delhi for less than $6. Astonishing as this feat sounds, it implies that many young travelers—people who'd been raised in the relative economic prosperity of the West—happily sought to exploit Asian hospitality in order to bolster their subcultural status.

A similar ethos reigned among Latin America's "Gringo Trail" wanderers of the same era. "Their conversation was predictable and was wholly concerned with prices, the exchange rate, the cheapest hotel, the cheapest bus," Paul Theroux observed in his 1979 book *The Old Patagonian Express*. "Their boast was always how long they had managed to hang on here in the Peruvian Andes and beat the system."

Being reflexively, self-aggrandizingly cheap is not a bygone hippie-era thing; it tends to recur most anywhere budget-minded travelers from wealthy countries begin to see journeys to less-than-rich countries as a pride-driven zero-sum financial endurance contest. "Too often money, and the process of saving money, becomes the entire point of traveling," Tim Cahill noted in his 2002 book *Hold the Enlightenment*. "If the nature of your quest is financial, stay home and get into arbitrage."

A BAD NIGHT'S SLEEP CAN BE A PART
OF THE ADVENTURE

Lousy hotels are more fun than good hotels, because you have to try harder to pretend you're not really there.
—Douglas Coupland, in his 2001 online book-tour journal

The most peculiar story chronicled in the New Testament's apocryphal Acts of John recounted a missionary excursion in Anatolia, when John's slumber at an inn on the road to Ephesus was ruined by bedbugs. "I say unto you, O bugs, leave this abode for one night," the exhausted apostle finally commanded. The next morning, John's companions awakened to find the insects dutifully lined up in the doorway, and the apostle, impressed by their respect for God's servants, allowed them to return to the bed.

Though this tale was meant to illustrate the miracles of faith, it spoke to the idiosyncrasies of travel in the ancient world, when roadside inns tended to be pest-infested shanties. A couple of millennia later, overnight lodging is a blessedly cleaner and more restful affair, though any engaged journey will, from time to time, yield a bad night's sleep. Home stays can be marred by incidental construction noise, seemingly quaint hotels can share street blocks with mosques blasting the call to prayer before dawn, and otherwise comfortable hostel bunkrooms can fill with chatty drunks past midnight.

Frustrating as it can be to lose sleep in unfamiliar settings, the best way to deal with this annoyance is to recognize it as part of the adventure that comes with seeking out new experiences. At a time when corporate chain hotel rooms are designed to be as interchangeably placeless as possible, the occasional bad night's sleep can be a sign that you're stretching your comfort zone into new directions, and seeking experiences unique to the place and the culture you're visiting.

AT TIMES, TRAVEL CAN BE A CRASH COURSE IN PATIENCE

Perhaps boredom is the distinctive quality of the modern Western mind. . . . In Africa, India, and Asia many people have a subsistence relation to time, taking it as it comes.
—Geoff Dyer, *Yoga for People Who Can't Be Bothered to Do It*
(2003)

In Vanuatu, the word *storian,* which refers to the act of exchanging stories to cement the bond of a relationship, evolved from the cultural necessity of patience. In this remote Pacific archipelago (where island-to-island flights can be delayed for days at a time, and a broken-down truck might require shipping a spare part in from Australia), *storian* serves as a bulwark against tedium and impatience. "[*Storian*] developed around waiting," wrote Bryan Webb in *The Sons of Cannibals.* "Something has to be done to keep that time from being wasted. . . . *Storian's* great benefit is that it turns waiting into a pleasant and useful experience. Some of the most amazing relationships I have had the privilege of having started with a long wait."

For travelers from the industrialized world, finding pleasure in waiting is a faintly absurd notion. In the West, we evoke the phrase "patience is a virtue" out of irritated resignation in the face of a delay; in much of the rest of the world, patience is the natural response to life's inevitable uncertainties and inefficiencies. Whereas at home we create routines that can make life feel more predictable, travel makes us more beholden to the fact that we can't optimize our own ideas of efficiency. In this way, the inevitable delays of a journey can become a crash course in the art of patience, and an ongoing invitation to seek pleasures in the task of waiting.

September 22

SPEND AT LEAST ONE FULL DAY
WALKING SOMEPLACE NEW

We travel too much in airplanes and cars. It's an existential quality that we are losing. It's almost like a credo of religion that we should walk.

—Werner Herzog, in a 1979 interview

In 2013, American journalist Paul Salopek embarked on what he called the "Out of Eden Walk," a twenty-one-thousand-mile ramble from Ethiopia to Tierra del Fuego, which aimed to retrace the early routes of human migration out of Africa. Thematic ambitions aside, the very act of moving from place to place on foot gave him a new perspective on travel. "Once you begin walking around the world," he said in a 2015 BBC interview, "traveling by sitting on your ass seems ridiculous."

Though few of us are likely to embark on journeys as extensive as Salopek's, he makes a valid point: In an age when you can literally circumnavigate the world strapped into airplanes and cars, walking returns you to a more essential form of travel. This in mind, resolve to spend at least one full day of your journey going someplace on foot. This can be as traditional as walking from *hütte* to *hütte* on the trails of the Swiss Alps, as quotidian as meandering from Brooklyn to the Bronx by way of Manhattan, or as casually purposeful as wandering from souk to souk in Cairo until your day finishes in the same place it started.

Regardless of where your daylong hike takes you, the very act of going on foot will transform your relationship to where you are: Instead of speeding through landscapes, you'll become a part of them; instead of focusing on where you're headed, you'll focus on where you are; instead of charting progress on an abstract itinerary, you'll feel that progress with each step you take.

NO PLACE IS "TIMELESS" (IN PART BECAUSE YOU'RE THERE)

> The perennial paradox of modern travel is that we want un-
> changed places and somewhere comfortable to stay—
> timelessness with a time limit.
>
> —Rebecca Willis, "The Timeless Orient" (1996)

A complication of seeking out "traditional" cultures in places like East Africa is that this task often comes with dishonest expectations. "Tourist discourse promises the tourist a total transformation of self, but the native is described as frozen in time," wrote tourist scholar Edward M. Bruner in a 1991 essay. "Despite these claims, the very opposite occurs in experience; the tourist self is changed very little by the tour, while the consequences of tourism for the native self are profound."

Bruner added that "tribal" displays in this part of the world were more about Western fantasies than on-the-ground realities among people who had already been affected by "colonialism, wars of independence, nationalism . . . and the entire production of modern technology, including automobiles, television, and Casio watches."

Several decades after Bruner made his observations, the tourist tendency to fetishize "timeless" aspects of local cultures has only been strengthened by the simplistic tropes of social media. In *Rediscovering Travel*, journalist Seth Kugel revealed that the reenactors in Eswatini's Mantenga Cultural Village—a "living museum" that replicates how the Swazi people lived in the 1850s—are often depicted as actual twenty-first-century villagers in Westerners' Instagram accounts ("#tribes in #africa #swaziland," reads a typical caption).

As often as not, the "authentic" traditions we seek out as travelers are less related to how people actually live in distant places than to our own desire for obvious and colorful cultural differences. Yet, as our very presence in these places suggests, life anywhere is far more global (and complex) than it might at first appear.

A JOURNEY CAN OFFER CONTEXT
FOR WHAT YOU BELIEVE

> I was angry with myself for not having taken the time to learn
> the orthodox prayer rituals before leaving America. . . . Imagine,
> being a Muslim minister . . . and not knowing the prayer ritual.
> —Malcolm X, from *The Autobiography of Malcolm X* (1965)

One of the more vulnerable moments in American activist Malcolm X's autobiography comes when he arrives in Saudi Arabia for his hajj pilgrimage and realizes he doesn't know the basic protocols of Islamic prayer. "I tried to do what [my guide] did," he recalled, describing his local escort's attempts to show him the proper invocation rituals. "I knew I wasn't doing it right. I could feel the other Muslims' eyes on me. . . . I refused to let myself think how ridiculous I must have looked to them."

In encountering an orthodox and culturally purer Arab form of his Americanized faith, Malcolm was joining a long line of travelers whose pilgrimage became a way of fine-tuning their personal beliefs. An entire tradition of Chinese travel writing revolved around Buddhist seekers—most notably Faxian in the fourth century, and Xuanzang in the seventh—making difficult journeys to India to collect sacred texts and clarify the foundation of their beliefs.

Getting a clearer perspective on one's own faith is, in fact, the very reason pilgrimages exist—though one doesn't need to be religious to use travel as a way to clarify one's conviction (as any vegetarian who's traveled through India or *capoeirista* who's visited Brazil will attest). In exposing us to the intricacies of cultural context, travel can allow us to develop a reinvigorated relationship with what we profess to believe.

September 25

FOREIGN PLACES CAN FEEL MORE LIKE HOME THAN WE'D LIKE

We look for Elysium in distant lands where there are no hamburger stands and satellite dishes and telephones—and yet all the while men have come before us and made where we are going just a little more like where we have just come from.
—Simon Winchester, in Martin Parr's *Small World* (1995)

When American artist Kirscha Kaechele first traveled by canoe to visit an *ayahuascero* shaman in the Peruvian Amazon, she was dazzled by how remote the region felt. Upon her arrival in the isolated village, the shaman welcomed her into this hut, blew flakes of dried snake's head at her, and misted her with a fragrant spray. Sensing a familiar smell, Kaechele looked closer and realized the shaman was holding a bottle of Eternity, a 1980s-era perfume popularized by American fashion designer Calvin Klein. "I was crushed," she recalled in a 2008 interview. "That was the perfume I wore every morning in junior high school. The sudden intrusion of the banal tainted my pure, exotic experience."

As it happens, longing for hermetic isolation and cultural purity in the places we visit can say more about our own fantasies as travelers than the places we visit. "As tourists, we have reason to hope that the quaint anachronism we have discovered will always remain 'unspoiled,' as fixed as a museum piece for our inspection," wrote Pico Iyer in *Video Night in Kathmandu*. "It is perilous, however, to assume that its inhabitants will long for the same."

Indeed, cultures have always existed in conversation with each other, and what seems impure about a place to us might be simple choice on the part of the people whose customs and rituals naturally adapt in ways that make sense to them, if not always to us.

ADVERSITY IS PART OF WHAT MAKES TRAVEL SO REWARDING

A total sense of dispossession connects the traveler to the beauty of motion. Journeys tend towards a hardship that sometimes contains happiness.

—Javier Sinay, *Camino al Este* (2019)

No discussion of global travel literature is complete without mention of seventeenth-century poet Matsuo Basho, whose writing blended prose and haiku to recount the walking journeys he took through Edo-era Japan. In *The Narrow Road to the Deep North*, which documents a fifteen-hundred-mile trek through the mountainous Tohoku region, Basho offsets moments of peace and beauty ("In absolute silence / A cicada's voice / Pierces the rock") with verses that underscore the miseries and difficulties of the journey ("Gnawed by fleas and lice / A horse pissing / Near my pillow"). Indeed, part of what makes Basho's walk across Japan's rugged north so rewarding for him is the fact that it is continually mixed in with hardship.

While adversity is often seen as something to avoid on a journey, it can actually make the achievements of travel resonate in a richer way. Early-nineteenth-century visitors to Niagara reported a sense of disappointment when newly built roads meant one could take a carriage to its massive waterfalls instead of hiking in along treacherous cliffsides from nearby settlements. "The effect produced upon us by any object of admiration is increased by the difficulties of approaching it," British traveler Francis Hall noted in his 1816 Niagara journal.

The difficulties of a journey are, in fact, what ultimately make its joys so satisfying. In embracing challenges rather than comforts—in welcoming difficulties rather than distractions—we find that no moment of instant gratification can compare to savoring an experience that has been earned by enduring the adversity that comes with it.

TRAVEL ATTUNES YOU TO WHAT YOU HAVE (AND OTHERS DON'T)

> Eighty percent of international tourists are citizens of the twenty richest nations. . . . They have the leisure time and discretionary income to make [travel] possible.
> —Sharon Bohn Gmelch, *Tourists and Tourism* (2009)

While cultivating a kind of poverty can afford us the freedom to travel, most journeys expose the relative prosperity that underpins our modern ability to wander. This often results in one of two compulsions: The first is to grow guilt-ridden and anxious as travelers, worrying that local people see us only in monetary terms; the other is to associate poverty with virtues, like voluntary non-materialism and spontaneity, that have more to do with sentimental projection than a true understanding of financial hardship.

In practice, the best response in the face of economic disparity is straightforward respect for (and engagement with) the people whose seeming poverty shines a mirror on our comparative wealth. Find ways to sidestep the tourist economy and overlap your journey with people whose lives seem poorer than your own: Ride the same buses, shop at the same markets, patronize the same businesses; get an honest sense for the needs and dreams that drive their lives.

Ultimately, interacting with less advantaged communities as a traveler can strengthen your appreciation of what in life is essential. When author Pico Iyer's home and possessions were incinerated in a 1990 California wildfire, for example, travel put his losses into perspective. "I could think back on all the people I had met, in Tibet and Morocco and Bolivia, who would still have thought of my life as luxurious," he said in a 2003 interview. "Many people one meets while traveling deal with more traumas every day than the privileged among us meet in a lifetime. That's how travel humbles and inspires."

A JOURNEY CAN CHANGE YOUR WAY OF BEING IN THE WORLD

One travels in order for things to happen and change; otherwise you might as well stay at home.
—Nicolas Bouvier, *The Way of the World* (1963)

In Hollywood storytelling, protagonists are defined by the fact that they need to change in ways that will ultimately serve to improve their lives and the lives of the people around them. "In a sense, stories are *about* change," wrote screenwriting guru Blake Snyder in his 2005 book *Save the Cat!* "And the measuring stick that tells us who succeeds and who doesn't is seen in the ability *to* change. Good guys are those who willingly accept change, and see it as a positive force."

Journeys are also defined by the ways they can transform the people taking them, though these changes are rarely so obvious as the ones in Hollywood movies. In fact, the most affecting changes travel offers aren't things that can be predicted before the journey, itemized en route, or tidily summarized afterward. Inevitably, this transformation is a quiet process that gradually leaves the traveler more generous and open-minded, less impatient and judgmental; more beholden to curiosity and vulnerability, less beholden to narcissism and stereotyping; more likely to confront fears and limitations, less likely to avoid them out of dull habit.

"The journey changes you," Anthony Bourdain wrote in his 2007 book *No Reservations*. "It should change you. It leaves marks on your memory, on your consciousness, on your heart, and on your body. You take something with you. Hopefully, you leave something good behind."

QUIETLY FIND WAYS TO PROLONG THE JOURNEY

> I have reversed the saying of Troubles are like Babies the more you nurse Them the bigger they grow so I have nursed the joys.
> —Juanita Harrison, *My Great, Wide, Beautiful World* (1936)

One of the most remarkable travel memoirs of the twentieth century was Juanita Harrison's *My Great, Wide, Beautiful World*, which recounted the author's journey through thirty-three countries in the 1920s and 1930s. Unlike other bestselling travel authors of that era, she was not an upper-middle-class white chap who'd studied literature at a fancy university. Harrison was a Mississippi-born African American woman who'd been working various domestic-labor jobs ever since her schooling ended at age ten.

Part of what makes *My Great, Wide, Beautiful World* so memorable is that Harrison doesn't harbor the typical middle-class anxieties about what is permissible or possible as a traveler—she just finds ways to make the journey happen, including finding overseas work as a nurse, nanny, and cleaning lady.

The most celebrated section of Harrison's book comes from a chapter devoted to Paris, where she sidesteps the admission fee at an exhibition of colonial African cultures by climbing over the fence. There, she proceeds to make friends with a group of Ubangi Congolese women as they perform a cooking demonstration. "They took a fancy to me," she noted. "I think they saw I had some of their blood." Later on, reflecting on the experience, Harrison wrote, "I have had a wonderful time in Paris. I think I love it best of all, but I can't help but love the last place best."

Thanks to her willingness to quietly create ways of prolonging the journey, Harrison continued to find new places to love—in a variety of cities and landscapes worldwide—for the next eight years.

TRAVEL REVEALS HOW "NORMAL" IS A RELATIVE CONCEPT

> One of the most important reasons to travel is to know what it feels like to be a foreigner.
>
> —A. A. Gill, *A. A. Gill Is Away* (2005)

In the early days of 2020, as the coronavirus reached pandemic proportions in the United States, hundreds of thousands of Americans rushed out and stockpiled toilet paper, resulting in a nationwide shortage. While newspapers and TV shows stateside debated the wisdom of hoarding a product that had little relation to how coronavirus was transmitted, media commentators in non-Western countries seemed puzzled as to why so many Americans felt compelled to use toilet paper in the first place.

Indeed, more than 70 percent of the world's population doesn't use toilet paper—a fact that I didn't properly appreciate until I traveled to India, where water is seen as a much more sensible (and hygienic) method of cleaning up in the toilet than smearing your butt with tissue paper. Cross-cultural travel is, in fact, an ongoing exercise in discovering how "normal" is a relative concept—from calculating out how much (if at all) to tip the bartender in Singapore, to figuring out when (if ever) to disobey pedestrian signals at empty crosswalks in Germany, to realizing that guinea pig can feature as a menu item in some parts of the Andes.

In this way, travel can be an ongoing encounter with all that we don't know about other places (which at times can feel like almost everything), and how making sense of these curious surprises can be a window into how other people conduct their daily lives. As the Australian travel writer Robyn Davidson said in her 1996 book *Desert Places*, "Real travel would be to see the world, for even an instant, with another's eyes."

JOURNEYS INVOLVE MINDSCAPES AS WELL AS LANDSCAPES

The freedom to daydream, to lose oneself in reveries, is part of travel's promise of freedom, part of the traveler's privilege.
—Peter D. Osborne, *Traveling Light* (2000)

Upon arriving by rental motorcycle at Lake Maninjau in western Sumatra, I confess that I didn't spend much time considering the nuances of its tectonic ecosystem or the ethnic Minangkabau culture along its shores. Instead, channeling the spirit of American movie protagonist Indiana Jones, I stripped down to my hiking shorts, jumped in the lake, and began swimming to the steep-sloped little island sitting half a kilometer across the water from my guesthouse cottage.

In his 1999 history of the modern vacation, Swedish ethnologist Orvar Lofgren noted that imagination plays a bigger part in our travels than most of us realize. "Perhaps the most important tourist experiments concern daydreaming and mindtraveling," he wrote. "Here, you learn to move simultaneously through landscapes and mindscapes, in time travel and flights of the mind."

In this way, my Lake Maninjau swim had less to do with an earnest embrace of the Indonesian landscape than a spectral connection to the person I was at age twelve, when I spent my summers competing for a youth swim team and I was besotted with Indiana Jones adventure movies. The best part of my island swim thus came not in its physical effort, but in the childlike thrill of not exactly knowing what I would find when I got there.

Though I arrived at the island to find little more than birds, fruit bats, and three bemused Indonesian fishermen, my strongest memory of the place is the simple reverie that took me there. As Kate Harris noted in *Lands of Lost Borders*: "Travel is perhaps one part geography, nine parts imagination."

October 2

TRAVEL CAN BE AN ONGOING EXERCISE IN HUMILITY

Traveling makes one modest—you see what a tiny place you occupy in the world.

—Gustave Flaubert, *Flaubert in Egypt* (1850)

Poet William Wordsworth is best known for helping launch English literature's Romantic Age, but he also gained renown as a long-distance walker. Beginning with a two-thousand-mile walk through Europe at age twenty, Wordsworth is thought to have walked more than a hundred thousand miles in his lifetime. Though the poet saw his treks as an act of aesthetic reverence, polite British society at the time considered long-distance walking a task for low-class peddlers and vagabonds. In throwing himself into a pastime thought to be reserved for less refined people, Wordsworth was actively attempting to reject social pretensions and embrace a humbler, more essential way of being in the world.

In taking us away from the assumptions of home, travel—be it on foot or otherwise—can become an ongoing exercise in modesty, as we navigate the uncertainty, naivety, and small embarrassments that come with being in an unfamiliar place. Away from everything and everyone familiar, journeys enable us to see ourselves not as we pretend to be, but as who we are—and who we might be—in the context of a much wider world.

Experiencing "a world different from their own, [travelers] realize their provincialism and recognize their ignorance," Paul Fussell noted in his 1987 introduction to *The Norton Book of Travel*. "Travelers learn not just foreign customs and curious cuisines. . . . They learn, if they are lucky, humility." This humility need not be humiliating. Coming to terms with our own relative imperfection and insignificance on the road allows us to return home with a deeper, more modest sense of who we are in relation to the rest of the world.

TRAVEL CAN REVEAL THE SPIRITUAL LIFE THAT UNDERPINS RELIGION

Religion has reduced everything down to concepts and ideas. And having the concept or idea short-circuits the transcendent experience.

—Joseph Campbell, *The Power of Myth* (1988)

When Australian radio commentator Sarah Macdonald first joined her journalist boyfriend for a two-year professional stint in India, she found herself overwhelmed by the crowds and noise and heat of New Delhi. Seeing that Indian people retained a sense of peace amid urban chaos, Macdonald, herself an atheist, sought to explore the religious faiths—Hinduism, Buddhism, Islam, Jainism, Sikhism, Zoroastrianism, Judaism, Christianity—that give spiritual significance to life in that part of the world. Though Macdonald didn't become attached to any single faith, she did leave India with a deeper sense of spiritual perspective. "I realize I don't have to be a Christian who follows the church, or a Buddhist nun in robes, or a convert to Judaism or Islam or Sikhism," she wrote in her 2002 book *Holy Cow*. "I can be a believer in something bigger than what I can touch."

Travel has always been intertwined with visits to religious sites, from the cathedrals and *wats* that feature on European and Southeast Asian itineraries to the Harlem church services frequented by sightseeing buses each Sunday in New York. Yet seeking to apprehend the religious textures of the places you visit is more effective when it isn't approached as a formal tourist endeavor. Places like churches and temples and mosques are welcoming by mandate, and attending services at sanctuaries that don't attract sightseeing buses can offer more than a glimpse at frescoes and icons and gospel choirs—it can offer you the chance to meet the people who worship in those places, and get a sense for how their faith enhances their lives.

HEALTHY CULTURES EVOLVE ON THEIR OWN TERMS

What is tradition? What is national character? Is there something inherent in our character that gave the Japanese predisposition to invent the kimono and wear it? What the hell is a kimono anyway?
—Ango Sakaguchi, "A Personal View of Japanese Culture" (1942)

As social scientists attempted to document the lifeways of traditional cultures in the early decades of the twentieth century, they were often frustrated by the fact that outsiders—people like missionaries and tourists—had already arrived and compromised the presumed "purity" of the societies they hoped to study.

As researchers gathered more data, however, they discovered two problems with their initial assumptions about cultural purity. First, even the most isolated societies they encountered were never monolithic, and had a great deal of individual diversity within them. Second, the culture of a given community tended to function as an internal conversation about what factors—outside influences included—best served the group's present-day needs.

"Thriving cultures are not set in stone," wrote scholar Philippe Legrain in a 2003 essay about the legacies of globalization. "They are forever changing from within and without. Each generation challenges the previous one. . . . By and large, people choose new ways because they are more relevant to their current needs, and offer new opportunities that the old ones did not." Or, as anthropologist Wade Davis mused in a 2008 *Discover* interview: "If I get my arm ripped off in an accident, I don't want to be taken to a shaman; no one else does either."

Like healthy people, healthy cultures are constantly growing and evolving in the face of an ever-changing world. To experience these cultures as travelers is more than a ritual of identifying unchanged traditions; it's a willingness to discern how those traditions are evolving to meet present-day needs.

EMBRACING "NOT KNOWING" ALLOWS FOR SERENDIPITY

As is often the case when I travel, my vulnerability—like not knowing what the hell I'm supposed to do upon arrival—makes me more open to outside interactions than I might otherwise be when I'm at home. . . . On the road, serendipity is given space to enter my life.

—Andrew McCarthy, *The Longest Way Home* (2012)

The word "freedom" is often used to describe the feeling of becoming immersed in a journey, though this is often understood as "freedom from," when in fact "freedom to" is what makes the act of travel feel so liberating. Indeed, finding freedom from the routines and responsibilities of home is ultimately less affecting than finding the freedom to explore new ways of thinking and living and doing. "Travelers perceive, often for the first time, a sense that they are in charge of their lives," wrote ethnographer Klaus Westerhausen in his 2002 book *Beyond the Beach*. "Rather than work or study imposing patterns on their time, the choice of what to do is now theirs."

At the outset of a journey, the choices you make as a traveler tend to be concrete, practical, and pegged to the task of getting from one part of the world to another and orienting yourself in a new place and culture. But as the journey stretches out and deepens, your best choice as a traveler might be to avoid making choices in advance—to leave your itinerary open to serendipity, and embrace vulnerability as your truest travel asset.

In not knowing exactly what will happen next, you'll be able to embrace the heady thrill of uncertainty; in not knowing exactly how you'll respond to new situations, you'll discover new ways of being yourself; in not knowing exactly where you're headed, you'll find ways of making the most of wherever you happen to be.

MISADVENTURES MAKE FOR MEMORABLE JOURNEYS

We travel to stretch ourselves, test ourselves, and unearth abilities we didn't know we had. . . . Bad trips make this possible.
—Eric Weiner, "Bad Trips Make for Great Stories" (2021)

One of the oldest recorded travel stories known to humankind tells the tale of a Pharaonic priest named Wenamun, who was dispatched to buy timber in Lebanon about three thousand years ago. Unlike such contemporary adventurers as Odysseus, Wenamun did not take a journey that involved triumph over adversity. Indeed, not long after leaving Egypt, he misplaced his letters of introduction, got robbed, and managed to insult his hosts in the Phoenician city of Dor. After enduring a hostile reception from the local king at Byblos, Wenamun broke down in a homesick fit of weeping.

Whereas most ancient travel tales depict aspirational heroism, Wenamun's journey stands out for its humble relatability. Most of us, after all, do not travel as exemplars of bravery, but as optimistic bumblers who are as prone to mistakes as we are to epiphanies. Fortunately, misadventures can be as memorable and edifying as our goal-driven accomplishments. In his 2019 book *Walking*, explorer Erling Kagge recounted the time he and his girlfriend got trapped without a tent or sleeping bags on Norway's third-highest mountain. "Spending the night together under such dramatic conditions made it stand out from other, easier evenings," he recalled. "When the sun rose and we helped each other descend to safety, we found those hours in the darkness had brought us closer together."

On the road, misadventures aren't merely the result of our own lack of preparation or competence—they often flow out of our simple willingness to try something different, and to make the most of (and grow from) what happens as a result.

REINVENT WHAT IT MEANS TO BE AN EXPLORER

Perhaps the great task of modern explorers is not to conquer but to connect, to reveal how any given thing leads to another.
—Kate Harris, *Lands of Lost Borders* (2018)

When Kate Harris was growing up in Canada, she felt destined for a life of exploration. The more she read about the swashbuckling explorer-philosophers of days gone by, however, the more she began to realize that planet Earth—and its rugged, inaccessible places—had long since been mapped. Demoralized by the limitations of terrestrial exploration, Kate decided that she was going to explore Mars instead.

Part of the conceit of our received notions of exploration and discovery is that even those storied explorers of days gone by typically carried out their physical feats in landscapes occupied by people who already lived there. Just as David Livingstone's purported "discovery" of Victoria Falls would have come as a surprise to the Africans who lived nearby, William Lewis and Meriwether Clark famously depended upon the assistance of indigenous North Americans as they explored North America.

Kate Harris has not (yet) been to Mars; she eventually decided to embrace exploration by reinventing her own notion of what it meant to be an explorer. Quitting a high-level but ultimately unsatisfying career in academic science research, she set off on an open-ended bicycle journey that wound up taking her nearly six thousand miles through Central Asia. Along the way, her experiences allowed her to make richer, humbler sense of her childhood dreams.

"Exploring is an attitude, really, a quality of attention to the world around you," she wrote in her book *Lands of Lost Borders*. "Exploration demands a refusal of all the usual maps: of the world, of how you're told to live your one and only life."

THE SUBTLER RISKS OF TRAVEL CARRY RICH REWARDS

Travel makes me a better person. It pushes me to be friendlier and humbler. There aren't a lot of chances for me to be vulnerable in my everyday life, so it's refreshing to let my guard down, to ask questions, and to put my trust in others.

—Maggie Downs, in a 2020 interview

The premise for Carl Hoffman's 2011 travel book *The Lunatic Express* was to sidestep the comforts of the tourism industry and circumnavigate the world using the same inexpensive transportation (rickety trains, crowded ferries, decrepit buses) that everyday people use to get around in their own countries. When his fellow passengers on a ramshackle third-class Indonesian ferry went out of their way to look after him on a five-day journey to the Molucca Islands, Hoffman resolved to follow the example of local travelers everywhere he went—even if it went against his instincts as a comparatively privileged American traveler.

"If they drank the tap water of Mumbai and Kolkata and Bangladesh, so would I," he wrote. "If they bought tea from street corner vendors, so would I. If they ate with their fingers, even if I was given utensils, I ate with my fingers. Doing so prompted an outpouring of generosity and curiosity that never ceased to amaze me; it opened the door, made people take me in. That I shared their food, their discomfort, their danger, fascinated and validated them in a powerful way."

On the road, the truest adventures don't involve purely physical risks: Often, they are a matter of lowering your cross-cultural social inhibitions, forgoing a few comforts and conveniences, and endeavoring to experience a place in ways people living there do.

THE JOURNEY ITSELF IS AS IMPORTANT AS ANY DESTINATION

We might say that one difference between pilgrims and tourists is that for pilgrims, the road to the site, the process of getting there, is as important as the arrival.
—Carol Becker, "Social Memory and the Making of Art" (2003)

When King Moses George of Nubia left Africa for Jerusalem in the late twelfth century, he went with the understanding that he wouldn't come back home. "He said that he wanted to go on pilgrimage to Rome, and from Rome to St. James, and then to Jerusalem, if he should live so long, and die there," wrote French chronicler Robert de Clari in 1216.

At the time Moses George was taking his journey, most Christians making the Jerusalem pilgrimage left home knowing their endeavor might not come full circle. The travel part of the pilgrimage was seen not as an inconvenience to be endured en route to the sacred place, but as a ritual act of penance and prayer that underpinned the spiritual significance of the journey. The transformation promised by pilgrimage lay not in the destination itself, but in the effort and challenges involved in seeking it.

Though modern travel isn't embraced with such a fatalistic spirit, it's useful to keep in mind these medieval pilgrims' conviction that destinations are only as meaningful as the efforts that take us there. As we make our way to dreamed-of places, the eventual joy of arrival is an outgrowth of the attention we give to the places we encounter on the way. Moreover, since travel inevitably brings us full circle to the place where we started—to home, and a new perspective on what that place is—arriving there transformed is inseparable from the attention we bring to each step of the journey itself.

October 10

TO TRULY EXPERIENCE A LANDSCAPE,
TRAVERSE IT ON FOOT

> Never have I thought so much, never have I realized my own existence so much, been so much alive, been so much myself, if I may venture to use the phrase, as in the journeys which I have made alone and afoot.
>
> —Jean-Jacques Rousseau, *Confessions* (1782)

When American author Pam Houston undertook a nine-day trek in the Bhutanese Himalayas, her deepest source of satisfaction came in the simple fact that the journey was accomplished under her own power, one step at a time. "One foot in front of the other, up to the top of the mountain pass and down," she wrote in her 1999 essay collection *A Little More About Me*. "There is something pure about it, unencumbered by gear or rules or devices, unaided by lifts or wheels or even currents; only the simple law of gravity working for or against me, only my mind and my body to speed me up or slow me down."

Indeed, while travel enables us to view the world's natural splendor firsthand, simply gazing upon mountains and forests is not nearly as rewarding as stowing a few essentials in a pack and navigating your way through those places on foot. Scores of classic hikes worldwide (from America's Appalachian Trail to New Zealand's Milford Track to Chile's Paine Circuit) feature on people's travel bucket lists, but a wilderness hike need not be famous to be worthwhile.

In simply removing yourself from the crowds and clamor of cities and committing yourself to walk in a wild landscape, you open yourself up to a quieter, more unplugged way of being in the world. "Of all the paths you take in life, make sure a few of them are dirt," goes a saying attributed to naturalist John Muir. This advice holds true for any journey.

LOSING ONESELF IN A PLACE IS NOT THE SAME AS BEING LOST

Not all those who wander are lost.
—J.R.R. Tolkien, *The Fellowship of the Ring* (1954)

In his 1932 memoir *Berlin Chronicle*, German Jewish philosopher Walter Benjamin explained how losing oneself in a place is not the same as getting lost there. "Not to find one's way in a city requires ignorance, nothing more," he wrote. "But to lose oneself in a city—as one loses oneself in a forest—that calls for quite a different schooling." In other words, losing oneself in a place is not a random error within the landscape; it's an active embrace of the landscape itself.

In English, the willingness to lose yourself can be expressed by a variety of synonyms—though in an age of GPS navigation and efficient autoroutes, Anglophones are less likely than ever to *meander,* or *traipse,* or *roam,* or *ramble,* or *wander*. Explorer Erling Kagge noted in his 2019 book *Walking* that the linguistic metaphors used for roving on foot have a deeper meaning in languages like Sanskrit or his native Norwegian, both of which imply that walking is a form of knowing. "The similarities between the meaning of these words follow the age-old kinships around the world," Kagge wrote, "and tell of the experiences that people have gathered as they have traveled."

In essence, the decision to wander through a new landscape—that is, to lose yourself in it—is a matter of trading the map you hold in your hands for the one you make with your feet. In this way, as you follow instincts rather than plans, you put yourself into a better position to discover what you hadn't expected to find.

YOU DON'T HAVE TO BE A PILGRIM TO ENJOY A PILGRIMAGE

A pilgrimage . . . is an old and corporeal kind of shock therapy, a structure that is maintained and promoted to help inspire an embodied sense of gratitude and wonder at the variety and generosity of the world, a world much bigger than our petty fears and desponds and regrets.

—Gideon Lewis-Kraus, *A Sense of Direction* (2012)

When I first set out to climb Adam's Peak some years ago, I didn't fully appreciate that the trail to the top of Sri Lanka's second-highest mountain has become a pilgrimage for adherents of the country's four biggest religions. Local Buddhists believe a rock atop the 7,359-foot summit bears the footprint of Lord Buddha; Hindus think the footprint belongs to Shiva; Christians and Muslims claim it bears the mark of Adam's first step after being exiled from the Garden of Eden.

As I made the six-hour predawn ascent to the summit, I came to savor the communal energy of my fellow Adam's Peak hikers: Some chanted hymns, others joked and posed for pictures; some toted offerings of fruit or money, others toted smartphones and texted messages to friends. Despite the various degrees of devotion, there was something deeply satisfying in the fact that—regardless of age, motivation, and nationality—we were all engaged in the same physical challenge on the same cool Sri Lankan morning.

Indeed, just as non-Catholics are encouraged to embark upon Spain's Camino de Santiago (and non-Buddhists can embrace the challenge of Japan's Shikoku Pilgrimage circuit), religious devotion isn't a prerequisite for ascending a place like Adam's Peak. Whether you are religious or not, sometimes the spiritual energy of a pilgrimage comes in the shared physical effort that no mediated experience can provide—the chance to see and smell and hear the ritual for yourself, in the company of others, and to feel happily exhausted when it's over.

PHOTOS HINT AT MORE COMPLEX TRAVEL STORIES

A photograph tells the story of two lives simultaneously, the one in front of the camera as well as the one behind.
—Pam Houston, *Waltzing the Cat* (1998)

In the early years of the twentieth century, as inexpensive point-and-shoot cameras like the Kodak Brownie made it possible for everyday folks to take photographs, critics marveled at the way "snapshots" promised to revolutionize the way people remembered their lives. "Our Kodak is the means by which we can penetrate visions that mysteriously deepen our life," wrote art critic Joseph August Lux in his 1908 book *Artistic Secrets of the Kodak*. "The picture speaks a universal language that tells more at a single glance than the swiftest stenographer could put on paper in hours," added journalist Frank Parker Stockbridge in a 1913 issue of *Popular Mechanics*. "Anyone intelligent enough to 'press the button' can write with his camera a story that everyone in the world can read."

While snapshot photography became more common in the decades that followed, the camera itself began to dictate which stories people sought to tell about ephemeral acts like travel. As having experiences on the road gradually became intertwined with taking photos, posing for photographs became the default reaction in the face of the world's wonders—a static ritual that stated, again and again, "I went here."

Though the ease of digital photography has allowed us to document our travels in more spontaneous and prolific ways, these snapshots still tell a simplified "I went here" story that can only hint at the richer contexts inherent in a journey. In this way, our travel photos tell private tales that go beyond what they depict; they serve as memory triggers for the richer stories that never fit into the frame.

ONE PERSON'S "ADVENTURE" IS ANOTHER'S VOCATIONAL DUTY

Adventure, in the good sense of the word, is a modern concept. For most of history, adventure was something inflicted on you, not something you sought out and certainly not something you paid for.

—Eric Weiner, *The Geography of Bliss* (2009)

Beryl Markham was best known as the first person to fly east to west across the Atlantic solo, but her 1942 memoir *West with the Night* is less about airplane travel than her coming of age in British East Africa. As the safari industry became popular in the 1920s, Markham marketed her nascent aviation skills to big-game hunters—though she harbored a faint disdain for wealthy clients who sought to showcase their masculinity by shooting lions and elephants in Africa.

"It is absurd for a man to kill an elephant," she wrote. "It is not brutal, it is not heroic, and certainly it is not easy; it is just one of those preposterous things that men do." Markham's ethnic Kamba colleagues, who tracked game for safari clients and preferred longbows to hunting rifles, expressed what she called "a kind of restrained contempt for that noisy and unwieldy piece of machinery with its devilish tendency to knock the untutored huntsman flat on his buttocks every time he pulls the trigger."

Though hunting safaris are far less common than they were a century ago, a certain segment of the travel industry still thrives by offering outsiders a taste of adventure in seemingly exotic landscapes. This is all well and good (I have myself enjoyed photo safaris in South Africa, mountain trekking in Peru, and horseback excursions in Mongolia), but it's wise to keep in mind, even as we post our "adventure" photos on social media, that these experiences are made safe and enjoyable by true adventurers—namely, the people who actually know and live (and carry our gear) in those places.

EXPLORE THE ART OF LINGERING
IN PLACES YOU LOVE

The experience of the duration, and not the number of experiences, makes a life full.
—Byung-Chul Han, *The Scent of Time* (2017)

Toward the end of a visit to Uruguay in 2015, I found myself in a conundrum. I loved the laid-back Latin American beach vibe of Punta del Diablo, but—apart from reading, swimming, and hiking along the shoreline looking for tegu lizards and burrowing owls—I hadn't really done anything during my one-week stay there. The list of attractions I'd researched before I went to Uruguay lay mostly unchecked, and this made me fear I hadn't properly experienced the country.

I needn't have worried. In his 2017 book *The Scent of Time,* Korean Swiss philosopher Byung-Chul Han argued that modern life has compelled us to throw ourselves into the *vita activa* (active life), which is ultimately less fulfilling than an equally intentional embrace of the *vita contemplativa* (contemplative life); the latter serves to counterbalance life experiences and reminds us of how best to spend our time. "The idea of accelerating life for its maximization is wrong," Han wrote. Doing twice as many things in life, he added, doesn't make life twice as fulfilling; rather, we make the most of life knowing when and where to linger in time and space.

Inevitably, the best part of travel comes in those moments when you give yourself permission to stop in a place that captures your imagination and get to know it a little better, devoid of goals and itineraries and hypothetical regrets.

I ended up staying one more week in Punta del Diablo, doing the same things I'd done there my first week. It remains one of my favorite memories of South America.

SOME GLOBAL STORIES REQUIRE A DIFFERENT KIND OF LISTENING

- -

> When we consider our own society, we use a system of values and a system of references which we have to abandon if we wish to reflect on other societies.
>
> —Claude Lévi-Strauss, in a 1969 interview

One of novelist Saul Bellow's more ignominious moments came in a 1988 *New York Times* interview, when he used a clumsy turn of phrase in an attempt to defend the traditional literary canon. "Who is the Tolstoy of the Zulus?" he rhetorized. "The Proust of the Papuans? I'd be glad to read them." In saying this, the American author wasn't just misrepresenting these authors' literary inheritance (Proust, after all, belonged to Papuans as much as he did to Chicagoans like Bellow); he was erroneously implying that storytelling is at heart an individualist undertaking. To suggest that Zulus or Papuans needed a Tolstoy or a Proust to be culturally relevant was to misconstrue collective storytelling traditions that went back thousands of years.

For people raised with the idea that stories are best shared in books, it can be disorienting to travel to societies where the most affecting stories are still shared in person. Moreover, to view history as a linear narrative is to misapprehend cultures that don't differentiate history from the rhythms of everyday life. "So-called primitive societies are surrounded by the substance of history and try to remain impervious to it," anthropologist Claude Lévi-Strauss once noted in a French radio interview. "Modern societies interiorize history, as it were, and turn it into the motive power of their development."

Realizing that there are integral differences in the way humans apprehend things like history and storytelling isn't just a matter of cross-cultural understanding; it's often the first step in taking one's cross-cultural journey to a new level of receptivity.

LIVING IN A FOREIGN CULTURE IS
A WINDOW INTO YOUR OWN

> If you want to know a man, the proverb goes, travel with him. If
> you want to know yourself, travel alone. If you want to know
> your own country, go make a home in another country.
>
> —Bob Shacochis, "Be an Expat" (2002)

In Ben Lerner's 2011 novel *Leaving the Atocha Station*, the neurotic young protagonist, living in Madrid on a poetry fellowship, becomes fixated on trying to avoid other Americans. "I would be congratulating myself on lunching . . . in a tourist-free restaurant," the protagonist comments, "congratulating myself on making contact with authentic Spain, which I only defined negatively as an American-free space, when I would catch the eyes of a man or woman at another table, early twenties to early thirties, surrounded by Spaniards, reticent compared to the rest of the company, and I knew—we would both know—that we were of a piece."

Lerner's coming-of-age-abroad novel is a self-conscious exploration of the way any attempt to linger in a foreign culture is at first inseparable from the assumptions and awareness of your own culture. When the protagonist says, "I reserved my most intense antipathy for those young Americans whose lives were structured by attempting to appear otherwise," he is in essence alluding to himself. As he tries to embed himself more fully into Spanish culture, he is exasperated to see evidence of his American self everywhere.

Choosing to live in a foreign place—as a study-abroad expatriate, a digital nomad, or just someone who's chosen to stay longer in an appealing place—can immerse you into that place, but this goes hand in hand with an intensified awareness of how entrenched your own cultural self can be. In embracing a foreign place, you thus gain a useful, humbling perspective on the place that formed you.

October 18

THE ROMANCE OF TRAVEL IS OFTEN
MIXED IN WITH ROMANCE ITSELF

Making love in novel environments, free from the censorship
and inhibitions of the familiar, is one of the headiest experiences
travel promises.

—Paul Fussell, *Abroad* (1980)

One of the most intriguing literary works to survive from the tenth century is Sei Shonagon's quirky and opinionated *The Pillow Book*, which blends poetry, anecdotes, and essays to describe Japanese court life. In a section describing a journey to Hase Temple in Nara Prefecture, Shonagon seemed to thrill in observing the flirtations among the pilgrims there. "The young men who visited the temple were apt to wander near the women's quarters and spend more time looking in that direction than at the Buddha," she mused. "Sometimes they would call for one of the sextons and, after a whispered consultation, set off for some other part of the temple. I saw nothing wrong in their behavior."

Romance between travelers was also common in the Christian pilgrimage tradition, causing writers like fourth-century mystic Gregory of Nyssa to express concerns about sexual misconduct. Even pilgrims who tried to abide by their vows, like Milanese nobleman Pietro Casola, remarked on the sensual temptations that came with visiting new places. "Venetian women, especially the pretty ones, try as much as possible in public to show their chests and shoulders," he wrote in his 1494 pilgrimage journal. "I cannot allow this to please me; I am a priest by way of the saints."

Though courtship between travelers and locals can be complicated (particularly when travelers from wealthy countries visit less-wealthy ones), romance between fellow travelers is a time-honored tradition—in part because, away from home, it is easy to embrace a more open-hearted worldview. Freed from familiar habits and inhibitions, travelers become uncommonly inspired to embrace romantic possibility.

SEEKING OUT MONUMENTS TO MORTALITY IS A COMMON TRAVEL RITE

- -

The race is not to the swift or the battle to the strong, nor does food come to the wise or wealth to the brilliant or favor to the learned; but time and chance happen to them all.

—Book of Ecclesiastes (c. 300 B.C.E.)

Quirky and macabre as cemetery tourism might sound, Mariana Enríquez's 2014 book *Alguien camina sobre tu tumba* (*Someone Walks on Your Grave*) delves into why it has become a common travel rite. Seeking out places like the Old Jewish Cemetery in Prague, Elvis Presley's mausoleum in Memphis, and the flooded ghost town of Villa Epecuén in her home country, Argentina, Enríquez explored what public cemeteries express about a given society, as well as the existential texture of graveyard visits. "There are many more dead people than alive," she wrote. "It is a simple truth, and we all end up in the ground."

Though it might seem odd to think of cemeteries as tourist attractions, that's exactly what famous ones have become over the years— from India's Taj Mahal (which is a mausoleum for a Mughal emperor and his wife) to Paris's exquisite Père Lachaise (final resting place of Colette, Proust, and Jim Morrison) to Washington's Arlington National Cemetery (which I visited as a teen on a junior high civics-class field trip). Nineteenth-century travelers were known to visit the Paris morgue (where as many as forty thousand visitors a day ogled recent fatalities); first-century Roman tourists sought out the embalming shops of Egypt (which mummified dozens of human corpses daily).

Respectfully walking among the graves of public cemeteries (even less-famous ones) can offer travelers a genuine perspective on the community that established them—and, in compelling us to ponder bygone eras (and our own mortality), invite us to embrace an introspective kind of time travel.

TRAVEL ENABLES YOU TO EXPERIENCE THE SUBLIME

There are all sorts of theories about what exactly is needed to have the experience of the sublime. But gathering them all together, essentially what lies at the center of the experience is a feeling of smallness.

—Alain de Botton, in a 2002 interview

One of the most unnerving stories in the Old Testament is that of a man named Job, whose life is ruined when God and Satan make a wager over whether or not tragedy will unravel the man's faith. Satan is allowed to systematically destroy Job's livestock, servants, children, and physical health, but Job refuses to curse God. Eventually God appears in a whirlwind, but instead of praising Job for his faith, God points out how humans understand almost nothing about the universe, and that man is insignificant in the context of creation.

Of the many insights offered by travel, a key epiphany often comes from encounters with the sublime—with the awe-inducing landscapes, raw vulnerabilities, and enervating challenges that remind the traveler of his own, Job-like insignificance in the greater scheme of the universe. On the road, the experience of the sublime might come from a solitary run through California's redwood forests, a difficult hike up a Greenlandic glacier, or a quiet sunrise over the broad expanse of ocean off the Mozambican coast.

The joy in these moments comes not from physical accomplishment, but from the realization that our humble little lives are not the measure of all things. As Alain de Botton noted in *The Art of Travel*, "We may come away from such places not crushed but inspired by what lies beyond us, privileged to be subject to such majestic necessities."

THE BIGGEST DISCOVERIES OF TRAVEL ARE OFTEN PERSONAL ONES

Sometimes I wonder if it's a biological need, perhaps a biological flaw, that compels me to seek the excitement and challenge that comes of being in a place where nobody knows me.
—Rita Golden Gelman, *Tales of a Female Nomad* (2001)

Author Michael Crichton is remembered for such action-oriented novels as *Jurassic Park* and *The Andromeda Strain,* but his lesser-known 1988 memoir *Travels* stands out for its introspective look into the life experiences that formed him. "Many of the most important changes in my life came about because of my travel experiences," he wrote. "Often I feel I go to some distant region of the world to be reminded of who I really am. . . . Stripped of your ordinary surroundings . . . you are forced into direct experience. . . . That's not always comfortable, but it is always invigorating."

As often as not, the most important self-discoveries you make as you travel are not the kinds of things you'd boast about on social media. As a journey's raw experiences compel you to make sense of where you are and who you are (in relation to who you hope to become), you develop a new relationship with the person who resides within your own skin—not in a way that makes you more comprehensible to other people, necessarily, but in a way that makes you more comprehensible to yourself.

In doing this, you will come into a deeper relationship with aspects of yourself that you didn't know existed before the journey began. "The two risks of travel are disappointment and transformation," Kate Harris wrote in *Lands of Lost Borders.* "The fear you'll be the same person when you go home, and the fear you won't."

October 22

TRAVEL OFFERS PERSPECTIVE ON THINGS YOU TAKE FOR GRANTED

Money itself isn't lost or made, it's simply transferred from one perception to another. That painting cost $60,000 ten years ago; I could sell it today for $600,000. The illusion has become real.

—Michael Douglas as Gordon Gekko, in Oliver Stone's *Wall Street* (1987)

I never thought much about the idiosyncrasies of paper money until the day I counted out small bills to buy a packet of toilet tissues during a bicycle journey through Myanmar. The Burmese *kyat* had recently suffered a jag of devaluation, and when I'd tallied up my tissue money, I noticed that it consisted of twelve small-denomination bills. Given that Burmese tissues came in packets of ten, I realized it would be more economical to just use the *kyat* as toilet paper and pocket the difference.

From that day forward, it always felt a little strange to use paper money. Even back home in the United States, I realized, a paper dollar had little inherent value beyond the fact that it was a part of the largest system of common faith in the world—an oddly metaphysical system that seemed as rooted in the ways of shared belief as in economic pragmatism.

Just as that moment in Myanmar helped me better understand the concept of money, travel through Italy has helped me appreciate a holistic approach to enjoying food, and my sojourn in Korea helped me apprehend more enlightened ways of treating the elderly. In taking you away from routines so familiar that you scarcely see them anymore—in seeing new concepts and routines as an outsider, and your own through outside eyes—travel has a way of giving you new perspectives on the things you might otherwise take for granted.

BEING ON THE ROAD SEEDS LIFE WITH A SENSE OF POSSIBILITY

To travel is to live in all the meaning of the word, to breathe the free air, feel the joy of living, to become an integral part of creation.

—Alexandre Dumas, *Travels in Switzerland* (1843)

When an English teenager named Patrick Leigh Fermor set out to walk across Europe in 1933, the journey imbued him with such a sense of possibility that he had trouble falling asleep at night. "Living in a yeasty ferment of excitement I grudged every second of sleep," he recalled in his journal. "All I saw, heard, smelt, touched and tasted or read was brand new. The intake, total and continuous, was crowding in to the bursting point." Thrilled to be living with an intensity he'd only thought existed in books, young Leigh Fermor stared up at the sky each night "in a coma of happiness."

As our journeys stretch out and deepen, part of the thrill of being on the road is less about accomplishing goals than savoring a heady openness to new experiences and delighting in the sense that anything can happen at any moment. With nothing to do beyond what a given day presents, you become attuned to new friendships, early mornings, late nights, and prolonged silences; newly receptive to who you might become, you're more inclined to let wonder and imagination guide your days.

"The freedom of being a stranger in a strange place, knowing no one, needing to know no one, with no obligations, elicits deep feelings of liberation," wrote Andrew McCarthy in *The Longest Way Home*. "Without an agenda, or company to distract me, I invariably feel a certain hopefulness that can appear contrary to my aimlessness. Perhaps it's just the simple joy of being alive."

LUXURY DIVERSIONS CAN PROVIDE A TRAVEL "TIME-OUT"

- -

The real place of the tourist is not the site of the exotic, but rather the noplace place (literally the "utopia") of . . . in-between space . . . —the industrial abstraction of the airport, or the machine-dimension of plane or bus.

—Hakim Bey, "Overcoming Tourism" (1994)

Growing up in the 1980s, I spent many listless Saturday nights watching *The Love Boat*, an ABC comedy/drama that featured a rotating cast of guests interacting with the crew of a Mexico-bound cruise ship. Though the characters occasionally took shore excursions in places like Acapulco and Mazatlán, they spent most of their time exploring romantic possibility on the ship itself. Comfortable and predictable, the titular "love boat" didn't evoke travel so much as it provided a parallel home environment—a cipher setting, where character-driven storylines could play out from week to week.

Many of the holiday settings that have been created for us by the travel industry, not just cruise ships, but places like beach resorts and safari lodges, are in fact designed to function as parallel home environments—places that create the aura of being someplace exotic while offering us all the comforts and conveniences of home.

While it's ironic that the travel industry has a way of standardizing the experience of faraway places into something that scarcely resembles travel, this doesn't mean these places need to be relegated to escape-minded vacationers. In the midst of an immersive long-term journey, choosing to occasionally splurge on luxury environments (as I've done in places like Bangkok's historic Mandarin Oriental, or Punta Cana's all-inclusive Barcelo Bavaro Palace) can serve as a respite from the rigors of independent travel—a travel-adjacent home setting, where one can put the trip on pause and indulge in a few self-contained comforts before returning to the joyful challenges of the real world.

WILDERNESS IMBUES A JOURNEY
WITH PERSPECTIVE

> To the desert go prophets and hermits; through deserts go pilgrims and exiles. Here the leaders of the great religions have sought the therapeutic and spiritual values of retreat, not to escape but to find reality.
>
> —Paul Shepard, *Man in the Landscape* (1967)

Some words that don't have a ready English equivalent were born out of the very geographies that gave rise to their uniqueness. *Waldeinsamkeit,* for example, which refers to the sublime feeling one gets while alone in the woods, is connected to Germany's forested landscape. *Dadirri,* the Ngan'gi indigenous term for quiet awareness and deep listening, emerged from the tropical savannas of northern Australia. *Kachou fuugetsu,* which refers to the personal discovery one feels while attuned to nature, is tied to the subtle changes of the four seasons in Japan. To truly experience the awareness evoked by these words is inseparable from immersing oneself in the wildernesses that inspired them.

In this sense, encountering most any wilderness—a Bolivian salt flat, an Uzbek desert, a Gabonese jungle—can make us feel sensations and consider perspectives we can't quite describe. The nature we behold in our travels can be gorgeous, but truly appreciating its grandeur goes beyond scenic viewpoints. Immersing ourselves for a time in a wilderness is something we feel in temperature shifts and insect bites; something we smell in the trees or swamp or ocean; something we hear in wind and birdsong.

Wilderness is, in short, something that makes us feel insignificant, even as it inspires us: It is a setting that allows us to leave the narcissisms of human-made environments and celebrate our own smallness in the context of a complex and humbling and intoxicatingly beautiful world.

ADVENTURES EXPLORE MORE THAN PHYSICAL TERRITORY

- -

A vacation is external. A pilgrimage is internal. An adventure combines them.

—Eddy L. Harris, *Mississippi Solo* (1988)

One interesting thing about reading ancient Chinese travel accounts is that they rarely feature the same "discovery" rhetoric as their European counterparts. Second-century B.C.E. envoy Zhang Qian, for example, visited wide swaths of India and Central Asia, but he is remembered in his homeland not for "exploring" these regions so much as for bringing their agricultural developments—things like the grapevine and alfalfa—back home to China. Subsequent generations of Chinese travelers didn't regard themselves as explorers of unknown territories so much as seekers and students of territories that were well known to the people living there, and then bringing those people's best innovations home.

The modern travel milieu reflexively uses terms like "discover" and "explore" to describe the actions of a journey, but it's useful to recognize the limitations of seeing travel purely in terms of unseen vistas and physical distances. British adventurer Alastair Humphreys bicycled around the world and rowed across the Atlantic Ocean early in his career, for instance, but as he approached middle age he realized that purely physical endeavors no longer made him feel vulnerable. Realizing that nothing terrified him more than performing a musical instrument in public, he decided to learn violin from scratch and fund a walking journey across Spain by busking in village squares. "If I wanted to keep living adventurously," he wrote in his 2019 book *My Midsummer Morning*, "I had to veer from what I was good at and search again for uncertainty."

Indeed, adventure can sometimes entail dazzling physical feats, but just as often it's a matter of stretching your comfort zone, following your curiosity, and enriching your life with the things you learn along the way.

October 27

TRAVEL IS A WAY OF LEARNING TO CHERISH OUR DAYS

The great measure of human maturation is the increasing understanding that we move through life in the blink of an eye . . . that we are simply passing through.

—David Whyte, *Consolations* (2014)

Africa's Skeleton Coast, just south of Namibia's border with Angola in the southwestern corner of the continent, has a mist-shrouded, rock-strewn, end-of-the-earth feel. Portuguese sailors attempting to navigate its winds in the sixteenth century called it "The Gates of Hell"; local Namibian Himba people dubbed it "The Land God Made in Anger." Apart from its desert-parched aura of isolation, its main draw for travelers is the rotting shipwrecks that litter the coastline.

Some of the shipwrecks I saw when I visited Namibia a few years ago evoked a haunted sense of grandeur, but many of them were scarcely identifiable as ships. The *Winston,* a South African trawler that ran aground north of Swakopmund in October 1970, had attracted Skeleton Coast sightseers for decades—but by the late 2010s the relentless churning of the Atlantic had reduced it to a few piles of rusting metal strewn along the beach. Given the fact that I was born in October 1970, it was confounding to see that the *Winston* had already eroded into indiscernible sea garbage.

Walking amid the detritus of the *Winston* was thus a poignant reminder that any attempt to more fully embrace life through travel is intertwined with the fact that life ultimately passes us by. "Recognizing impermanence allows us to cherish the days and hours that are given to us," Thich Nhat Hanh wrote in his 2017 book *The Art of Living.* "The insight of impermanence has the power to liberate us: We can be at peace living our life to the fullest."

TO TRAVEL IS TO EXPERIENCE THE LIMITS OF NATIONAL IDENTITY

And I resented this: resented being called an American (and resented resenting it) because it seemed to make me nothing more than that, whatever that was; and I resented being called not an American because it seemed to make me nothing.

—James Baldwin, *Giovanni's Room* (1956)

After James Baldwin moved his life to Paris from New York in the late 1940s, his writing began to subtly examine the limitations of national identity. In his 1956 novel *Giovanni's Room*, the protagonist, a white American named David, loathed being stereotyped by his nationality in Europe, even as he found himself stereotyping the other Americans he encountered there. In the 1955 essay collection *Notes of a Native Son*, Baldwin chafed at French sympathy over American racism, noting that such news-headline-driven compassion viewed Black Americans as little more than victims living in "a place which one has never seen or visited, which never has existed, and which never can exist." For Baldwin, any attempt to reduce a person to the size of their national identity invariably overlooked the subtleties and specificities of that person's actual hopes and integrity.

In a way, nationality is a kind of shorthand we all use as a starting point to make sense of human differences across the sprawl of the world's geography. Part of the point of travel is to look past the constraints of national identity, yet, even as we try our best to do this, it can be frustrating to find ourselves beholden to stereotyped notions of our own nationality. Getting past such stereotypes (in both directions) is an imperfect process that involves patience, respect, and the optimistic conviction that travel is a chance to represent your nationality in a nuanced way, even as you seek out nuances in your host nation.

TRAVELERS CREATE THEIR OWN DISTINCT GLOBAL CULTURE

Culture is no longer bound to place or ethnicity, but is also re-flective of the processes and encounters that link different places and diverse people.

—Erve Chambers, *Native Tours* (1999)

The most unsettling scene in Pegi Vail's 2013 documentary *Gringo Trails* is a simple juxtaposition that illustrates backpacker travel culture at its worst: Having just displayed a veteran traveler's photos of Thailand's Haad Rin Beach as a beautiful and pristine backwater in 1979, the film cuts to the same beach crusted with beer bottles, plastic bags, cast-off glow sticks, vomit, and passed-out backpackers the morning after thousands of travelers had attended the island's 2010 "Full Moon Party."

Events like full-moon parties are unique to a global subculture that defines itself through travel, although—as the subtler scenes in *Gringo Trails* illustrate—this nation of world-wanderers represents far more than its self-indulgent excesses. United by the fact that they are far from their own homes, travelers invariably find common ground as peripatetic outsiders, and share an uncommon openness to each other as they try to stay open to the places they visit. Many places around the world (including Ubud in Bali, Lamu in Kenya, Ibiza in Spain, Panajachel in Guatemala, and Byron Bay in Australia) have, over the years, become so popular with travelers that they can feel like laid-back sister cities on the global vagabonding circuit.

Indeed, even as we aim to engage with host cultures (and avoid destructive beach party scenes) as mindful travelers, it's not uncommon to befriend, say, Germans in Laos, Brazilians in New Zealand, Nigerians in China, Arizonans in Korea, or Koreans in Arizona. In this way, a journey can offer engaged global connections in ways that reach beyond the places we'd meant to experience.

EVEN IMMERSED IN A CULTURE, YOU'RE STILL AN OUTSIDER

"When in Rome, do as the Romans do" is okay advice, but don't expect anyone to think that you're Roman just because you're trying to do whatever it is that Romans do. You're a tourist, baby, and everything about you will announce it to the world.
—Ed Buryn, *Vagabonding in Europe and North Africa* (1971)

In the late 1960s, India became a hotspot for wanderers hoping to shed the materialistic trappings of modern society. Trading jeans and T-shirts for dhotis and saris, scores of Westerners (including, famously, the Beatles) moved to places like Rishikesh and Goa seeking spiritual enlightenment. The 2001 documentary *Last Hippie Standing* investigated what had become of these counterculture pilgrims, interviewing aging travelers with names like "Swami William" and "Goa Gil," as well as Indian officials. While the Westerners dressed like sadhus and waxed lyrical about Hindu non-materialism, the Indians seemed puzzled by their presence. "We have enough poverty," one government minister said. "We want visitors who can spend money."

This tendency for travelers to drape themselves in traditional fashions and cherry-pick local spiritualities is sometimes characterized as "going native"—a faintly derisive term that applies to people who embrace a half-understood devotion to the cultures they encounter on a journey. Though travelers from centuries past adopted local customs for utilitarian reasons, "going native" is a modern phenomenon that is as much a reaction to the perceived constraints of one's home culture as it is an embrace of local ones.

Enthusiasm for different cultural traditions is part of the joy of travel, of course, but it's good to maintain a sense of perspective. If in doubt, balance your affinity for exotic spiritual and sartorial practices with a humble attention to human contexts you're only just beginning to understand.

REST DAYS ARE KEY TO THE LONG-TERM TRAVEL EXPERIENCE

> Schedule a day of rest every now and then. Contrary to what you might read, sudden insights seldom happen at the summit of a mountain. . . . Exhaustion seldom engenders insight.
> —Tim Cahill, *Hold the Enlightenment* (2002)

Of the many places I've traveled around the world, a handful stand out for the fact that I didn't "travel" once I'd arrived there. That is, instead of going on hikes or visiting historical monuments or interacting with local people, I just took naps and read books and stared off into the middle distance. Hence, there are certain corners of the world (Hvolsvöllur in Iceland and Ponta do Ouro in Mozambique both immediately come to mind) that I remember fondly because I did absolutely nothing there. Or, to be more precise, I enjoyed those places because they allowed me to take a rest.

When I first started traveling long-term, I didn't realize how essential rest days can be when it comes to making the most of a journey. On my first true vagabonding trip—an eight-month van journey around North America at age twenty-three—I was so enamored by the classic sights of the United States that I tried to pack as many of them into my journey as possible. Years later, I remember Utah's Uinta National Forest with a wistfulness that rivals my memories of Yellowstone and New York City—not because I accomplished great things in the Uinta wilderness, but because I accomplished little there beyond sitting in the sun and reading a few books.

Since then, I've come to realize that the key to enjoying a long-term journey often lies in those moments when you give yourself a few days to rest up, absorb the journey, and anticipate the possibilities of where you'll go next.

THE EXTENDED JOURNEY (AND THE JOURNEY HOME)

FIGURE OUT WHAT YOU'VE BEEN OVERLOOKING IN PLACES

[Travelers'] limited acquaintance with the environment, and consequent inability to grasp anything but the most obvious and easily recognizable features of it, necessarily . . . [leads] to stereotyping.
—Erik Cohen, "Stranger-Local Interaction in Photography" (1992)

Some of my favorite road trips growing up played out on the backroads of western Kansas, in the company of my science-teacher father. Travelers passing through this stretch of the high plains tended to stop at Dodge City's Boot Hill Museum and then move on—but Dad found every aspect of the landscape fascinating. As a biology instructor, he knew that what looked like monotone prairie in fact consisted of several distinct geophysical regions. The richest aspect of these grassland biomes, he told me, lay beneath the soil, where the roots of bluestem and buffalo grass might stretch ten or twenty times deeper than their height (and beneath that topsoil, he added, one could find mosasaur and plesiosaur fossils, evidence of Kansas's oceanic prehistory).

Decades later, the Kansas grasslands have become my metaphor for what I might be overlooking when I visit new places. It makes sense to seek out iconic attractions early on in a journey, but the longer you travel, the more it behooves you to consider what lies beneath a place's touristic surface. In Paris, this could involve moving beyond the brasseries of the Latin Quarter, and seeking out Senegalese or Ivorian food in the Eighteenth Arrondissement; in Cambodia, it might entail venturing beyond Angkor Wat and visiting such lesser-known Khmer temples as Koh Ker and Banteay Chhmar.

In this way, developing an instinct to venture beyond the obvious on the road allows you to see places not merely as checklists of sights to be visited—but as mysteries to be investigated.

November 2

GIVE YOURSELF OVER TO THE FLOW OF THE JOURNEY ITSELF

One of the highest pleasures is to be unconscious of one's own existence, to be absorbed in interesting sights, sounds, places, and people.

—Alan Watts, *The Wisdom of Insecurity* (1951)

In his 1990 book *Flow: The Psychology of Optimal Experience,* Hungarian American psychologist Mihaly Csikszentmihalyi theorized that people are happiest when they become so fully absorbed in the activity at hand that nothing else seems to matter. "The ego falls away," Csikszentmihalyi noted. "Time flies. Every action, movement, and thought follows inevitably from the previous one. . . . Your whole being is involved, and you're using your skills to the utmost."

Though this idea of "flow" naturally applies to creatives such as dancers and painters, Csikszentmihalyi actually borrowed the term from a mountain climber. "The purpose of flow is to keep on flowing," the climber told him, "not looking for a peak or utopia but staying in the flow. . . . There is no possible reason for climbing except the climbing itself." Once a person becomes fully absorbed in such a flow, "clock time" disappears and the activity becomes inseparable from the simple act of doing it.

Though travel is not always as singularly focused as climbing a mountain or dancing, it too can lend itself to immersive flow experiences. Absorbed in the sights and sounds and smells of a given moment on the road, you forget that you're in a new place; you just are where you are, independent of the motivations and goals that brought you there.

Late in her life, the French philosopher Simone de Beauvoir observed that travel allowed her to be at peace in a way she was not at home. "I forget my own existence," she wrote. "I live in a moment that embraces eternity."

THE MOST AFFECTING ADVENTURES
AREN'T ARBITRARY ONES

> Men who go looking for the source of a river are merely looking
> for the source of something missing in themselves, and never
> finding it.
>
> —Richard Francis Burton, quoted in his biography
> *The Devil Drives* (1967)

One of the ironies of Jon Krakauer's 1996 book *Into the Wild* is that its protagonist, Christopher McCandless, might never have become an adventure icon had he survived his Alaska endeavor and written his own memoir. But Chris's lonesome death in an abandoned bus a few hundred miles south of the Arctic Circle presented Krakauer with the challenge of deciphering why the young man had embraced such an arbitrary adventure to begin with. "McCandless yearned to find a blank spot on the map," he wrote. "In 1992, however, there were no more blank spots on the map—not in Alaska, not anywhere. But Chris, with his idiosyncratic logic, came up with an elegant solution to this dilemma: He simply got rid of the map."

Into the Wild is appealing in part because McCandless's desire to escape the superfluities of modern life is a relatable one. His biggest mistake may have come in seeking physical isolation rather than creating an engaged and immersive adventure that took other humans into account. "A lot of what people call adventure is bull," wrote journalist Robert Young Pelton in a 2002 article about post-9/11 tourism. "Travelers seek experiences that have a cachet of risk, but it's isolated from cultural reality. Travelers go someplace seeking adventure, then basically ignore the people that live in that place."

Creating life-affecting adventures is often a matter of embracing the full cultural context of your journey—of mixing physical endeavors with human engagement to create an experience that challenges you to look beyond yourself.

THE VAGABOND'S WAY – 323

MISFORTUNES ON THE ROAD OFFER A SENSE OF PERSPECTIVE

> In the difficult and dangerous journey, the self of the traveler is impoverished and reduced to its essentials, allowing one to see what those essentials are.
>
> —Eric J. Leed, *The Mind of the Traveler* (1991)

For all the presumed and imagined dangers that await modern travelers, the twenty-first-century journey is downright benign compared to the hazards of previous eras. In his 1617 travel account *Itinerary*, English traveler Fynes Moryson detailed his creative attempts to conceal his money from highwaymen in the French countryside. When he got robbed at gunpoint near Burgundy, his assailants found the gold he'd quilted into his doublet, but they overlooked the sixteen crowns he'd stashed in a box daubed with "stinking ointment for scabs." "Smelling the stink of the ointment, they cast it away on the ground," he recalled. "By the grace of God, I had some money left, to keep me from begging in a strange country."

A willingness to encounter and learn from misfortune was, in fact, an essential attitude among travelers of previous centuries. When the great Chinese traveler Xuanzang made the arduous Buddhist pilgrimage to India in the seventh century, he dealt with all kinds of difficulties, including Taklamakan Desert sandstorms, Himalayan snowstorms, and all manner of bandits. When sword-wielding desperados robbed him in Punjab, Xuanzang took it in stride. "Why lament the few garments and possessions we have lost?" he recounted later. "We are alive; let us rejoice that we have our greatest treasure."

Though our own journeys are unlikely to involve such melodramatic misfortunes, it's useful to keep in mind that the travails of the road—even small frustrations, like sickness and swindles and stolen luggage—are negligible compared with the privilege of traveling out into the world and risking new experiences.

TRAVEL MAKES YOU RECONSIDER
THE NOTION OF VALUE

- -

Speaking of presents and articles for payment, as of money, it is essential to have a great quantity and variety of *small change*, wherewith the traveler can pay for small services. . . . Beads, shells, tobacco, needles, awls, cotton caps, handkerchiefs, clasp knives, small axes, spear and arrow heads, generally answer this purpose.

—Francis Galton, *The Art of Travel* (1855)

One of the more poignant moments in Daniel Defoe's 1719 novel *Robinson Crusoe* comes when the protagonist, washed ashore on a forlorn island off the coast of South America, finds a bit of money while salvaging items from his wrecked ship. "What art thou good for?" he despairs. "Thou art not worth to me, no, not the taking off of the ground; one of those knives is worth all this heap; I have no manner of use for thee."

Two centuries later, the most plaintive moment of Nicolas Bouvier's *The Way of the World* came not when the young Swiss traveler damaged his car or ran low on money, but when his travel journal got tossed out with the hotel trash in Quetta, compelling the author to spend a day digging through cigarette butts, melon rinds, betel-juice-stained rags, and layers of "ashy and acidic paste" in a futile attempt to find it in the detritus of a Pakistani municipal dump.

Indeed, carrying out a journey can put us into a more practical relationship with what we consider valuable. At home, we might not think much about earplugs, power adapters, waterproof gear bags, or passports, whereas at moments on the road they can become the most essential things we possess. By reducing what we own to what we can carry—and by making our experiences (and our manner of documenting them) count for more than our possessions—travel compels us to reconsider the notion of value itself.

SEEING OTHER PEOPLE'S VALUES HELPS US MAKE SENSE OF OUR OWN

Travel can be good for us because otherness is good for us. . . .
Considering new and unfamiliar things forces us to expand and
rethink what we know.
　　　　　　　—Emily Thomas, *The Meaning of Travel* (2020)

Years ago, while traveling around Southeast Asia, I met an American engineer named Doug, with whom I spent the better part of an afternoon at a café in Phnom Penh. Doug seemed to be enjoying his time volunteering in a Cambodian village forty miles from the capital—but he talked less about the rural wells he was installing than the way fathers interacted with children in the village.

Doug sheepishly admitted that his own approach to fatherhood back in Oregon—with its micromanaged schedule of art lessons and soccer practices and mealtimes—felt soulless compared to how he saw Cambodian fathers relate to their kids. "Nothing they do is planned because there's no sense of separation," he told me. "They have a fraction of the money that we do in the U.S., but their family lives are so much richer. They're just naturally present in their kids' lives."

In pointing this out, Doug wasn't suggesting that he'd been a bad father to his own kids; he was just reflecting on the way that experiencing a different culture had given him a useful perspective on the ways he could enlarge his own approach to fatherhood. At its best, travel can thus give us a sense of context for the life choices we make at home, and—by exposing us to other ways of living—help us fine-tune those choices in a way that makes our home life fuller.

TRAVEL OFFERS A NEW WAY OF DEFINING WHO YOU ARE

Should the reader think strange that I could find pleasure in these curious and strange places . . . he must bear in mind that those are the only places and streams where flows the tide of curiosity.

—David F. Dorr, *A Colored Man Round the World* (1858)

When David F. Dorr published his travel memoir in 1858, his narrative occasionally alluded to his travel companion— a New Orleans native named "Cornelius"—as it detailed a sojourn through places like England, Italy, Greece, and Egypt. Though Dorr seemed fond enough of his sidekick, Cornelius comes off as something of a minor character in the book—a bumbler who proves inept at managing money and incompetent at dealing with beggars.

The delicious irony here is that Dorr hadn't traveled as Cornelius's friend; he'd traveled as Cornelius's domestic slave. Of the many new perspectives Dorr gained by being in Europe, the most significant was a reconstituted sense of self-worth—and his first act upon returning to the United States with Cornelius was to escape slavery in New Orleans and make his way to freedom in Cincinnati.

At the time, abolitionists promoted their cause by encouraging former slaves to record dramatic accounts of their escape from bondage, but for Dorr, escaping slavery was incidental to a more self-defining adventure in the capitals of Europe and the Near East. Writing *A Colored Man Round the World* thus served not to dramatize an escape from his worst life experiences, but to celebrate the creation of his best ones.

Though our present-day journeys don't carry the same stakes as they did for Dorr, they do give us the opportunity to regard ourselves in a new light as we visit other places—and to let that understanding shape our lives when we return home.

A JOURNEY OFFERS YOU A NEW
RELATIONSHIP WITH YOURSELF

- -

I've told the world that it can do what it wants with me if only,
by the end, I have learned something further. A bargain, then.
The journey, my teacher.

—Kira Salak, *Cruelest Journey* (2004)

Growing up in suburban Stockholm in the early part of the nineteenth century, Fredrika Bremer never felt she measured up to her mother's standards of feminine perfection. Though she dreamed of travel to distant lands, family obligations meant she wasn't able to travel in earnest until—having found success as a novelist in middle age—she took a two-year journey through North America in her late forties.

"My life, both in and with this New World, has assumed a romantic form," Bremer wrote in her 1853 book *Homes of the New World*. "I have found here a heart, a living spirit, which meets me in it." Invigorated by the transformation she felt as she experienced new cultures and landscapes, Bremer continued to travel the world (exploring places like Britain, Greece, and the Holy Land), and write about it, into her sixties.

As Bremer discovered, travel has a way of offering not just new sights and experiences, but of offering one the opportunity to become a more engaged and complete person. A journey doesn't just take us to new lands; it stirs us up, and encourages us to try out new versions of who we might be. In taking us away from the habits and restrictions of home, travel can thus help us grow into fuller versions of ourselves.

"Travel is more than the seeing of sights," historian Miriam Beard wrote in her 1930 book *Realism in Romantic Japan*. "It is a change that goes on, deep and permanent, in the ideas of living."

ON THE ROAD, THE QUEST FOR "AUTHENTICITY" IS OFTEN INWARD

Travel often provides situations and contexts where people confront alternative possibilities for belonging to the world and others that differ from everyday life. Indeed, part of the promise of travel is to live and know the self in other ways.
                    —Mark Neumann, "The Trail Through Experience" (1992)

In the late twentieth century, as urbanization and telecommunication technology made people's lives feel less rooted to a single landscape, tourism scholars reported that travelers were increasingly motivated by a search for places that felt more "authentic" than their home societies. The more researchers investigated this trend, however, the more they discovered that most travelers weren't looking for authenticity in specific places so much as they were seeking a *feeling* of authenticity in themselves.

"Tourists are not merely searching for authenticity of the *Other*," Chinese sociologist Ning Wang wrote in a 1999 *Annals of Tourism Research* article. "They also search for the authenticity of, and between, *themselves*. . . . People feel they themselves are more authentic and more freely self-expressed than in everyday life . . . free from the constraints of the daily."

Wang went on to note that travelers, in finding themselves away from the routines and social constraints of home, consider themselves to be "freer, more spontaneous" and "less serious, less utilitarian" than they are in domestic life. "[Travel] idealizes the ways of life in which people are supposed as freer, more innocent, more spontaneous, purer, and truer to themselves than usual," he wrote. "Such ways of life are usually supposed to exist in the past or in childhood."

Indeed, as travelers we are less equipped to identify objective authenticity in the places we visit than we are to revisit subtler forms of authenticity within ourselves. Removed from the expectations and obligations of home life, we discover that we can live in ways that are truer to our own instincts.

SOME OF THE BEST TRAVEL EXPERIENCES ARE THEIR OWN REWARD

There are many reasons to travel: for instance, to travel.
—Graffiti spotted in Madrid's Atocha railway station, 2018

Psychologists studying creativity have determined that there are two general approaches to the activities we plan for ourselves. "Telic" activities revolve around goals, and don't carry a lot of meaning beyond the specific outcomes of those goals; "autotelic" activities, on the other hand, are focused on the intrinsic rewards of the activity itself. Hence, going on a daylong hike with a telic mindset might find significance in accomplishing a certain number of miles in a certain number of hours, whereas taking a hike for autotelic reasons would find significance in enjoying each step of the hike itself.

While we're often focused on telic motivations at the outset of our travels (visiting ten new countries, for example, or growing our social media following with photos of ourselves in dazzling places), our journey becomes more and more autotelic as we attune ourselves to the serendipities and surprises we encounter along the way. As we become more focused on appreciation and less fixated on achievement—as we revel in questions rather than answers—the journey has a way of becoming its own, ever-deepening destination.

STAYING LONGER IN PLACES ENRICHES THE JOURNEY

> If you fall into the tourist traps . . . you can appear to the local population kind of like locusts. . . . You've only consumed. You've only taken from them. When you stay awhile, you balance those scales.
>
> —Matt Kepnes, *Ten Years a Nomad* (2019)

I wrote my first book, *Vagabonding,* in a guesthouse apartment in the southern Thailand border town of Ranong. The woman who owned the guesthouse, Wilaiwan, had a policy of letting travelers oversee the downstairs coffee shop, and when I first arrived it was managed by a young Swedish couple named Astrid and Sten. Though Ranong was a rainy estuary port that mainly attracted backpackers on visa runs to Myanmar, the Swedes enjoyed its provincial vibe. "We liked the beach we stayed at on Koh Samui, but all the travelers there made it feel like we were in some tropical version of Europe," Astrid told me. "In this place, we feel like we're finally in Thailand."

When Astrid and Sten weren't working in the coffee shop, they would head to the Ranong public market to shop for ingredients, or go off for hikes in the nearby rainforest. Their easygoing charisma made their café popular not just with backpackers, but also with middle-class Thais, who would invite the Swedes to banquets and religious festivals around town. Wherever Astrid and Sten are living now, I'd like to think that they cherish their memories of the time they wandered away from a beach resort and wound up running a coffee shop in a sleepy little Thai border town.

One appeal of traveling long-term is that it can offer you the opportunity to move through places you'd previously only dreamed about. A sure way to deepen that journey is to linger somewhere, and find ways to let a place move through you.

EMBRACE THE EXALTED ART OF DOING NOTHING

It is a disease to be doing something always, as if one could never sit quietly and lose oneself in mystery and wonder.

—Freya Stark, *The Journey's Echo* (1963)

In the eighteenth century, a Grand Tour tutor named Dr. John Moore recalled an English student whose strategy for seeing Rome was to rent a carriage before dawn and race past the city's "churches, palaces, villas and ruins, with all possible expedition." In this way, Moore noted, his young countryman was able to cover more in two days of scurrying through Rome than his own students were able to see in six weeks. "I found afterwards," noted Moore, "by the list he kept of what he had seen, that we had not the advantage of him in a single picture, or the most mutilated remnant of statue."

Though there is a hint of absurdity in Moore's anecdote, the student was simply employing an extreme distillation of how countless tourists approach Italy to this day. Faced with the sheer wealth of attractions, travelers speed through Italy in an attempt to see as much as possible. In doing so, they don't properly see Italy—in part because this strategy goes against the Italian virtue of *dolce far niente*.

Literally translated as "sweet idleness," *dolce far niente* is the experience of finding pleasure in doing nothing—of getting lost in your thoughts over a cappuccino, or observing the buzz of life on a street after a meal, or simply reveling in the exquisite simplicity of an indolent moment.

Though culturally Italian, *dolce far niente* can be exported to most any travel setting where you forgo the obligations of your to-do list for the more blissful task of savoring exactly where you are.

REVERIE AND IMAGINATION FEED INTO THE JOY OF TRAVEL

> What we perceive in ruins is the impossibility of imagining completely what they would have represented to those who saw them before they crumbled. They speak not of history but of time, *pure time.*
>
> —Marc Augé, *Non-Places* (1995)

My favorite moment in Ibn Battuta's fourteenth-century *Travels* comes when the great Moroccan wanderer sails through the Maldives. "We came to a little island in which there was but one house, occupied by a weaver," Battuta wrote. "He had . . . a few coco-palms and a small boat, with which he used to fish and cross over to any of the islands he wished to visit. . . . I swear I envied that man, and wished that the island had been mine, that I might have made it my retreat until the inevitable hour should befall me."

This detail feels vividly human and relatable, since in my own travels—sparked by things I see, or people I meet along the way—I often lapse into unrealistic fantasies about alternative existences. Sometimes these daydreams are the result of genuine cross-cultural empathy—but just as often they are pure reverie, as I imagine myself living out the rest of my life in places that capture my fancy.

This kind of imaginative travel tends to blur the present with a sense for the past and future, which could explain why ruins (in places like Stonehenge, Angkor Wat, or the Great Wall of China) hold such appeal to travelers. Gazing on the remnants of eras and cultures that seem so rooted in the past as to feel incomprehensible, we give ourselves whimsical permission to imagine ourselves living there—and to imagine what people living in future eras might make of our own.

SEEN FROM THE OUTSIDE, TOURISM CAN SEEM PERPLEXING

> Don't you know that all the guidebooks say: "Don't act like a tourist"?
>
> —Cary Grant to Grace Kelly in Hitchcock's *To Catch a Thief* (1955)

In the years after World War II, English novelist Nancy Mitford wrote her books while she was based in places like Venice and Versailles. Living in places popular with tourists gave her a keen perspective on their behavior: how they tended to be noisy and oblivious; how they were picky and unimaginative about food, even in places with exquisite culinary traditions; how they crowded around the same obvious attractions, even as they complained about other tourists. "One thing about tourists is that it is very easy to get away from them," Mitford mused in a 1959 essay. "Like ants they follow a trail, and a few yards each side of that trail there are none."

Even in isolated places, visitor behavior can be perplexing to the visited. When I reported a travel story from Uluru, one Pitjantjatjara elder told me that when tourists first arrived in central Australia, indigenous residents were befuddled by their presence. "People of my great-grandparents' generation assumed there were people in the world whose job was tourist," she told me, "and whose purpose in life was to travel around and take photos and argue about how much stuff cost."

Though it's easy to dissociate oneself from the worst tourist behavior, it can be useful to consider the perspective of residents in places where—as a traveler—you are literally out of place. Sometimes the easiest way to do this is to slow down, rent a room for a while, create a simple routine, and learn what the place feels like when you aren't just passing through.

SEEK THE STORIES A PLACE ISN'T TELLING ABOUT ITSELF

> How we are engaging history has everything to do with how we
> would like our identities to be seen in the present.
>
> —Salamishah Tillet, in a 2019 interview

For generations, visitors to Virginia's Mount Vernon were taught the story of its onetime owner, American president George Washington, whose forebears first acquired the land in 1674. Tourists were encouraged to stroll its gardens, interpretive guides explained the plantation's agricultural operations, and the gift shop sold things like Christmas ornaments and vintage playing cards. What the estate didn't describe in much detail was the fact that Mount Vernon's fields and facilities had been maintained by 317 enslaved people. In being shown a Mount Vernon that didn't depict slavery, visitors weren't being told its full story.

In 2012, a Philadelphia-based enterprise called Monument Lab was founded to broaden the narratives that are being told at America's historical sites. Noting that only two historically identifiable women were represented in Philadelphia's fifteen hundred public sculptures—and that the city had a statue depicting a fictional hometown boxing legend (Rocky Balboa), yet none honoring its real one (Joe Frazier)—the project explored ways of sharing underappreciated historical narratives. Using downloadable smartphone apps and alternative tour operators, Monument Lab enabled visitors seeking facts at, say, Philadelphia's 1790s-era President's House to learn not just the story of Washington, but also the story of Oney Judge, an enslaved woman who'd escaped the residence in 1796.

Historical sites anywhere in the world invariably present a limited perspective on the events that imbued those places with significance. Seeking ways to learn what stories aren't being told isn't just a creative challenge for engaged travelers—it's also a window into a fuller understanding of what happened in those places.

ENJOY THE PRIVILEGE OF SAYING
"I DON'T KNOW"

The master of the monastery asked Fayan why he was making the pilgrimage. "I don't know," said Fayan, to which the master responded, "Good. Not knowing is most intimate."
—Wansong Xingxiu, *Book of Equanimity* (1224)

When Mary Kingsley's memoir *Travels in West Africa* debuted in 1897, editors at *The Times* of London refused to review it, since its narrative was at odds with British imperialistic assumptions about cultures in that part of the world. Whereas Kingsley's male contemporaries went to great pains to establish their scholarly credentials and scientific erudition, Kingsley readily admitted her own ignorance, as well as the inherent limits of received information about Africa. "One by one I took my old ideas derived from books and thoughts based on imperfect knowledge and weighed them against the real life around me," she wrote, "and found them either worthless or wanting."

As travelers, we're often fixated on identifying certainties about the places we visit—particularly at the outset of the journey, when knowing exchange rates and bus routes and cultural norms helps orient us in unfamiliar environments. As the journey deepens, however, it's useful to admit the limits of what we know—and can know—about the places we visit. Whereas, at home, knowledge is central to our sense of esteem and status, admitting what we don't know as outsiders is often the most essential step in making ourselves vulnerable to new places.

In doing so, we leave ourselves receptive to a humbler, more curious understanding of a complicated world. "What we recognize and applaud as honesty and transparency in an individual is actually the humble demeanor of the apprentice," wrote poet David Whyte in *Consolations*, "someone paying extreme attention . . . someone who does not have all the answers but who is attempting to learn what they can, about themselves and those with whom they share the journey."

NOMADIC LIFE REFLECTS HUMANKIND'S ORIGINAL CONDITION

The urge to migrate, to quest, to go on a journey, is deep-seated—ancestral, essential and instinctive. . . . Living your whole life in the village, town or city of your birth is a relatively recent, anomalous development.

—Felix Marquardt, *The New Nomads* (2021)

An initial cause of anxiety for some readers of my 2003 book *Vagabonding* was its advice to showcase long-term travel on one's résumé instead of hiding it from potential employers. By the end of the 2000s, nervous reader emails had ceased—in part because economic shifts were upending traditional employment practices, but also because the ubiquity of Wi-Fi and digital videoconferencing had made it easier to blend work with long-term journeys. In 2009 *The Economist* noted that flexibility and a willingness to travel made young people more employable, and by the mid-2010s the term "digital nomad" was being used to describe people who used telecommunications technologies to enable location-independent work.

Digital nomadism is, in fact, just the latest manifestation of a human tendency to prize mobility. In 1868 the rise of railroads and steamships compelled *Putnam's Monthly* to declare, "If the social history of the world is ever written, the era in which we live will be called the nomadic period." This glib pronouncement overlooked the fact that, prior to about twelve thousand years ago, nomadism was the essential condition of humankind. Early hunter-gatherers and pastoralists didn't possess much material wealth, but their geographical flexibility made them healthier, less patriarchal, and safer from invasion and natural disasters than people who lived in settled communities.

Regardless of whether or not you elect to mix your travels with work, taking one's life on the road isn't something that is done in defiance of conventional civilization; it's a modern expression of the way people have always lived.

TRAVEL FIRST, THEN (IF YOU WANT) BECOME A DIGITAL NOMAD

> It is mobility, consumption, communication, and leisure—not labor or work—that create meaning and identity for nomadic peoples.
>
> —Eric J. Leed, *The Mind of the Traveler* (1991)

When the rise of location-independent work became a media "trend" in the late 2010s, many stories focused on travelers who were said to be driving up prices, straining infrastructure, and socializing in English-speaking bubbles that excluded locals in digital nomad hotspots like Tulum and Bali. Many of these problems were tied to the fact that a growing percentage of digital nomads were moving directly from North America to co-living spaces full of North Americans in Chiang Mai and Tbilisi and Medellín.

Economic and infrastructural complications aside, one risk of embracing digital nomadism before first immersing oneself in open-ended cross-cultural travel is that workers tend to superimpose their old habits and assumptions onto a new place—often working longer hours abroad than they do back home. This is in fact at odds with thousands of years of traditional nomadic practice. "Leisure, rather than labor, is a primary value in nomadic societies," wrote historian Eric J. Leed in *The Mind of the Traveler,* noting that many nomads met their subsistence needs with less than three person-days of work per week. "All observers of such societies have been impressed by how little work hunter-gatherers and pastoralists do."

Though new technologies have made nomadic life as varied and far-flung as ever, don't restrict your cross-cultural engagement and recreational off-time in distant places to the hypothetical life you advertise on social media. When in doubt, travel the world before you become a digital nomad—not just to create separation from your home life, but to get a fuller sense for where in the world you might want to stay for a while.

BECOME AN EXPATRIATE AT SOME POINT IN YOUR TRAVEL LIFE

Paris was a fine place to be quite young in, and a necessary part of a man's education.

—Ernest Hemingway, "A Paris Letter" (1933)

One of the more resonant bits of travel-related advice I read in the glossy-magazine era was part of a "60 Things a Man Must Do in His Lifetime" feature in a bygone issue of *Men's Journal*. There, amid admonitions to master the art of woodworking and learn to tie a proper Windsor knot, was a mini-essay entitled "Be an Expat" by novelist and former Peace Corps volunteer Bob Shacochis. "Go among strangers in strange lands," he wrote. "Sniff, lick, and swallow the mysteries. Learn to say clearly in an unpronounceable language, 'Please, I very much need a toilet. A doctor. Change for a 500,000 note. I very much need a friend.' . . . Stop at a crossroads where nothing is familiar . . . and the vibes are just plain alien, and stay long enough to truly be there."

Becoming an expatriate—that is, committing yourself to live in a foreign country for an extended period of time—puts you into an intensified relationship with places that goes beyond travel. Indeed, the two years I spent teaching English in Busan in my twenties were more than just a way for me to experience Korean culture: It became, as critic Malcolm Cowley said of Paris in the 1920s, "a great machine for stimulating the nerves and sharpening the senses."

Living as an expatriate offers you a new perspective not just on a foreign environment, but on yourself. "You'll learn to engage the world, not fear it, or at least not to be paralyzed by your fear of it," Shacochis wrote. "When you come back home, it's never quite all the way."

COUNTERBALANCE YOUR JOURNEY
WITH STILLNESS

> In some ways, the very movement of the world around us en-
> forces the need for stillness. Movement is almost the first act of
> a symphony that stillness must complete.
> —Pico Iyer, "A New Kind of Travel for a New Kind of World" (2006)

Toward the end of his 2012 travel memoir *The Longest Way Home*, actor and writer Andrew McCarthy ruminated on the way his global journeys have made him appreciate parts of himself that lie beyond the act of travel itself. "There is a pure, still place in me that remains mine alone," McCarthy wrote. "It is that place I first encountered as a child in my front yard, under the stars, it is the place from which I move out into the world, the place from which so much that is good in my life has sprung."

For all the movement that characterizes travel, sometimes the most potent realizations of a journey come not from motion, but from stillness. That is, instead of finding things to do as we move through the world, it can behoove us to simply find ways to *be*—to pause for a moment and let the world move through us. Travel thus has an ironic way of underscoring stillness, since when we're at home—immersed in routines and rote obligations and multitasking and technological distraction—we are profoundly uncomfortable with the notion of not being busy.

Indeed, at a certain point in your travels it becomes useful to focus your journey less on achievements than appreciation—to slow down, listen more, look longer, and learn to savor exactly where you are. As Pico Iyer noted in the speech that inspired his 2014 book *The Art of Stillness*, "A journey is only as meaningful as the stillness that underwrites it."

SEEK A NEW KIND OF SILENCE AS YOU TRAVEL

Wherever you are is called Here,
And you must treat it as a powerful stranger,
Must ask permission to know it and be known.
. . . Stand still. The forest knows
Where you are.
You must let it find you.

—David Wagoner, "Lost" (1999)

American avant-garde musician John Cage is best known for
$4'33''$, his 1952 composition wherein performers are instructed to
not play their instruments for a duration of four minutes and thirty-
three seconds. Initially assumed to be about silence, $4'33''$ was in fact
about attuning oneself to sounds that haven't been created for our
consumption. "There's no such thing as silence," Cage told an interviewer in 1968. "What we think is silence is full of accidental sounds."
Indeed, as audiences sat through Cage's composition, they became attuned to the ambient room noises they'd previously never listened for.
In a sense, $4'33''$ wasn't about absolute silence, but what happens when
we stop creating noise.

At home, "creating noise" is one of the ways we seek to occupy the
time we're otherwise unsure what to do with. Faced with an empty
moment, we invariably fill it with passive entertainments and social
media distractions. Instead of leaving space for silence, we fill our
emptinesses with comforting chatter. On the road, where each day
puts us into conversation with new places, we're given the opportunity to not just hear, but listen—to forgo the diversions of compulsive
chatter and leave space for what we might otherwise have never
known was there.

TRAVEL IS AN INHERENTLY SPIRITUAL UNDERTAKING

That is key to the idea of pilgrimage. You can't just press a button, download an app, send out a tweet and get through a particularly dark moment in your life. You have to go on a journey.
—Bruce Feiler, "You Have to Go on a Journey" (2015)

The rite of pilgrimage has, over the millennia, become an expression of religious faith not because it's required for belief, but because the very act of taking a journey compels one to put belief into perspective. In moving away from home to seek the sacred, pilgrims of various faiths have found themselves in a liminal state that goes beyond theology. Belonging to no single place for the duration of the journey, the corporeal act of travel forces pilgrims to reflect on the passing nature of life itself. "The geographical pilgrimage is the symbolic acting out of an inner journey," wrote Thomas Merton in his 1967 book *Mystics and Zen Masters*. "One can have one without the other. It is best to have both."

Modern travel, whether or not it's consciously undertaken as a pilgrimage, can become a spiritual undertaking by the very act of transposing your inner journey with a physical one. Since material things only serve to weigh you down as you travel, you want and need less. Away from the familiar, you're forced to make sense of what is not familiar; away from comforts, you're forced to deal with discomforts; away from what you know, you're forced to come to terms with what you don't know. Your senses are heightened and your ego is leavened in the ongoing experience of new contexts. Even in moments of difficulty, you become more attuned to the here and now, and more receptive to gratitude and wonder.

TRAVEL CAN BE A WAY OF IMMERSING YOU IN THE MOMENT

Now is your life. Live it. Love it. That's all you can do. You won't get anything else. You won't get another moment.
—Ryan Holiday, "Never Wish Away a Minute of Your Life" (2021)

In the 1920s, as an economic boom had Americans working harder than ever, a cottage resort industry sprang up in New York's Catskill Mountains. For stressed-out city dwellers, spending a week immersed in nature became an unexpectedly spiritual experience. "At the little hill farm, we bathe our souls in a delicious now," one visitor reported. "The straining forward for a better tomorrow is stopped a bit."

As much as ever, travel continues to be an opportunity to experience the "delicious now"—to cast off concerns about the future (and regrets about the past), and embrace life as it is happening in real time. Far from home, encountering novelties that we don't fully understand, we're more compelled to just exist in the moment. This is something we do naturally in childhood, before the duties of life condition a spontaneous sense of wonder out of us. On the road, we can find ourselves steered back—often by utter surprise—into a naive sense of presence.

Since it is not wise to restrict notions of peace and happiness to the past or the future, the experience of the present moment is a sacred ideal in most all spiritual traditions. Yet developing this heightened sense of presence also carries the utilitarian objective of not letting us take our days for granted. As travel brings us into a state of increased attention to the moments we encounter, it compels us to contemplate rather than react, to ponder instead of plan, and to pay fuller attention to the miracle of life itself.

AT A CERTAIN POINT IN THE JOURNEY, THE ROAD BECOMES HOME

> Birds in flight, claims the architect Vincenzo Volentieri, are not *between* places, they carry their places with them. We never wonder where they live: they are at home in the sky, in flight. Flight is their way of being in the world.
>
> —Geoff Dyer, *Out of Sheer Rage* (1997)

In describing his early-nineteenth-century journey from Serbia to Egypt on horseback, English traveler Alexander Kinglake spoke of a moment in Turkey when he felt like the road itself had become his home. "[Travel] becomes your mode of life, and you ride, eat, drink, and curse the mosquitoes as systematically as your friends in England eat, drink, and sleep," he wrote in his book *Eothen*. "If you are wise, you will not look upon the long period of time thus occupied in actual movement as the mere gulf dividing you from the end of your journey, but rather as one of those rare and plastic seasons of your life from which . . . you may love to date the molding of your character—that is, your very identity. Once feel this, and you will soon grow happy and contented in your saddle-home."

Most extended journeys have a way, in time, of blurring the instinctive line between the home you left behind and the place where you find yourself on a given day. The notion of home becomes an internalized concept as you begin to feel somewhat at home everywhere—or, at least, you begin to enjoy a heightened sense of comfort and normalcy amid the ongoing unfamiliarity of travel.

"Travel is at its most rewarding," wrote Paul Theroux in *Ghost Train to the Eastern Star,* "when it ceases to be about your reaching a destination and becomes indistinguishable from living your life."

TRAVEL CAN LEAVE YOU WITH GRATITUDE FOR LIFE

Travel! Set out and head for pastures new—
Life tastes the richer when you've road-worn feet.
No water that stagnates is fit to drink,
for only that which flows is truly sweet.

—Imam al-Shafi'i, *Al-Risala* (c. 820)

Amid my first vagabonding trip across North America at age twenty-three, I was intrigued by a public ritual I found in Florida's Key West. At the end of each day, a group of people would gather in Mallory Square and break into applause as the sun sank down into the seascape west of the island. At the time, I was so impressed by this rite that I attempted to practice it each day for the rest of my journey. Even if I didn't clap out loud, I tried to give my full attention to the sunset, and savor the day I had just experienced. I loved the idea that I could take time at the end of each day and celebrate a moment I might otherwise have ignored; in my journal, I referred to it as "exercising my awe muscle."

I have since learned that applauding the sunset isn't unique to Key West: In Brazil, folks did it at Rio's Arpoador Rock; on the Greek island of Santorini, I witnessed the ritual in the cliffside village of Oia. While the popularity of this rite might make it seem less special (indeed, one backpacker I met in Oia called it "that corny tourist thing"), clapping at sunsets isn't the only way to honor the heightened sense of attention a journey can give us. In teaching us to appreciate rather than accumulate—to seek awe rather than outcomes—travel can be an ongoing exercise in gratitude.

November 26

RETURNING TO PLACES IS A
PLEASURE OF TRAVEL

> Returning to a place is one of the little pleasures of travel: you
> perceive it differently over the years, and it reminds you of who
> you once were, and often enough the whole experience spills
> over into a thoroughly pleasant melancholy.
> —Richard Todd, "Las Vegas, 'Tis of Thee" (2001)

Sinclair Lewis's 1929 novel *Dodsworth,* which satirized the European travel habits of middle-class Americans, asserted that a person doesn't properly experience a place until he pays it a return visit.
"He who has seen one cathedral ten times has seen something; he
who has seen ten cathedrals once has seen but little; and he who has
spent half an hour in each of a hundred cathedrals has seen nothing
at all," he noted. "Four hundred pictures all on a wall are four hundred
times less interesting than one picture; and no one knows a cafe till he
has gone there often enough to know the names of the waiters. These
are the laws of travel."

Though Lewis's observation was framed as a takedown of tourism,
it hinted at the very real merit of returning to a place to get to know it
better. Indeed, for all the joys of seeking out new places on the road,
returning to a place that has captured your imagination is one of the
keenest pleasures of travel. Even when you can't replicate the energy
of your initial visit, returning allows you to seek subtleties and serendipities you may have missed before.

Revisiting a place you've come to love is, in a way, like revisiting a
part of yourself: Though it feels familiar in many ways, it can still surprise you, and yield deeper understandings as it leavens cherished
memories with new perspectives.

IT'S OKAY TO FEEL TRAVEL BURNOUT SOMETIMES

The truth is that our travel anticipations, and our memories, have a way of holding only the most striking parts of an experience—the parts that don't cause burnout.

—Matt Kepnes, *Ten Years a Nomad* (2019)

Toward the end of his long-term travel memoir *Ten Years a Nomad*, blogger Matt Kepnes pinpointed the moment when—amid his multiyear global journey—he began to feel weary of travel. "Burnout can seem like the ultimate in ingratitude," Kepnes wrote. "What's there to be tired of? . . . You are seeing famous attractions, meeting people from all over the world trying new cuisine. . . . You get to do whatever you want, whenever you want. . . . And what, you're *over it*? So you'll ask yourself, like I asked myself: *Why am I not enjoying this more? What's wrong with my trip? What's wrong with me?*"

The condition Kepnes described is not a new one. In 49 C.E., the Roman philosopher Seneca skewered travelers whose wanderings begin to bore them. "They make one journey after another and change spectacle for spectacle," he wrote. "We must realize that our difficulty is not the fault of the places but of ourselves." For Kepnes, burnout was tied to his early assumption that travel's epiphanies wouldn't be offset by a host of workaday hassles and banalities. "When you're planning a trip, all you see is excitement," he wrote. "You forget that travel can settle into a routine just as easily as office life can."

Indeed, one reason travel can be fatiguing is that it's a part of life—and life itself has its ups and downs. Ultimately, it's good to know when to slow down, to linger in one place—or even to go home and save your energy for a time when you get the desire to travel again.

INDEFINITE WANDERING CAN YIELD DIMINISHING RETURNS

We've never managed, either one of us, to get all the way into life. We're hanging on to the outside for all we're worth, convinced we're going to fall off at the next bump.
—Port to Kit, in Paul Bowles's *The Sheltering Sky* (1949)

One of the most quoted lines about the tourist/traveler dichotomy comes from Paul Bowles's postwar existentialist novel, *The Sheltering Sky*. "Whereas the tourist generally hurries back home at the end of a few weeks or months," Bowles wrote, "the traveler, belonging no more to one place than to the next, moves slowly, over periods of years, from one part of the earth to another." This line refers to the book's protagonists, a privileged American couple named Port and Kit, who have just arrived in North Africa after having traveled from place to place (Europe, the Near East, South America) for most of their twelve-year marriage.

Though Bowles's tourist/traveler line is usually quoted approvingly (I have done so myself), Port and Kit do not prove to be exemplary travelers. Ignorant of North African culture, rudderless in their meanderings, and burdened with too much luggage, the Americans' idealized, self-congratulatory notion of travel doesn't match up to the ongoing reality of horrible meals, filthy hotels, and questionable companions. Both Port and Kit prove sexually unfaithful to each other; Port dies of typhus, and Kit disappears into the streets of an Algerian coastal city after suffering a mental breakdown.

Grim and pitiless, *The Sheltering Sky* isn't a celebration of being a "traveler" so much as it is an illustration of the alienation that can result from too many years of aimlessness; a warning that travel for travel's sake yields diminishing returns when it becomes unmoored from any sense of community or continuity.

HOME IS SOMETIMES THE NEXT OBVIOUS DESTINATION

> You couldn't travel forever. When you stopped seeing, when you lost your curiosity and openness to the world, it was time to return to your starting point and see where you stood.
>
> —Carl Hoffman, *The Lunatic Express* (2010)

Back in the 1990s, before the rise of blogs and social media, I researched my travels on a Usenet newsgroup called travel.rec. In addition to practical tips, I enjoyed the humor posts, where users poked fun at travelers suffering from ailments like "Exaggeritis" and "Inflamed Spirituality." Years later, when I'd accumulated more vagabonding experience, I came to realize that such chronic maladies as "Constipated Payment Disorder" (aggressive haggling for already cheap items) and "Eternal Friendship Delusion" (intense bonding between people who will never see each other again) tended to recur among travelers who'd been on the road for too long.

Part of the reason people overextend a journey is tied into the initial thrill of being on the road—of realizing how much there is to see in the world, how cheap and easy it is to keep traveling, and how there might not be a better time to do it. Yet the point of a long-term journey isn't to travel indefinitely: The point is to travel in such a way that it deepens and diversifies your life.

If there comes a point when the sense of novelty and discovery is not as strong as it felt earlier in the journey, sometimes the best way to sharpen these enthusiasms is to head back home. Travel is not an endurance contest, after all, and there are times when the best way to maintain a lifelong relationship with travel is to take the journey back to familiar ground and renew your sense for what makes it special.

COMING FULL CIRCLE IS PART OF THE POINT OF A JOURNEY

> A man travels the world over in search of what he needs and returns home to find it.
>
> —George Moore, *The Brook Kerith* (1916)

Of all the strangeness that one encounters on a journey, sometimes the strangest travel experience of all is coming back home and seeing that once-familiar place with new eyes. "The only way to [see one's home] is to go somewhere else: and that is the real object of travel," wrote English author G. K. Chesterton in his 1909 book *Tremendous Trifles*. "The whole object of travel is not to set foot on foreign land; it is at last to set foot on one's own country as a foreign land."

Part of the reason home can seem like a new place when we return to it at the end of a journey is tied to the awakened spirit of travel itself. Having been away from the routines that once defined our lives, we reenter those home routines with a new sense of perspective; having experienced time in a slower way on the road, we're less likely to let a day slip by; having become comfortable with traveling within faraway cultures, being back in our home culture feels strangely exotic.

What feels novel about home has less to do with how it has changed than with how *we* have changed. In coming full circle, we haven't finished the journey so much as found a way to bring its lessons into a specific context, one that finds itself in humble conversation with the greater world. As a saying attributed to thirteenth-century Persian poet Rumi put it: "It may be that the satisfaction I need depends on my going away, so that when I've gone and come back, I'll find it at home."

THE MOST IMPORTANT DISTANCE TRAVELED
IS WITHIN ONESELF

Where we had thought to travel outward, we will come to the center of our own existence.
—Joseph Campbell, *The Power of Myth* (1988)

The ritual of travel has been considered a signifier of social status since the days it was first done for pleasure, but its biggest gift has always been the way it offers the traveler possibilities for belonging to the world (and to the people in it) in ways that wouldn't have revealed themselves at home.

I got my first sense for this when I returned stateside from my earliest international journeys. To my mild disappointment, few of the folks I reunited with back home were interested in hearing me hold forth in granular detail about my travels—but, curiously, most all of them made offhand observations to the effect that I seemed more grounded and self-possessed than I had been when they'd last seen me.

Ultimately, travel isn't about creating a worldlier persona that you project on others; it's about realigning your values through action, and rediscovering a fuller sense of self. Travel isn't about embracing cutting-edge destination trends; it's about embracing parts of your being that you didn't previously know existed. Travel isn't about fine-tuning your self-presentation; it's about breaking open a more personal love of the world, and a deeper love of yourself.

In this way, travel allows one to move beyond what philosopher Jean-Jacques Rousseau called *amour-propre* (that is, the kind of self-love that hinges on the opinions of others) and embrace *amour-de-soi*, the self-love that arises from a life that is lived on its own terms. The irony here is that in creating a life unique to yourself—free of others' opinions—you are more likely to win the esteem of other people.

DON'T SET LIMITS ON WHEN THE FORMAL JOURNEY ENDS

The surprises, liberations, and clarifications of travel can sometimes be garnered by going around the block as well as going around the world.

—Rebecca Solnit, *Wanderlust* (2000)

One great thing about returning home from a soul-enriching journey is that you can take the openness and engagement of your travel attitude and apply it to the life you live at home. On the road, you naturally "play games" with your day: watching, waiting, listening; allowing things to happen. And the more you become accustomed to doing this in distant places, the more you enable yourself to embrace the same attitude at home.

Oftentimes, bringing the attitude of travel back home is a matter of pushing back against the dull fears and routines that might have limited the life you lived before you sought out a more far-flung sense for the world—and the open-to-anything confidence you sharpen on the road can be utilized to rejuvenate relationships with friends and family, explore new concepts and strategies in a business setting, or simply meet new people and seek out new places in your hometown.

Just as the open horizons of travel compel you to break old habits and test out new facets of your personality on the road, seeking open horizons in the landscape of home can ensure that the journey never truly ends. Indeed, in refusing to set limits for what is possible on a given day (even at home) you open yourself up to an entire new world of possibility.

ONE RETURNS FROM A JOURNEY WITH NEW PERSPECTIVE

In outer space you develop an instant global consciousness, a people orientation, an intense dissatisfaction with the state of the world, and a compulsion to do something about it.
—Astronaut Edgar Mitchell, in a 1974 interview

American writer Ken Ilgunas felt a twinge of anger when, in his early twenties, he beheld the sublime splendor of Alaska's night sky for the first time. "It was as if I'd just learned of an inheritance that had been stolen from me," he wrote in his 2013 book *Walden on Wheels*. "If it wasn't for Alaska, I might have gone my whole life without knowing what a real sky was supposed to look like, which made me wonder: If I'd gone the first quarter of my life without seeing a real sky, what other sensations, what other glories . . . had the foul cloud of civilization hid from my view?"

The existential context that Ilgunas gained by looking into an unpolluted starscape echoes the lessons of "Icaromenippus, an Aerial Expedition," a dialogue by second-century Greek poet Lucian, in which the narrator flies into the sky and views the world from above. Gazing down from the heavens, he sees how comically small even the richest citizens and settlements now appeared. "What men and cities suggested to me was so many ant-hills," he marvels. "The proudest of our rich men, methought, was the cultivator of an Epicurean atom."

Though modern travel allows us to view both the heavens and the earth from intoxicating new vantage points, the epiphanies evoked by Ilgunas and Lucian might best be understood in a more metaphorical sense: In taking us away from our own familiar comforts and routines, a journey allows us to come back with a profound new perspective on what in our lives is important.

TRAVEL ALLOWS YOU TO SEE HOME AS A NEW DESTINATION

We travel long roads and cross water to see what we disregard when it is under our eyes.

—Pliny the Younger, *Epistulae VIII* (106 C.E.)

When the German poet Johann Wolfgang von Goethe visited Italy's Lake Garda in 1786, he was so impressed by the beauty of a fortress overlooking the water that he immediately sat down and began to sketch it. Local villagers, not used to seeing anyone take such a fascination with their castle, assumed he was an Austrian spy and placed him under arrest. Goethe defended his actions not by clarifying his geopolitical loyalties, but by extolling the splendor of the medieval buildings that lay before them. In declaring his exuberant good intentions, Goethe thus helped the locals appreciate the value of a landscape they had, out of workaday habit, ceased to see. Chastened, they set him free.

The inability to appreciate the familiar landscapes of home is a conundrum that goes back at least to the time of the first century, when Pliny the Younger noted how jaded Roman citizens had become to the splendors of their own city. "Whatever the reason," he wrote, "there are numbers of things in this city of ours and its environs which we have not even heard of, much less seen; yet, if they were in Greece or Egypt or Asia . . . we could have heard all about them, read all about them, looked over all there was to see."

This in mind, travel to distant places should allow us to regard the return home not as the disappointing end of the journey, but as a new destination. Unburdening us of day-to-day routines and familiarities, travel thus allows us to rediscover and explore these once-familiar places in a whole new way.

COMING HOME CAN BE A DIFFICULT PART OF THE JOURNEY

When you return home, you miss being a stranger in a strange land. You find it lonesome to be out in public and receive no extra attention or hospitality.

—Bart Schaneman, in *The Week* (2016)

For all the challenges of long-term travel, the final step—coming home—can be a curiously difficult part of the journey. When English adventurer Jason Lewis completed his record-setting human-powered circumnavigation of the globe in 2007, he found it unsettling to arrive back where he'd started. "When I came home, it was a huge anticlimax," he told writer Dave Seminara. "I felt like one of those cartoon characters who falls off a cliff but their legs keep turning." For some travelers, this anticlimax is so acute that it can bleed into the journey itself, as Seminara himself admitted in his 2021 book *Mad Travelers*. "Midway through a trip, I start to lose sleep," he wrote, "because I'm already dreading going home."

The ongoing stimulation and serendipities that come with immersive travel have a way of making home seem like an alien place. Old rituals that used to bring low-stakes pleasure—indulging in your favorite snacks, or mindlessly surfing the internet—no longer have the same appeal, and the friends and family you left behind hardly know what to ask about your trip, let alone appreciate its subtler epiphanies.

For travelers experiencing this for the first time, it can feel like something fundamental about home has changed, but the most significant change has typically taken place in the traveler herself. The best way to confront this altered sense of self is to embrace your own home as an exotic new stop on a journey that hasn't fully ended.

December 6

TRAVEL CAN DEEPEN ONE'S APPRECIATION FOR HOME

Surely one advantage of traveling is that, while it removes much prejudice against foreigners and their customs, it intensifies ten-fold one's appreciation of the good at home.

—Isabella Bird, *A Lady's Life in the Rocky Mountains* (1879)

In the 1939 MGM movie *The Wizard of Oz*, Dorothy's fantastical adventures along the Yellow Brick Road to Emerald City culminate in the heroine finding her way back to the place where she started. "Oh, Auntie Em, there's no place like home!" Dorothy exclaims in the movie's final scene, nestled in her Kansas bedroom.

When I was growing up in Kansas decades later, many of my classmates had a far less sentimental attitude about home. A popular T-shirt when I was in middle school read: "Dear Aunt Em: Hate You! Hate Kansas! Taking the Dog. Dorothy." Part of my classmates' frustration with Kansas was that it felt provincial and boring, yet when I moved to the West Coast years later, many of my university classmates—people from cool-seeming places like Seattle and Anchorage and Boise—also expressed feeling limited by life in the places where they grew up.

Indeed, part of one's relationship with home, particularly early in life, is the insistent desire to leave it. Yet traveling away from it, especially for an extended time, is a great way to appreciate it in a deeper and richer way. In taking you away from your own nation, travel allows you to enjoy the comforts and privileges (things as basic as clean water and consistent electricity, old friends and community connections) that you had previously taken for granted. In taking you full circle to reexperience these privileges, travel becomes a way of appreciating them in a new way.

COMING HOME ALLOWS YOU TO REINVENT WHAT HOME IS

> The question of where one lives or dwells . . . is not a simple
> matter of residential geography. It is also a matter of emotional
> geography.
>
> —Naomi Rosh White, *Home and Away* (2007)

One of my most satisfying travel acts since I departed on my first long-term journey nearly three decades ago was not some intrepid feat on a distant continent: It came in the spring of 2005, through the simple act of getting a house of my own, on thirty acres of prairie near my family in north-central Kansas. Domestic as this gesture might seem, I consider it a key moment in my global journey.

In his 2011 book *Falling Upward* Franciscan friar (and native Kansan) Richard Rohr noted that, for all the modern connotations of the word *odyssey*, Homer's ancient story of Odysseus's far-flung adventures is at heart about a man trying to find his way back to a familiar place. "The whole story is set in the matrix of seeking to find home and then to return there," Rohr wrote, "and thus refining and defining what home really is."

In a globalized world, where we are no longer bound to geographical places like previous generations were, the task of defining and refining home has become a more fluid and emotional process—one that can be clarified by the process of travel. Even if you already have a concrete sense for home before your travels, a journey can help you redefine and reappreciate your relationship to that home. And one amazing thing that travel teaches you is that coming home—or finding home—after a long trip doesn't spell the end to your wandering; it simply deepens your relationship to adventures still to come.

TRAVEL OFFERS NEW PERSPECTIVES ON THE FAMILIAR

> The Westerner, of course, took his riches and wonder for granted, just as I had never noticed the enchantment of the East or its mystery. . . . As with the Westerner, the Easterner was never so bored as he was when on his own shores.
>
> —Nguyen Viet Thanh, *The Sympathizer* (2015)

When I was younger, I used to get irritated at the stereotypes visitors brought to Kansas. Sensitive to my home state's reputation for being more provincial and conservative (and far less exciting) than states that boasted beaches, national parks, and sprawling metropolises, I bristled at people's naive observations about a place I felt I knew well. It wasn't until I began traveling in earnest—and became aware of the naive point of view I took to other places—that I began to appreciate their perspective.

In Nguyen Viet Thanh's novel *The Sympathizer,* the Vietnam-born narrator becomes perplexed when he reads about his own country in *Fodor's Southeast Asia.* "Everything my guidebook said was true and also meaningless. Yes, the East was vast, teeming, and infinitely complex, but wasn't the West also? . . . But what did I know? I had only lived there, and people who live in a given place may have difficulty seeing its charms as well as its faults, both of which are easily available to the tourist's freshly peeled eyes."

Several decades into my travel career, having once again made Kansas my home, I have come to realize that the fresh eyes of my visitors often remind me of things I've stopped appreciating. While some guests note the same dull stereotypes that irritated me years ago, their perspective also reminds me to appreciate the merits of my home state (big skies, friendly neighbors, a slow-paced way of living) that I might otherwise take for granted.

SEE FAMILIAR MOMENTS IN THE SPIRIT OF EXOTIC ONES

Life isn't short. We just waste it. We waste it wishing for things to be otherwise. We waste it by ignoring what's in front of us.
—Ryan Holiday, "Never Wish Away a Minute of Your Life" (2021)

The most indelible memory I have of the bicycle journey I took across Myanmar in my late twenties involves a nighttime ferry ride across the Irrawaddy River. Since the journey involved a number of river crossings in places that didn't appear on my map, I'm not sure where exactly I was; all I know was that, in the dim light, with the stars glowing above and the moon glittering across the water, I felt unmoored from past and future. Fully present, I felt fully alive.

Perhaps it was because I wasn't exactly sure where I was when this happened that I recall it as a special moment in my life. I have since come to realize that travel is not the only time I can feel this way. Thich Nhat Hanh's 1975 book *The Miracle of Mindfulness* asserts that even a task so ordinary as washing dishes can be an exercise in being fully alive. "At first glance, that might seem a little silly," he wrote. "Why put so much stress on a simple thing? But that's precisely the point. The fact that I am standing there and washing these bowls is a wondrous reality."

Ever since reading this, I have come to regard the act of washing my own dishes as a kind of homebound travel exercise—a reminder that life itself is an ongoing journey, and the ever-present goal of the traveler is to appreciate the simple (and eternal) resonance of whatever task is before him.

December 10

AVOID BEING A PRETENTIOUS
RETURNED TRAVELER

> We wish to learn all the curious, outlandish ways of all the dif-
> ferent countries, so that we can "show off" and astonish people
> when we get home. . . . The gentle reader will never, never know
> what a consummate ass he can become until he goes abroad.
> —Mark Twain, *The Innocents Abroad* (1869)

One of the harshest critics of travel as a form of education was the
Scottish economist Adam Smith. In his 1776 treatise *The Wealth
of Nations,* Smith digressed from economics to complain about how
Grand Tour journeys were turning Britain's young aristocrats into
pretentious nitwits. "The traveler commonly returns home more con-
ceited," he wrote, "more unprincipled, more dissipated, and more in-
capable of any serious application . . . than he could well have become
in so short a time had he lived at home."

As it happened, Smith had recently spent thirty-two months traveling the Continent as a Grand Tour tutor, and the experience allowed
him to meet the greatest philosophers of his time. Whenever he blus-
tered to his colleagues about meeting Voltaire in Geneva or Benjamin
Franklin in Paris, Smith was indulging in his own flavor of traveler's
pretension.

One century later, American humorist Mark Twain took a more
self-deprecating approach by admitting that one can turn into a "consummate ass" in enthusing about one's travels. "I speak now in the
supposition that the gentle reader has not been abroad and therefore
is not already a consummate ass," he wrote in *The Innocents Abroad.*
"If the case be otherwise, I beg his pardon and extend to him the cordial hand of fellowship and call him brother."

Often, what is seen as pretension to folks back home feels like innocent enthusiasm to the returned traveler himself. After the journey
is over, enthusing about your travels counts for less with folks back
home than quietly showing how the experience has deepened your
life.

DON'T FLAUNT YOUR JOURNEY; INTERNALIZE IT

> When a traveler returneth home, let him not leave the countries where he hath traveled altogether behind him . . . and let his travel appear rather in his discourse than in his apparel or gesture.
>
> —Francis Bacon, "Of Travel" (1625)

As travel advice goes, philosopher Francis Bacon's suggestions to Englishmen taking the seventeenth-century Grand Tour across Europe are curiously relevant to modern-day travelers. Historical differences in customs and conveyance notwithstanding, the insights in his 1625 essay "Of Travel" readily apply to twenty-first-century wanderers: Seek a mix of scenic, artistic, and cultural sights in a place, he advises; find travel companions who aren't petty and quarrelsome; embrace a variety of experiences within a single location; mix a good guidebook with local sources of information; keep a detailed travel journal; learn from your experiences each day as you go.

Some of Bacon's most astute advice doesn't apply to travel itself so much as to how one should let the journey inform life when one arrives back home. Making the most of a long-term journey isn't a matter of showcasing flashy new souvenirs and mannerisms, but of quietly incorporating a broadened perspective into one's daily life. In internalizing the lessons of travel, Bacon advises the traveler not to boast of his new perspective in social settings, "but only prick in some flowers of that he hath learned abroad into the customs of his own country."

Though long-term travel to distant countries is no longer a signifier of aristocratic prestige, it's useful to embrace Bacon's attitude of engaged humbleness when you return home from a journey. As was the case half a millennium ago, the truest accomplishments of travel come not in the way we compare to our neighbors, but in the more assured way we relate to ourselves.

TRAVEL MAKES "HOME" A MORE DYNAMIC PLACE

Home brings together memory and longing, . . . the affective and the physical, the spatial and the temporal, the local and global.

—Nigel Rapport, *Migrants of Identity* (1998)

One of my all-time favorite Spanish words is *querencia,* which refers to the affection one feels for home, and the centered, rejuvenated feeling that results when one returns there to embrace its renewal and well-being. In feeling an attachment to one tiny corner of the world, *querencia* allows a person to develop a stronger sense for how human attachment to place reveals itself in other corners of the world.

As author Suzannah Lessard wrote in her 1977 *New Yorker* essay about *querencia,* the concept "is in many ways the opposite of patriotism; it is a humble, creaturely symbiosis unrelated to governments or power." Traveling to distant places to witness how other people create their lives at home thus gives us a stronger sense for our own connection to home. "Separation most effectively enlarges its meaning," Lessard noted.

Ultimately, for all the exciting possibilities one encounters when traveling to distant places, *querencia* allows a person to counterbalance ongoing movement with a lingering connection to home. In seeing how other people define and manifest home in faraway parts of the planet, one thus gains a stronger sense for what is essential about one's own home. In the process, travel allows one to return to that familiar place with a stronger sense for what in life is truly important.

TRAVEL MAKES "AWAY" A MORE DYNAMIC PLACE

After traveling long and far enough every mountain reminds you of another mountain. Every river summons another river. And you learn enough landmarks by which to love the whole world.
—Kate Harris, *Lands of Lost Borders* (2018)

A curious counterpoint to the feeling of *querencia* is the experience of topophilia, a concept popularized by a 1974 book of the same name by Chinese American geographer Yi-Fu Tuan. Whereas *querencia* is an intuitive attachment to one's home place, topophilia is an intuitive appreciation of all the places that have made you who you are. "Diffuse as a concept, vivid and concrete as a personal experience," Tuan wrote, "*topophilia* . . . [is] the affective bond between people and place or setting."

Importantly, topophilia isn't something you can piece together from watching travel videos or accumulating sightseeing encounters—it's the result of actively navigating your way through a variety of landscapes and growing attached to the places that move you. Topophilia can emerge from most any life experience, but we are particularly susceptible to it as we travel. In bringing home a deepened appreciation for places we encounter on distant journeys, we put them into a conversation with all the other places that have given our lives meaning.

In a sense, topophilia might be understood as a kind of nostalgia for places that are invoked by the specific sensations—the smell of rain, the taste of jackfruit, the sound of a flute, the rumble of a passing train, the tingle in your muscles as you crest a hill, the chill of the air on an autumn day—that remind you of being in those places. In synthesizing the world's diverse textures into your experience of the ongoing moment, you're embracing a more dynamic way of being alive.

December 14

DON'T LET ROUTINES DIM THE EXPERIENCE OF HOME

> Wherever we live, to be on this planet at all is an extraordinary gift. The best way to show our gratitude is to learn as much as we can about where we live . . . since it's all a part of us.
> —Sophfronia Scott, *The Seeker and the Monk* (2021)

In his 1972 book *Invisible Cities*, novelist Italo Calvino wrote of a fantastical city called Phyllis, whose balustrades and onion domes dazzle upon first arrival, but begin to fade once the traveler begins to live there. "Like all of Phyllis's inhabitants, you follow zigzag lines from one street to another," Calvino wrote. "Phyllis is a space in which routes are drawn between points suspended in the void. . . . All the rest of the city is invisible. . . . Many are the cities like Phyllis, which elude the gaze of all, except the man who catches them by surprise."

Though Calvino's Phyllis is a fictional metropolis, he is alluding to the very real way that routine has a way of rendering places invisible. In allowing yourself to ignore the familiar parts of where you live, you thus run the risk of overlooking the subtle wonders and serendipities of your own life.

Fortunately, the best way of staying open to the nuances of home-adjacent places is to bring the attitude of travel into the life you live at home. This can be as simple as taking a new route to work each day, or as involved as formally studying the cultural history of your own neighborhood. The surprises you find along the way won't just make your days at home more interesting—they will also leave you with a sharpened sense of receptiveness for your eventual return to more distant places.

December 15

EMBRACE A TRAVEL-WON SENSE
OF SIMPLICITY AT HOME

> One does not accumulate but eliminate. It is not daily increase
> but daily decrease. The height of cultivation always runs to sim-
> plicity.
>
> —Bruce Lee, *Tao of Jeet Kune Do* (1975)

Life on the road naturally lends itself to simplicity, since travel
forces you to reduce your day-to-day possessions to a few select
items that fit in your suitcase or backpack. Moreover, since it's difficult
to accumulate new things as you travel, you tend to accumulate new
experiences and friendships instead—and these enhance your life in
ways mere "things" cannot.

Taking the attitude of simplicity back home can be a life-enriching
souvenir of the travel experience. If nothing else, abiding by the principles of simplicity can help you live in a more deliberate and time-
rich way. How much of what you buy and own at home really improves
the quality of your life? Are you accumulating new things out of necessity or out of compulsion? Do the things you own enable you to
live more vividly, or do they merely clutter up your life?

Once you reintegrate into your home routines, keep in mind how
the experiences of travel—not the things you collected along the
way—are usually what make the journey so memorable and rewarding.

This in mind, find ways to invest in new activities and relationships (rather than new possessions) in the life you live at home. A less
materialistic state of mind will not just make your home life more
engaged and satisfying; it will also help you save money as you begin
to dream up your next journey.

December 16

FIND WAYS TO HAVE TRAVEL ADVENTURES AT HOME

I began to turn closer to home looking for adventure. Searching for opportunities rather than groaning at the limitations in my life. I found short, local escapes that were compatible with real life. I called them microadventures.

—Alastair Humphreys, *My Midsummer Morning* (2019)

When I first met my wife, Kiki, we often talked about the distant places we dreamed of traveling to together—places like England, Kenya, Alaska, Borneo, and Vanuatu. Unfortunately, I'd met Kiki in the middle of the 2020 coronavirus pandemic, which meant that we couldn't travel very far. Kiki has Scandinavian ancestry, and I was intrigued by the adventures she'd had visiting her cousins in Norway. Since international travel wasn't possible, we elected to seek out Scandinavia in our home state of Kansas—specifically Lindsborg, an old immigrant town known as "Little Sweden."

Though Kiki and I had both visited Lindsborg before, this time we decided to travel the twenty-two miles there on foot. Hiking all day on dirt backroads, we wandered through prairie vistas we'd never seen before, and savored the simple task of taking things slow under a warm winter sun. We arrived on the *dala*-horse-fringed main street of Little Sweden just after sundown—exhausted and happy and marveling at how satisfying it was to spend seven hours immersed in the curiously exotic landscape that lay just beyond our home.

British adventurer and author Alastair Humphreys calls these close-to-home travels "microadventures"—simple, inexpensive initiatives (be it sleeping in your backyard or sipping whiskey with strangers at a nearby inn) that compel you to explore the world just beyond your front door. " 'Adventure' is not only crossing deserts and climbing mountains," Humphreys wrote. "Adventure can be found everywhere, every day, and it is up to us to seek it out."

GOING OUT TO EAT IS A WAY TO REVISIT THE JOURNEY

On speculating in which cultural surroundings Chinese food tastes best, the answer is not necessarily "China." . . . A global world city . . . operates like a reproductive machine that relatively swiftly multiplies any local attribute of one particular city in all other cities around the world.

—Boris Groys, "The City in the Age of Touristic Reproduction" (2006)

Perhaps the most elegant testament to the way that travel has transformed the world over the course of human history comes in the food we eat each day. A picnic spread at a typical North American barbecue (a word deriving from the Caribbean Arawak word *barabicu*) might include foods originally domesticated in Europe (beef and strawberries), China (chicken and peaches), the Middle East (wheat and almonds), India (cucumbers and limes), South America (peanuts and potatoes), Africa (watermelon and coffee), and Mexico (corn and chocolate).

Specific ingredients aside, ethnic dishes are often our first window into the flavors of distant places (rarely does one taste her first taco in Mexico, lasagna in Italy, or pho in Vietnam), and food can be a fun way to recall those places when we get home. Most any world city will feature a host of international dining options—Turkish *köfte* on offer in the same neighborhoods as Thai *tom yum* and Brazilian *galinhada*—and the local variations of these dishes tell an intriguing global story. As an aficionado of Korean food, for example, I can attest that the *bulgogi* one eats in Beaverton, Wichita, or Queens evokes aspects of those American places, each in a slightly different way, even as it recalls the flavors of Korea.

Seeking out these culinary subtleties—and comparing them to what you once tasted in distant lands—is one of the best ways to revisit the global journey.

GOING ON WALKS IS A WAY TO REVISIT THE JOURNEY

[Walking] stretches time and prolongs life. Walking makes the world much bigger and thus more interesting.
—Edward Abbey, *The Journey Home* (1977)

A curiously simple way to reintegrate the serendipity and discovery of the journey once you return home is by going for walks. In *Wanderlust*, her 2000 philosophical exploration of walking, Rebecca Solnit's case for striking out on foot near one's home is a matter of freeing oneself from the inherent isolation of indoor environments. "On foot everything stays connected, for while walking one occupies the spaces between those interiors in the same way one occupies those interiors," she wrote. "One lives in the whole world rather than in interiors built up against it."

Indeed, in an 1851 essay about walking, Henry David Thoreau pointed out that the English word *saunter* is related to the French phrase *sans terre*, which literally translates as "without land" but implies that one is equally at home everywhere. This in mind, going for a walk, even a short distance from home, re-creates the openhearted spirit of travel. "Two or three hours' walking will carry me to as strange a country as I expect ever to see," he wrote. "There is in fact a sort of harmony discoverable between the capabilities of the landscape within . . . the limits of an afternoon walk, and the threescore years and ten of human life. It will never become quite familiar to you."

December 19

EMBRACE THE KIND OF HOSPITALITY
YOU ONCE ENJOYED

What we learn of the world is never simply a result of how often
or how far we travel. It is just as intimately related to how sin-
cerely we receive strangers amongst us.
—Erve Chambers, "Can the Anthropology of Tourism Make Us Better
Travelers?" (2005)

Historically, the rite of hospitality—that is, of making strangers
welcome in your own community—has been underpinned by
two primary motivations. The first has to do with the fact that outsiders invariably make life at home more interesting. "The traveler [has
been seen as] a source of entertainment, of novelties, of comic relief,
as well as of new conceits and designs," Eric J. Leed wrote in his 1991
book *The Mind of the Traveler*. "Certain species of travelers—singers
of tales, bards (called *griots* in Africa), minstrels, comic actors,
mountebanks—specialized in these functions and were welcome and
honored guests."

The second major motivation for hospitality has been the simple
spirit of reciprocity—of offering generosity to outsiders in the faith
that the favor might be returned if you ever find yourself in a strange
land. For this reason, nomadic societies—cultures like the Bedouin of
the Arabian Desert, the Maasai of Nilotic Africa, and the Mongolians
of the Central Asian steppe—are famously hospitable. Knowing that a
life of constant travel occasionally leaves a person in need of assistance, nomads see offering food, drink, and shelter to strangers as a
core human virtue.

Returning from a journey has a way of attuning you to the kind of
hospitality you enjoyed when you were yourself a stranger in strange
lands. In making travelers feel welcome in your own home community, you are keeping the spirit of that journey alive.

DON'T SET LIMITS ON WHAT IS WORTH SEEING AT HOME

Savoring the moment, examining things closely, reminiscing—
these practices are not strictly for use on the road. They're for
everyday life, anywhere.
—Stephanie Rosenbloom, *Alone Time* (2018)

Back when I was a track athlete in high school, some of my favorite workouts involved keeping pace with my teammates Joey and Paul as they ran through their own neighborhood in Wichita's North End. Whereas the streets south of our school were leafy and residential, the North End was laced with railyards and hulking industrial structures like the Beachner Grain Elevator. I savored running there, in part because its working-class vibe made me feel like a character from *Rocky,* and in part because I got to see a part of my hometown that I'd never thought to visit before.

Thirty years after my teenage running excursions, the massive concrete flank of the Beachner Grain Elevator became the canvas for *El Sueño Original,* the world's largest mural painted by a single artist. The colorful images celebrated the Mexican migrants (people like Joey and Paul's grandparents) who'd done the hard labor of the city's agricultural-industrial economy for more than a century. Originally created in the interest of neighborhood beautification, *El Sueño Original* wound up transforming Wichita's North End into something of a tourist destination.

El Sueño Original underscored how most any part of a city—even its grittier industrial corners—can be filled with would-be attractions. Sometimes murals or interpretive signs will remind us of these workaday monuments' significance; usually, we have to figure this out on our own. In returning home after farther-flung travels, the next stage of the journey is often found in simply keeping your curiosity wide open, and seeking out parts of your hometown that you'd previously overlooked.

December 21

BE A WITNESS TO THE WORLD
WHEN YOU'RE HOME

It's important that we leave each other and the comfort of it and circle away, even though it's hard sometimes, so that we can come back and swap information about what we've learnt even if what we do changes us and we risk not recognizing each other when we return.

—Robyn Davidson, *Tracks* (1980)

Spanish explorer Álvar Núñez Cabeza de Vaca took a curious route to becoming an advocate of indigenous American rights in Europe. Traveling to North America as a member of Spain's disastrous 1527 Narváez expedition to Florida, Cabeza de Vaca was eventually captured by the Karankawa people in what is now Texas. In eight years of wandering the American Southwest with his captors, he worked as a trader and healer in the region's indigenous communities before reconnecting with the Spanish in northern Mexico in 1536.

Whereas his fellow Spanish colonialists saw indigenous people as little more than potential slaves, Cabeza de Vaca had learned to regard them as members of diverse and dynamic cultures, entitled to the same rights Europeans claimed for themselves. He eventually returned to Spain, where he wrote memoirs that described America's indigenous traditions with a sense of compassion and respect, arguing against the cruelties of Spanish practices in the region.

Though we no longer live in complete isolation from (and utter ignorance of) peoples in distant parts of the world, travel is still a way to experience those places in a way that goes beyond lazy cultural stereotypes and media generalizations. In returning to our home communities from these faraway places, we are in a unique position to bear witness to their human complexity. "Make a broader perspective your favorite souvenir," wrote Rick Steves in his 2009 book *Travel as a Political Act*. "Back home, be evangelical about your newly expanded global viewpoint. . . . Then make a difference."

SLOW DOWN AND EMBRACE NON-TRAVEL EXPERIENCES TOO

Make the most of today. Time waits for no man. Today is a gift. That's why it is called the present.
—Alice Morse Earle, *Sun Dials and Roses of Yesterday* (1902)

One of the advantages of an engaged journey is that it allows us to slow down and let things happen as we find new experiences on the road. Freed from inflexible expectations, we begin to discover the kinds of things and meet the kinds of people that itinerary-driven travelers might overlook in their haste to tick attractions off a list.

All too often, however, when we return home, we fall back into a compulsion for "efficiency"—we rush to work, we rush through meals, we multitask when we're hanging out with friends. Unless we learn to pace ourselves and savor our daily experiences (even our work commutes and our noontime meals), we'll be cheating our days out of small moments of leisure, discovery, and joy.

If one of the gifts of travel is the way it enables us to savor moments that feel extraordinary, a key gift of homecoming is the way journeys ultimately teach us to savor *all* moments, extraordinary or not.

"The here and now is the only time and place where life is available," Thich Nhat Hanh noted in his 2017 book *The Art of Living*, "and where we can find everything we are looking for, including love, freedom, peace, and well-being." This applies as readily to life at home as it does to life on the road.

SOUVENIRS INVOKE THE JOURNEY THAT WAS

> The evocative power of souvenirs rests in their seeming un-changeability, all those objects that have no other function than to store memories. Cups that are not for drinking out of, painted cutting boards that never come near a loaf of bread . . . they are vessels for travel back in time and space.
>
> —Orvar Lofgren, *On Holiday* (1999)

Travel souvenirs are sometimes regarded as tacky objects—cheap ephemera from some random gift shop on the other side of the world—but their function shares a history with the cherished relics pilgrims have carted home from sacred places for millennia. Hindu pilgrims returning from Varanasi's Shiva temples brought back glass phalluses, *linga,* to evoke the journey; Buddhists returning from Bodh Gaya brought miniature dried-clay stupas; Muslims returning from Mecca brought myrrh, frankincense, and jewelry; Christians returning from Jerusalem brought engraved medallions, silver bells, and palm-frond crosses.

As with these pilgrimage relics, the souvenirs we bring home from the journey can transport us back to a heightened time in our own lives. "People feel the need to bring things home from a sacred, extraordinary time and space, for home is equated with ordinary, mundane time and space," scholar Beverly Gordon observed in a 1986 essay about souvenirs. "They can't hold on to the non-ordinary experience, for it is by nature ephemeral, but they can hold on to a tangible piece of it, an object that came from it."

In French the word *souvenir* means "to get back to myself," or "to remember"—and often the things we bring home from our travels become part of a lifelong conversation we have with ourselves. In this way, souvenirs—be they artisanal handicrafts, found seashells, or cheap plastic trinkets embossed with the name of a destination—become objects in a museum of the personal that we can visit when we want to recall our bygone journeys.

SMALL DETAILS CAN REMIND YOU OF DISTANT PLACES

To know another country well is both a gain and a loss—for the rest of your life, there is always somewhere you could be but are not.

—Anne P. Beatty, "You Don't Have to Be Here" (2018)

In Claude McKay's 1922 poem "The Tropics in New York," the Jamaican author recalls how the sight of tropical fruit in a Harlem store window gave him an intense sense of yearning for his homeland:

Bananas ripe and green, and ginger-root . . .
Set in the window, bringing memories
of fruit-trees laden by low-singing rills,
And dewy dawns, and mystical blue skies
In benediction over nun-like hills.

For McKay, the sight of Caribbean produce didn't just remind him of Jamaican fruit; it made him long for every aspect of the landscape he'd left behind when he came to work in New York.

McKay's poem was about the visceral power of homesickness, but its language also evokes the reverse-homesickness that can seize you when you return home from a journey. As often as not, this longing is something that takes you by surprise: Catching the scent of cardamom in a supermarket, you're transported to the morning you sipped Arabic coffee as the sun brightened over Byblos; hearing the sound of tablas in a pop song on the radio, you find yourself missing the warm winter day you spent lakeside in Udaipur; biting into a black cherry in your own kitchen, you yearn for the day you ate a whole sack of them in a Marseille market.

As much as any physical souvenir, these sensations can evoke memories of old journeys, inspire visions of new ones, and remind you of the world's ever-wondrous riches.

YOUR TRAVELS ARE CONTEXT FOR THE SPAN OF YOUR LIFE

> Persuade yourself that each new day that dawns will be your
> last; then you will receive each unexpected hour with gratitude.
> —Horace, *Odes* (23 B.C.E.)

One of the classic metaphors human cultures have used to evoke life's transience is the cycle of the seasons, which mirrors the cycles of one's life. For this reason, the sacred festivals that take place around the world each winter—most notably Christmas—underpin the importance of hope and faith in the face of mortality. As days shorten in tandem with the winter solstice, we are reminded to be thankful for the blessing of light; as the seasons cycle across the span of our years, we are reminded to be grateful for the blessing of life. In marking the transience of seasons, we are compelled to live in a way that honors the time we've been given.

The other iconic metaphor for the transience of life is the journey: Knowing that life is impermanent, departure can be celebrated as a symbolic embrace of life's possibility; the route of the journey, with its challenges and surprises, mirrors the progression of our days. In seeking the unfamiliar, embracing change, and coming to terms with impermanence, travel reminds us to live in the moment—to actively seek each day as an adventure, to practice kindness to our fellow humans, and to develop a deepened appreciation for what home might become.

In this way, our travels—both the journeys we've completed and the journeys yet to come—remind us to not take anything for granted, to pay attention to the precious gift of time, and to honor the miraculousness of our days.

December 26

EVEN AT HOME THE JOURNEY IS
THE DESTINATION

> Truth be told, I missed the adventure of the road too. If so much
> can happen in such a short time, then what are we doing with
> most of our lives, just going on from day to day with so little
> variation and excitement?
>
> —Andrew McCarthy, *Just Fly Away* (2017)

When French military officer Xavier de Maistre was imprisoned
in the citadel of Turin in 1794, he decided to stave off boredom by writing *A Journey Around My Room*, which described the
contents of his cell (a "parallelogram of thirty-six steps around") in
the manner of a travelogue. Declaring that travel was a state of mind
as much as a physical activity, he wrote about his room as if it were an
enchanting foreign land. "Room journeys . . . don't explore exotic, far-
off places, but instead remain in immediate surroundings," German
scholar Bernd Stiegler wrote in his 2010 book *Traveling in Place*. "Yet
these spaces can transform themselves . . . into genuine realms of experience that have been previously hidden or consumed by the gray
mildew of the everyday."

Though de Maistre's tale is an extreme case of seeking the exotic in
the familiar, it can serve as an example of how to maintain the spirit
of travel in everyday life. Returning from a journey, we can let the
lingering buzz of life on the road imbue our home lives with the same
attention we brought to more far-flung surroundings.

Experiencing home as part of the journey is an attitude as much as
anything—a matter of seeking in-person interactions rather than digital distractions, walking home the long way, lingering longer over
meals, and wandering outside to look up at the night sky. It's a matter
of being curious about the smallest details of daily life, and embracing
the unexpected in a place that feels familiar.

December 27

SOME ASPECTS OF THE JOURNEY CAN'T
BE BROUGHT HOME

> You can't bring the crackle or the soul-swell or the revelation of
> the journey home. . . . This reality used to sting me, but, many
> journeys later, I know it as something the traveler has to get
> over.
> —Colleen Kinder, "To the Stranger from the Silver Hour" (2016)

For all of his far-flung sojourns as a scholar and diplomat, American president Thomas Jefferson was hesitant to recommend travel to younger generations. "Traveling makes men wiser, but less happy," he noted in a 1787 letter to his nephew. "When men of sober age travel, they gather knowledge, . . . [but] they learn new habits which cannot be gratified when they return home. . . . Their eyes are forever turned back to the object they have lost, and its recollection poisons the residue of their lives."

While Jefferson's prognostication might sound grim, he was simply trying to make sense of the letdown one can feel at home after an extended bout of travel. Indeed, even when one tries to carry the openhearted attitude of a journey into one's home life, there are certain aspects of life on the road—in particular the ongoing sense of novelty and expectation—that can't be replicated amid familiar sights and routines.

This need not be seen as a bad thing. Having fond associations with distant places doesn't have to devolve into "poisonous" recollections of what can never be replicated at home, and some of the pleasures one finds on a journey are inevitably inseparable from the ongoing stimulation of travel itself. If in doubt, make peace with the quiet banalities of domestic familiarity, and let memories of past journeys blend with dreams of future ones.

December 28

LIFE, LIKE TRAVEL, LIES IN
THE JOURNEY ITSELF

Keep Ithaka always in your mind.
Arriving there is what you're destined for.
But don't hurry the journey at all.

—C. P. Cavafy, "Ithaka" (1911)

When I first read "Ithaka" by the Greek Egyptian poet Constantine Cavafy, I was so enamored by its philosophical spin on Odysseus's homeward travels that I wrote the phrase "Life's a journey, not a destination" into my journal. Though I later realized that this exact phrase also happened to be an Aerosmith rock lyric popular when I was in college, I was nonetheless inspired by the idea that travel can be a metaphor for how we experience life itself.

Indeed, just as the existence of Ithaka gave Odysseus a pretext to set out on the adventure that gave him the travel-won experiences that came to define him, the goals that motivate our day-to-day lives are less essential than what we encounter and learn as we live out those days in real time. When we return home from our far-flung journeys to rediscover the Ithakas that once defined us, we can use the buoyant aliveness we experienced amid those travels to more actively embrace the life we live at home.

As Ralph Waldo Emerson noted in his 1844 essay "Experience," it is by fully engaging the ongoing moment that we make the most of life, wherever life happens to find us. "To fill the hour—that is happiness," he wrote. "To finish the moment, to find the journey's end in every step of the road, to live the greatest number of good hours, is wisdom."

YOUR JOURNEY THROUGH THE WORLD DEEPENS AS YOU AGE

Trying to hang on to youth, trying to hang on to what was really great twenty years ago, throws you totally off. You've got to go with it and seek the abundance that's in this new thing.

—Joseph Campbell, in *The Hero's Journey* (1990)

In his 1994 book *The Gutenberg Elegies*, American essayist Sven Birkerts noted that the books we read affect us in different ways at different points in life. "When I reread *On the Road* a few years back I was shocked to find how much of the pith had gone out of the novel," he wrote. "It had a tremendous effect—more than any single thing it guided my attitudes and actions for a time in my late teens—but whatever magic had been there now survived as only a memory of magic."

The same might be said for the author of *On the Road*, Jack Kerouac, who was frustrated by his fans' desire to see him exude the novel's youthful energy as he grew into middle age. In being expected to perform the travel-manic version of his younger self, Kerouac found it difficult to reconcile the person he had become with the novelistic persona his readers had come to love.

A common mistake many travelers make as they age is attempting to re-create the energy and excitement that characterized their initial journeys, when in fact the journey of life itself allows us to experience the world in deeper and richer ways as we grow older. Instead of looking to remember old experiences, we get to create new ones, revisiting old places with changed eyes, and seeking out new experiences with road-won humility and wisdom.

Whereas our earliest travels help us figure out who we are, our ongoing journey allows us to enjoy being that person as we discover newer, subtler ways to enjoy a still-magical world.

THE BEST JOURNEYS NEVER FULLY END

The perfect journey is never finished, the goal is always just across the next river, round the shoulder of the next mountain. There is always one more track to follow, one more mirage to explore. Achievement is the price which the wanderer pays for the right to venture.

—Rosita Forbes, *From Red Sea to Blue Nile* (1925)

My first long-term journey, across North America by van at age twenty-three, was in part designed to get travel out of my system before I embraced the responsibilities of adulthood. That never quite worked out, in part because adult life need not be uncoupled from the joys of open-ended travel, and in part because I am, in a very real way, still on that journey.

In discovering that travel need not be as difficult, dangerous, or expensive as I'd initially feared, those early meanderings emboldened me to seek more far-flung horizons. The more I traveled, the more confident I became about seeing the world's wonders. To this day, I can't read global news without thinking about people I've met in places where those events are happening; I can't watch the Olympics without rooting for athletes from countries I've come to love (or wish to visit next); I can't walk through an airport without seeing each row of departure gates as a bewitching menu of possibilities.

"A journey, after all, neither begins in the instant we set out, nor ends when we have reached our doorstep once again," wrote Ryszard Kapuscinski in his 2008 book *Travels with Herodotus*. "It starts much earlier and is really never over, because the film of memory continues running on inside of us long after we have come to a physical standstill. Indeed, there exists something like a contagion of travel, and the disease is essentially incurable."

YOUR NEXT JOURNEY BEGINS WHEN
YOU RESOLVE TO TAKE IT

Scope eludes my grasp, that there is no finality of vision,
that I have perceived nothing completely,
that tomorrow a new walk is a new walk.
—A. R. Ammons, "Corsons Inlet" (1965)

New Year's resolutions are said to have originated more than four thousand years ago with the Babylonian festival of Akitu, which marked the beginning of the barley-planting season each spring in Mesopotamia. Promising to the gods that they would repay their debts and return what they had borrowed, Babylonian citizens hoped to ensure a rich harvest in the coming year. Part of the point of these promises was that such oaths held people publicly accountable to their neighbors. By contrast, modern New Year's resolutions are mainly tied to personal goals (often involving health, self-discipline, or productivity), and sharing these ambitions is a way of making ourselves accountable to our ambitions.

The first step of your next journey is the resolution to one day make it a reality. In scanning maps and dreaming of distant places—in holding oneself accountable to one day balancing those dreams with real-life endeavors—you are cultivating an attitude that will yield unseen harvests. Even at home, the desire to travel can attune you to life's possibilities, and keep you from taking your apportioned days for granted.

"There should always be a healthy tension between the life we have settled for and the desires that still call us," John O'Donohue wrote in *To Bless the Space Between Us*. "In this sense, our desires are the messengers of our unlived life, calling us to attention and action while we still have time here to explore fields where the treasure dwells."

ACKNOWLEDGMENTS

A big thanks to Steve Hanselman for helping me initiate this project, and to Mary Reynics for helping me see it to its finish. Kristin Van Tassel was generous with her insights (as was Derek Van Becelaere with his research) well before I knew what form this book would take. Tim Ferriss gave me the right advice at the right moment, and Ryan Holiday (in tandem with Steve H.) provided the template for this book's eventual format. For years of technical, website, and podcast assistance, a big thanks goes to Mike Marlett, as well as Justin Glow. Jorge Luis Flores Hernández and Beatriz Herrera helped me translate assorted Latin American travel texts not available in English; Don George helped me interpret certain Basho haikus; George Potts helped me fact-check scientific allusions. This book is dedicated to Kiki Bush, who gives me her love, more precious than money. May she travel with me as long as we live.

FURTHER READING

Assembling a book of this nature put me into conversation with hundreds of authors, spanning dozens of centuries. I quoted a few specific writers multiple times in the preceding pages, each on the power of their prose and the clarity of their insight. This included a number of travel writers, such as Dervla Murphy, Tim Cahill, and Thomas Swick, as well as novelists, critics, and philosophers, including James Baldwin, Susan Sontag, and Thich Nhat Hanh.

Every section of this book is rich with quotes and allusions that might inspire further reading. For a brief sampling of what to read next, any one of the following travel books—each of which was cited several times in these pages—might offer a great place to start.

Matsuo Basho, *The Narrow Road to the Deep North* (1702)
Basho's account of an ambitious walking journey through northern Japan mixes poetry and prose to explore the spiritual resonance of travel on foot.

Ibn Battuta, *The Travels* (1355)
This medieval Moroccan travel masterpiece is a fascinating (and, at times, delightfully quirky) account of a sprawling thirty-year journey across Africa and Asia.

Nicolas Bouvier, *The Way of the World* (1963)
Bouvier's insightful travelogue evokes the thrills, surprises, and illuminations of a youthful automobile journey from Geneva to the Khyber Pass.

William Finnegan, *Barbarian Days: A Surfing Life* (2015)
Technically a surfing memoir, Finnegan's book reveals the joys

of traveling around the world through the lens of a single obsession.

Eddy L. Harris, *Native Stranger: A Black American's Journey into the Heart of Africa* (1992)
This underappreciated travel classic stands out for its aphoristic prose, taut storytelling, and nuanced perspective in describing an overland journey across Africa.

Kate Harris, *Lands of Lost Borders: Out of Bounds on the Silk Road* (2018)
Harris's travel memoir mixes science, philosophy, and history to evoke the exuberant, meditative experience of a bicycle expedition through Central Asia.

Pico Iyer, *Video Night in Kathmandu and Other Reports from the Not-So-Far East* (1988)
Iyer's Asia-themed essays illustrate how travel's truest revelations lie in the intimate (and often comical) cross-cultural discoveries that arise from an ever-shrinking world.

Nanjala Nyabola, *Traveling While Black: Essays Inspired by a Life on the Move* (2020)
Kenya-born Nyabola reports from places like Haiti, New York, and Botswana in this engaging and wide-ranging collection of essays about travel, migration, and identity.

Rebecca Solnit, *Wanderlust: A History of Walking* (2001)
Solnit's philosophical history of walking is an erudite meditation on the task of traveling by foot through a rich variety of settings, landscapes, and eras.

Paul Theroux, *The Tao of Travel: Enlightenments from Lives on the Road* (2011)
America's most celebrated travel author aggregates and reflects upon a wide range of travel books that influenced his career and his understanding of the world.

For a centralized and comprehensive list of all of the works referenced in the book, itemized by topic, visit rolfpotts.com/vagabond books.

NOTES ON THE TEXT

The quotes in these pages reflect decades of reading and notetaking in assorted libraries, streetside cafés, train compartments, hostel lounges, and jungle hammocks around the world. I tried to avoid culling online quotes (in part because such outtakes tend to be unreliable), and I've taken pains to cite original sources. A smattering of my own prose in these pages took original form in such venues as the *Los Angeles Review of Books*, *The Guardian*, *World Hum*, *The Atlantic*, and rolfpotts.com.

I aimed to be global in my travel literature allusions, though this often left me beholden to what has been translated into English (which meant my Asian sources skew Japanese and Chinese, and my Latin American sources skew Mexican and Argentine). If Sumatra and Namibia anecdotes seem particularly abundant, it's because those places dazzled me not long before I wrote this book; if Kenya and Norway allusions abound in various chapters, it's because I was dreaming of vagabonding through those places next. Kansas, Korea, Thailand, Myanmar, Egypt, and Paris were all formative in my development as a traveler, hence their recurring anecdotal prominence here.

Citing three thousand years of travel literature to inspire and inform twenty-first-century journeys has no doubt resulted in the occasional individualist or "presentist" interpretation of ancient sources (investigate the context of most any allusion in this book, and you're liable to enter a delightful rabbit hole of global-historical complexity). I did my best to balance the original sensibility of older texts with the needs and realities of modern-day travelers.

For a rundown of pragmatic, nuts-and-bolts travel tools, check out the online resources I maintain at Vagabonding.net.

ROLF POTTS is the author of five books, including the bestselling *Vagabonding: An Uncommon Guide to the Art of Long-Term World Travel.* His adventures have taken him to six continents, and he has reported from more than sixty countries for *National Geographic Traveler, The New Yorker, Slate, Outside, The New York Times Magazine, The Believer, Sports Illustrated,* and the Travel Channel. Rolf's stories have appeared in numerous literary anthologies, and more than twenty of his essays have been selected as "Notable Mentions" in *The Best American Essays, The Best American Non-Required Reading,* and *The Best American Travel Writing.* His podcast, *Deviate,* has been recommended by such venues as *The New York Times* and *The Washington Post* for its counterintuitive travel conversations. He is based in north-central Kansas, where he keeps a small farmhouse on thirty acres with his wife, Kansas-born actress Kristen Bush.

rolfpotts.com

ABOUT THE TYPE

This book was set in Minion, a 1990 Adobe Originals typeface by Robert Slimbach. Minion is inspired by classical, old-style typefaces of the late Renaissance, a period of elegant and beautiful type designs. Created primarily for text setting, Minion combines the aesthetic and functional qualities that make text type highly readable with the versatility of digital technology.